Ties That Bind

Ties That
Bind

THE BLACK FAMILY IN
POST-SLAVERY JAMAICA,
1834–1882

Jenny M. Jemmott

THE UNIVERSITY OF THE WEST INDIES PRESS
Jamaica • Barbados • Trinidad and Tobago

The University of the West Indies Press
7A Gibraltar Hall Road, Mona
Kingston 7, Jamaica
www.uwipress.com

A catalogue record of this book is available
from the National Library of Jamaica.

ISBN: 978-976-640-506-9 (print)
978-976-640-518-2 (Kindle)
978-976-640-529-8 (ePub)

Cover image: *Native Family at Home, Jamaica*, Cousins Hereward Postcard Collection,
reprinted courtesy of the University of the West Indies Library, Mona

Book and cover design by Robert Harris
Set in Adobe Garamond Pro 11/14.5 x 27
Printed in the United States of America

For Donald and Elma Smith, who have enriched my life with their legacy, and for David, Craig, Julie-Ann and Patrick, who remain my inspiration

Contents

Illustrations

Preface

SEVERAL YEARS AGO, THE IDEA for a quantitative study of the family in post-slavery Jamaica was suggested to me by Barry Higman, and so began a journey of many twists and turns, but one which eventually led me to the successful completion of the work that is the subject of this book. My research took me on a somewhat different path from the one suggested by Professor Higman as I came to realize my own incapacity to deal with the mass of quantitative data analysis that was required to produce a demographic study on the black family in post-slavery Jamaica. But the seeds of an idea were sown, and these have come to fruition in the present work, which is centred instead on the experiences of black families in post-slavery Jamaica as they acted individually and collectively to keep familial bonds together, at times under the most challenging of circumstances. So it is to Barry Higman that I offer my first thoughts of gratitude for setting me on this path.

It was while browsing the vast and varied resources of the West Indies Collection of the Main Library at the University of the West Indies, Mona, that I encountered a wealth of primary material which allowed me to ground my research in the experiences of post-slavery black families. From the outset, it was clear to me that they had an amazing narrative of their own to convey, albeit through the records generated by the powerful. In this respect I am profoundly grateful to so many members of the staff of the Main Library, particularly of the West Indies Collection, past and present, for accommodating me so warmly and for being so very helpful for the extended duration of my research. Special words of thanks are reserved for Patricia Dunn, former head of section, and Frances Salmon for their expert guidance, and to Leona Bobb-Semple and

Cherry-Ann Smart for their invaluable assistance. I am grateful, too, to the staff of the National Library and the Jamaica Archives for facilitating my work.

I have been indeed fortunate to have been the beneficiary of the insightful, supportive and expert guidance provided by Swithin Wilmot, who was my supervisor for most of this journey. His passion for the post-slavery experiences of ordinary Jamaicans proved infectious as well as inspirational. I thank Dr Wilmot as well as Verene Shepherd and Barbara Bush for their humbling vote of confidence in my work. I am grateful to Bridget Brereton, who read my dissertation and offered very useful comments for the way forward, and to Waibinte Wariboko for his helpful suggestions on the West African aspects of this work.

My thanks to dear friends and colleagues from the Department of History and Archaeology, at Mona, Aleric Josephs and Kathleen Monteith, who have encouraged me along the way, and to my son, David, for his unfailing support and technical assistance.

At the end of this journey, I extend special thanks to Linda Speth and her team at the University of the West Indies Press for their endorsement of my work and for agreeing to bring this aspect of the black experience to a wider audience.

Jenny M. Jemmott

Introduction

"We will support dem – as how dey brought us up when we was pickaninny, and now we come trong, must care for dem."
  – Excerpt from an interview between visiting abolitionists James A. Thome and J. Horace Kimball and a group of fifteen apprenticed head boilers and constables drawn from twelve estates in St Thomas-in-the-East[1]

IN A HISTORIOGRAPHICAL CONTEXT, MUCH of the discussion on the black family in the anglophone Caribbean and in the United States has focused on the enslaved family. In this regard, the emphasis has been on an examination of the household types and family forms which emerged during slavery. Sociological and anthropological assessments of the Caribbean family in the contexts of both slavery and post-slavery, such as those of Michael G. Smith, Franklin Frazier and Fernando Henriques, cited the adverse and formative influence of slavery and the consequent predominance of what the authors of these studies perceived as "disorganized" and chaotic family units, which were for the most part matriarchal or female-headed units.[2] Early historical assessment of the enslaved family structure in the Caribbean was similar to these sociological and anthropological perspectives. Elsa Goveia, using the Western construct of the nuclear family as the norm and the prerequisite for stability, concluded that in the Leewards, the female-headed family type was predominant and that slavery accounted for either the marginalization or the non-existence of the male in the household unit, an issue which is discussed later in this introduction.[3] Similarly influenced by the concept of the nuclear family as the ideal, sociologist Orlando Patterson concluded that "the nuclear family could hardly exist within the context of slavery".[4] A parallel perspective emerged in the United States,

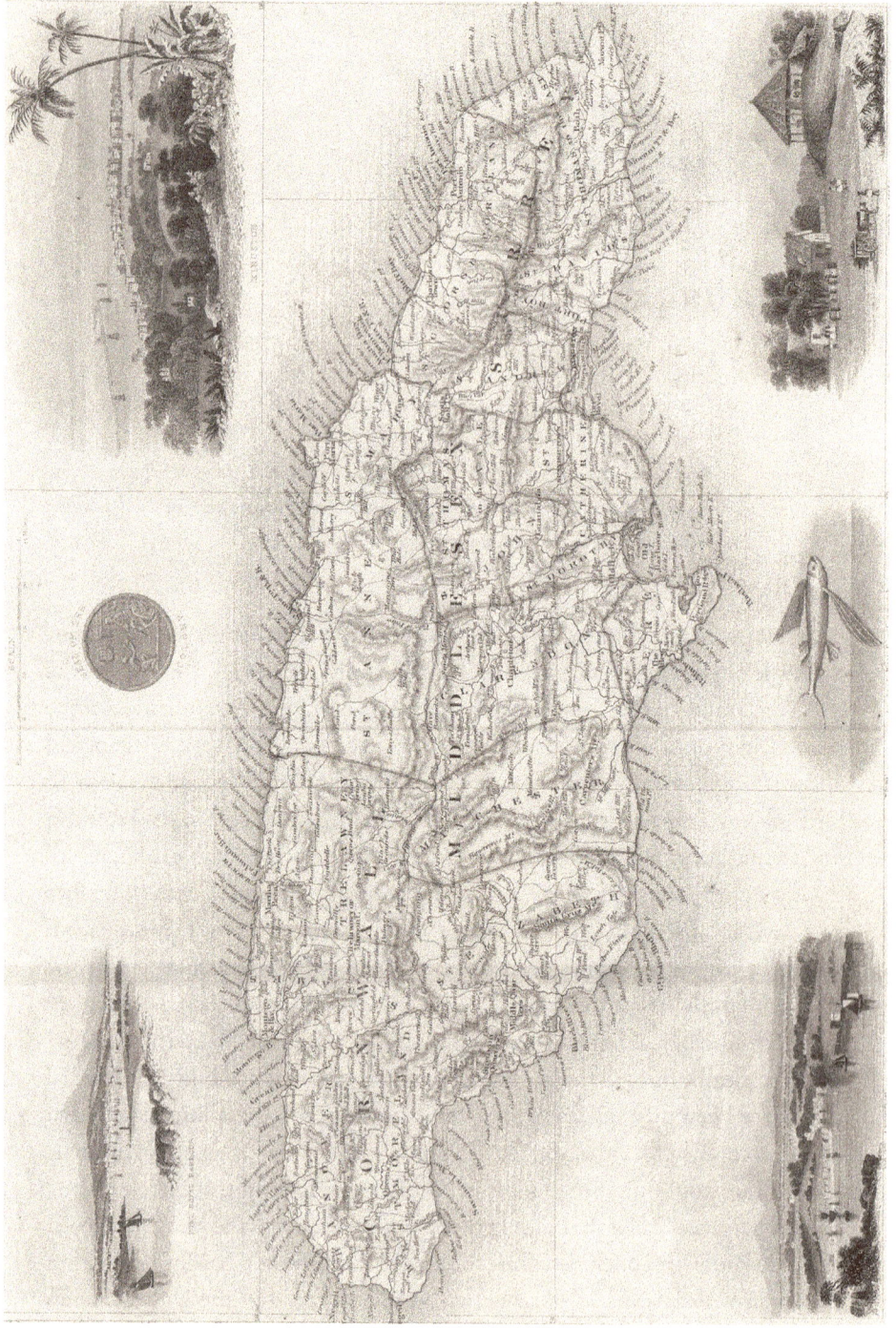

Figure 1. Map of Jamaica, 1851, by J. Rapkin. Reprinted courtesy of the National Library of Jamaica.

where the historiography of the antebellum period in particular represented the black family as "disorganized, unstable and matriarchal".[5]

Developments in quantitative methods during the 1970s enabled American historians such as Herbert Gutman, Robert Fogel and Stanley Engerman to provide convincing studies of the stability of family units among the enslaved population. Gutman, for example, showed that nuclear family units were extensive in this group and that the enslaved exhibited strong familial ties.[6]

In Caribbean historiography, Barry Higman's seminal application of quantitative methods to the study of the enslaved family produced a different assessment from the previous perspectives provided by Patterson and Goveia. His groundbreaking work on the early nineteenth-century enslaved population of Jamaica and Trinidad demonstrated that the most common family unit was the nuclear family, which by Higman's definition consisted of "a man, his wife, and their children". Higman emphasized that it could not be ascertained whether the couples in these nuclear family forms were bound by legal marriage.[7] Given the restricted influence of missionaries during slavery, it is possible that most, though certainly not all, of Higman's nuclear family types would have had their raison d'être in their African-derived commitments (discussed in chapter 1) rather than in Euro-Christian forms of legal marriage. Regardless of whether these enslaved couples were united in Christian, legal marriage or not, Higman's findings presented convincing evidence of elements of stability and durability among the enslaved population that he studied which challenged earlier assertions that nuclear-type family groupings "could hardly exist" within the confines of slavery.[8]

In his assessment of Caribbean historiography of slavery and emancipation, Francisco Scarano, while emphasizing that "no single portrayal of 'the family under slavery' can do justice to the richness of forms one finds across space and time", also underscored the need for historians to move the discussion on the family (in freedom as well as in slavery) beyond the traditional focus on structure. Indicating the rationale for this call, Scarano pointed out that "we are now keenly aware that any discussion of 'family forms' tends to conceal a great deal about the human interactions that actually occurred in family and community contexts".[9] In affirming the significance of examining "human interactions" in the study of family history, David Sabean argued that the preoccupation with the study of the household and family forms has tended, over time, to relegate family history to "a statistical artefact". Thus, Sabean urged historians of the family to "deal with the relational aspects of family life".[10] This book, which focuses on the black family in Jamaica from the inception of the apprenticeship system to 1882, has been written precisely because of this need to shift the historiographical emphasis away from the traditional focus on family forms and household structure. It therefore builds on the pioneering contribution of Higman's works on the enslaved family in two important ways. First, it shifts the focal point of historical investigation on the family from the time period of slavery into the evolving landscape of post-slavery Jamaica. Second, by uncovering, assessing and prioritizing the interactions within the black family and between freed families and communities, the book signals an important departure in the study of family history, particularly black family history in Jamaica, precisely because it chronicles those "relational aspects of family life" of which Sabean writes.

No historical study of black family forms and structure equivalent to Higman's work on family structure among the enslaved has been done for the post-slavery period in Jamaica, and it is perhaps necessary. This book is not intended as a sequel to Higman's sterling assessments of family structure during the period of slavery, nor should it be construed as such. While it is at times necessary to discuss post-slavery family forms, for the purposes of conceptual clarification and historical analysis of efforts by the colonial state to mould black family unions to European norms, the emphasis throughout this book is on black familial values and interrelationships rather than on family structure. With this in mind, it is vital, in order to uncover some of these family interactions of which Scarano and Sabean have written, to assess, for example, how black families strove to promote the welfare of their members and, in so doing, to discover how they perceived themselves and their rights as free persons. Such an analysis is all the more warranted in the absence of any major historical evaluation on the black family in Jamaica for the period 1834–82. In this respect, Patrick Bryan's *The Jamaican People, 1880–1902: Race, Class and Social Control*, in devoting a chapter to marriage and family, provides useful insights into late nineteenth-century attitudes to marriage, patterns of sexual behaviour, concubinage and courtship among the different social classes in Jamaica, but lacks a singular focus on the black family. In their work *Neither Led nor Driven: Contesting British Cultural Imperialism in Jamaica, 1865–1920*, Brian L. Moore and Michele A. Johnson also dedicate a chapter to "Sex, Marriage and Family", which presents a fine analysis of the attempt to exert "cultural imperialism" in the realm of family life of "Afro-Jamaicans".[11] However, neither of these chapters is intended to be an in-depth historical investigation of the black family, with its rich and diverse tapestry of challenges and advocacy on behalf of kin. Importantly, both of these works are focused on the Jamaica of the late nineteenth and early twentieth centuries. Therefore, in starting the historical assessment of the black family in 1834, when slavery was terminated, and extending the analysis to 1882, when Jamaica experienced the final years of pure Crown Colony government, *Ties That Bind* breaks ground both in terms of the period it covers and its thematic focus. In so doing, this work makes an important contribution to the historiography of Jamaica and, by extension, that of the Caribbean. In highlighting the historiographical importance of engaging with the relational aspects of family history, Scarano notes that "unearthing those interactions, discovering what they meant to those who lived them, and assessing their social and cultural implications remains an exciting frontier in Caribbean studies".[12]

This work presents evidence which challenges and indeed overturns several stereotypical misrepresentations of the attitudes which blacks had towards their families. In particular, this undertaking is replete with cases of black parents, mothers and fathers, who by dint of their own persistence and sacrifice ensured that their children had access to health care and education and maintained their freedom at any cost. This evidence challenges contemporary stereotyping of black parents as irresponsible and neglectful by writers such as Edward Long, Mrs A.C. Carmichael and Bryan Edwards.[13] After 1834, these stereotypes continued to inform the plantocratic, governmental and judicial perspectives, especially those of the stipendiary magistracy. Not surprisingly, the 1879 *Report of the Commissioners of Inquiry upon the Condition of the Juvenile Population of Jamaica* indicted black parents as irresponsible, careless and at times absent.[14]

It is a premise of this analysis that the abundant evidence of black paternal as well as maternal activism, apparent throughout the entire period being examined, challenges these negative assumptions of a disinterested and even non-existent black parenthood. This work further contends that this wide-spread evidence of parents' support for their children's welfare is indicative of the continued significance of African-derived kinship bonds, especially those between mother and child, in informing the black experience in the post-slavery period. This work demonstrates that by both their statements and their actions, the formerly enslaved indicated that they viewed freedom as an opportunity to pursue the welfare of their families – a conclusion endorsed by Rebecca Scott, Bridget Brereton and Nigel Bolland, who have all indicated that freed people often accorded primacy to family-oriented goals over individual concerns.[15] Chronicled throughout this book are the issues which were intrinsic to freed people's notions of family well-being, including the reconstitution of members separated by slavery, attainment of secure shelter, access to land and income, education for their children, assertion of parental control, autonomy over family labour and liberty, and the pursuit of recognition of the dignity of family members.

Foundational to all traditional West African societies was the significance attached to ties of kinship. The evidence of black activism on behalf of family that is examined throughout this work is a testament to the durability of this cultural tradition. Clearly, the severing of kinship ties by forced migration did not erase the importance of bonds of kinship from the collective memories of enslaved Africans and their descendants, as they recreated kinship networks inclusive of "fictive kin" in their altered circumstances.[16] While recognizing that the importance attached to kinship was not unique to African societies, this work postulates that the African-derived centrality of kinship, both real and fictive, proved to be a cardinal feature of a familial culture embraced by many black Jamaicans in the period under study. The importance of kindred was embodied in the fierce demonstration of both maternal and paternal advocacy apparent under apprenticeship and thereafter, in the efforts made by freed blacks to reunite family members separated by enslavement, in the ample evidence of other forms of black family advocacy detailed in chapter 2 and in the persistent use of kinship networks as safety and support mechanisms during periods of crisis, such as occurred in the aftermath of the Morant Bay uprising. This work also takes into consideration the fact that not all black Jamaicans displayed this commitment to family and kinship ties, and that these bonds of kinship would have been severely challenged by factors such as the deteriorating socio-economic environment of the 1850s and 1860s. Nevertheless, this analysis demonstrates that the social ills facing the black family in this period did not negate the activism undertaken by so many in advancing the welfare of their own. Rather, the fact that so many blacks engaged in some form of family advocacy in the worst of times as well as the best of times constitutes an affirmation of the extent and the endurance of the kinship ties which they so valued and by which they were bound and defined.

Central to the project of unearthing the human interactions within the family is the crucial issue of the "marginalization of the black male", especially within the context of the family. Conceptually, to marginalize means "to make or treat as insignificant".[17] The assessment of the view of the male as marginal in relation to the black family constitutes a critical and timely centrepiece of this work. In today's context, in which social researchers and commentators are still focused on trying to find the "invisible and marginal" black male in family settings, this work seeks to make a substantial contribution to the discourse, and to Jamaican and indeed Caribbean historiography, as it presents important evidence of black male activism on behalf of family in the period under consideration here, 1834 to 1882. Indeed, the testimony locates the black male in this period not as peripheral, but as a significant and central father, husband or partner, grandfather, son, grandson and brother, both in terms of his image of self and in the activation of these familial roles. It is anticipated that this work will provide greater visibility to the importance of the black male in familial contexts, thereby addressing this historiographical imbalance. This issue is discussed further in chapter 1 of this work.

Efforts undertaken by black men and women, especially during the apprenticeship, to affirm the dignity and integrity of their family members were part of a wider black mission to emphasize self-worth in the aftermath of slavery's dehumanizing experience. This work treats this endeavour as thematic and pivotal to the realization of the true meaning of freedom in the context of family relationships. Thus, when confronted with the persistence of demeaning treatment after 1834, especially of female family members, blacks sought to "recover or re-establish a lost birthright . . . that included notions of . . . personhood".[18] Building on the work done by Brereton on family strategies such as the withdrawal of female labour from the estates and pens, this study extends the arena of family strategies[19] to include the widespread family-based activism intended to assert the right of family members to be treated with dignity and honour.

A hallmark of freed societies across the Americas, and certainly one of the clearest indicators of black people's commitment to familial goals in Jamaica after 1 August 1834, was their persistent efforts to reunite and consolidate family members separated by slavery. Both Edward (Kamau) Brathwaite and Bush have emphasized the existence under slavery of attempts, albeit restricted, at effecting family reunions, evidenced by episodes of running away and "night rambling", while Woodville Marshall has established the unfettered reunification and consolidation of families as a major black expectation of freedom.[20] This theme was further developed by Swithin Wilmot and Brereton, both of whom viewed decisions by freedwomen to focus their labour on family economic activities as indicative of their interest in consolidating their families (among other motives).[21] However, within the anglophone Caribbean, and certainly in Jamaica, the historiographical assessment has not ventured much beyond an acknowledgement of the primacy to blacks of this objective of reconstituting their families in the post-slavery period. It is therefore expected that this work will make a significant contribution to Jamaican and, by extension, Caribbean historiography through its extensive analysis of black efforts to reconstitute and consolidate families from 1834 onwards. Against the backdrop of a post-slavery resurrection of the trade in human beings, this undertaking also breaks ground by assessing the attempts by some family members, aided by colonial authorities, to achieve reunion with relatives abducted from Jamaica's shores for the purpose of enslavement abroad. In his telling commentary on the significance to American blacks of these attempts at reuniting families, Leon Litwack underscores the historiographical importance of this issue to the reconstruction of the interactions within the black family: "In their eyes the work of emancipation was incomplete until the families which had been dispersed by slavery were reunited."[22]

John Lean and Trevor Burnard, in accentuating the historiographical value of the project to "examine the past from perspectives other than those of the mighty", have reminded us of the need to "hear the voices of other sorts of people – the excluded, the weak, the . . . marginalized".[23] Certainly within the anglophone Caribbean, this task has been given impetus by the work of historians such as Alvin Thompson, who has utilized the testimony of enslaved persons to allow us a window into the world of Crown slaves in Berbice; Wilmot, who has highlighted voices of protest and political activism in post-slavery Jamaica; and Verene Shepherd, who has been involved in gaining access to the voices of the enslaved and indentured in the colonial Caribbean.[24] This work on the black family facilitates engagement with this project through its extensive utilization of blacks' testimonies about their familial goals and concerns. In so doing, it makes a significant contribution to the ongoing effort to give voice to the black experience, particularly in the anglophone Caribbean in the post-slavery period. For this reason, it is perhaps instructive to make a few observations about the sources used for this work.

Although blacks left no lengthy accounts of their family lives during this period, the data are certainly not as restricted as might be initially concluded. Beginning with apprenticeship and continuing throughout the entire period under study here, blacks gave depositions and affidavits, wrote or had petitions written for them, gave evidence before commissions of inquiry, gave interviews to missionaries and visiting abolitionists, communicated their views to stipendiary magistrates and addressed public gatherings. Specifically, reliance upon the minutes of evidence taken before commissions of inquiry such as that convened at Brown's Town (1837) and the Jamaica Royal Commission (1866) had inherent source limitations. Despite these limitations relative to intent or motive, possible coaching, linguistic or cultural misinterpretation, exaggeration and bias, the fact remains that these sources conveyed significant insights into blacks' familial goals, aspirations and advocacy on behalf of their families. In the use of sources such as testimonies before commissions of inquiry, careful methodological scrutiny with its attendant tests of internal and external validity were applied. When we combine what blacks did with what so many of them said by way of testimony, we gain an even greater insight into black families during this period. Ultimately, the aforementioned limitations and the possible shortcomings of individual witnesses do not alter the validity of the general images and messages generated by such testimonies.

The evidential base for this work rests predominantly with the correspondence between the governors and the Colonial Office (CO 137) for the period 1834–82. Careful scrutiny of this correspondence revealed a variety of sources, such as reports of stipendiary magistrates or special magistrates, petitions, court cases, education reports, missionaries' observations, laws and Foreign Office correspondence, which provided valuable material. As with other documents of record and official correspondence, the Colonial Office and governors' correspondence have the obvious limitation of being written from the cultural perspective of the colonial authorities, and reflect their own agendas. This aside, the contents of these despatches and their enclosures revealed an abundance of material on black families, through both "witting" and, to an even greater degree, "unwitting" testimony.[25] One of the most helpful sources contained in the governors' correspondence was the reports of the stipendiary magistrates, who, as intermediaries between the plantocracy and the formerly enslaved, were ideally placed to hear the voices of blacks on familial issues, even if the blacks' messages did not always meet with their approval. Being strategically placed in such interactive positions created opportunities for these officials to comment on black familial aspirations and culture and thus transmit to us, albeit within their Eurocentric parameters, unwitting testimony about blacks in familial contexts. The reports of the stipendiary magistracy have the advantage of comparative longevity, having been made, with some interruptions, until 1860, and therefore provide a great deal of raw material for understanding the goals and activism of freed families.

An assessment of black family life in Jamaica from 1834 to 1882 raises the practical as well as interpretive issue of how to determine "blackness" in the sources. In evaluating data on the apprenticeship period, this task was facilitated by the general observation that most, though clearly not all, apprentices were black. The relatively frequent inclusion of the terms "negro" and "black" in sources from the period expedited this determination. However, ascertaining "blackness" in the sources assumed more challenging proportions in the years after 1838, primarily because the largely black population of former slaves became subsumed under the general population, along with people of mixed race, poor whites and immigrants from Asia. Isolating references to blacks was usually possible through a process of elimination, as the observed trend in the sources was the use of terms including "immigrants", "indentured immigrants", "coolies" or "coolie labourers" to refer to immigrants and "persons of colour", "coloured" or "brown" for people of mixed race or coloureds. An interpretive approach was used to verify whether references were indeed being made to blacks. Whereas all-inclusive terms such as "the poor", "the people", "the mass of the population", "the lower orders", "labourers" and "the labouring class" do not, on their own, allow us to form valid conclusions about the race or ethnicity of the subjects being alluded to, an examination of the context in which the terms are used usually does. For example, an initial reference to "the people" in a document was clarified when the same source made mention of the need to end the prejudice of "the people" against agricultural labour "arising out of its peculiar connection with slavery".[26] Contextual analysis also indicated that phrases such as "the mountain people" or "country people" were generally references to the black majority.

In several important ways, 1834 heralded a watershed for black families, facilitating the start of reconstruction and consolidation, and therefore this analysis of the black family begins then. The evaluation terminates in 1882, when, in the final years of pure Crown Colony government, the legislative effort to shape the "morality" of the black family reached its apex. The general objective of this work is to demonstrate that from 1834 to 1882, despite persistent hegemonic attempts to wield control, black families, through their constant activism, resilience and commitment to kin, were in some respects able to shape their own reality, endure crisis and change, and generally emerge as the basis on which meaningful black communities could be established.

It is intended that this work will make a much-needed contribution to the historiographical dimensions of the project on the emancipated peoples of the Caribbean through its focus on the agency of black families in the maintenance of freedom on their terms, a vision which for many was closely linked to the protection of familial rights and well-being. As this analysis explores the theme of black familial activism throughout the period under consideration, it is also intended to highlight the salient contributions of both black men and women to the welfare of their families; to dispel the stereotypical notions of the black family as dysfunctional, disorganized and unstable; and to challenge claims of irresponsible black parenthood in general and the marginality of the black male in the historical context in particular. Finally, by lending greater visibility to black testimonies on familial issues, it is hoped that this undertaking will make a contribution to the ongoing project of giving voice to the historical aspects of the black experience in Jamaica and the Caribbean as a whole.

Chapter 1

Conceptualizing the Black Family

LEGACIES, FORMS AND RELATIONSHIPS

Most of the Africans who were captured and brought to America arrived without members of their families, but they brought with them the societal codes they had learned regarding family life. To argue that the trans-Atlantic voyage and the trauma of enslavement made them forget, or rendered useless their memories of how they had been brought up or how they had lived before their capture, is to argue from premises laden with myths about the Black experience.

– Niara Sudarkasa, "Interpreting the African Heritage in Afro-American Family Organization" [1]

A HISTORICAL EXAMINATION OF THE black family in post-slavery Jamaica must take cognizance of the cultural legacies and formative influences which helped to shape the values and attitudes that were intrinsic to the relational aspects of such families. Post-slavery developments within the black family in the anglophone Caribbean were in some respects linked to antecedents present during slavery. Significantly, too, black familial forms and values evident both in the period of slavery and in the post-slavery context exhibited some relational linkage to the West African cultural environment from which they derived. The extent to which black family life continued to reflect traditional West African cultural forms during the period of enslavement and through the post-slavery era to 1882 was conditioned by various factors, including the constraints imposed by the system of enslavement, the impact of the related forces of creolization and cultural adaptation to Eurocentric norms and values, generational separation from the cultural locus of West Africa and socio-economic conditions in the post-slavery period. This chapter will explore these factors as well as the rich variety of family forms that were evident in Jamaica in this period, conceptualizing the term "family" as the freed people did: as all-inclusive and encompassing of all these forms. Importantly, this chapter also highlights some of the fundamental issues which were pivotal to relationships within the family during the post-slavery period and which, to a significant extent, became the hallmarks of the black family in the evolving environment of free Jamaica.

The West African Heritage and the Shaping of Black Family Life in Jamaica

Historiographical and sociological assessment of the role of African derivatives in enslaved and, by extension, free black familial culture is far from unanimous. Franklin Frazier theorized that West African culture was obliterated by the experiences of New World enslavement.[2] In keeping with this exclusionary model, George W. Roberts asserted that forced migration meant that the enslaved population of Jamaica "inevitably experienced a dissolution of their traditional family forms".[3] West African influence on the structure of Caribbean family patterns was similarly discounted from the mid-1950s onwards by a group of anthropologists and sociologists influenced by structural functionalism.[4] Accordingly, Fernando Henriques, Edith Clarke, Judith Blake, M.G. Smith, Sidney Greenfield and Raymond Smith[5] all explained Caribbean family structure as a "functional response to the disorganizing effects of contemporary socio-economic conditions in Caribbean village communities" and posited the nuclear and co-resident family as the norm.[6]

The Frazierian thesis and the perspective of the structural functionalists stood in sharp contrast to the view which emphasized the formative influence of West African cultural traditions on black American and Caribbean familial forms and values. Melville Herskovits emerged as the principal early supporter of the impact of African retentions on black family life in this region, albeit conceding modifications by the experience of enslavement.[7] Orlando Patterson's groundbreaking research on the culture of enslaved people in Jamaica failed to explore the impact of West African culture on the enslaved family itself because the Pattersonian concept of family, restricted as it was to the Western construct of the conjugal couple united by Christian, legal marriage, allowed him to conclude that the family (nuclear, by his definition) could hardly have been evident within the confines of slavery.[8]

Certainly one of the most prolific advocates of the link between traditional West African culture and the forms of black familial organization and value systems which emerged in New World societies during slavery and in freedom has been Niara Sudarkasa. She has emphasized the continuity of African familial principles and values, which facilitated the emergence of "variants of African family life in the form of the extended families" found among enslaved and free black communities.[9] Endorsing this theme of the legacy of Africa in the Caribbean, Barbara Bush points out that in spite of the repressive circumstances of enslavement, the enslaved sought to perpetuate "traditional attitudes to family, children and kin, even where this involved resistance to European cultural impositions, as in the case of Christian marriage".[10] While acknowledging the disruptive impact of slavery on the black family and kinship organization through separation of kin, restricted movement beyond estate boundaries and the wielding of plantocratic power through "sexual intervention", Barry Higman nevertheless asserts that "there is evidence of strong family bonds within the slave community . . . subtle variations of family patterns having their origin in Africa".[11]

The historiographical divide between the Frazierian proponents of negation of African culture and the Herskovitsian advocates of African continuities in black family life was bridged beginning with the seminal contribution of Edward (Kamau) Brathwaite to the development of the concept of a creolization of culture in Jamaican slave society. Although influenced by Herskovits's theory, Brathwaite argues that there was within the Jamaican setting a cultural blending of African and European traditions which resulted in the creolization of the region's cultural forms. According to this model, therefore, the familial norms and values of the enslaved and, by extension, the freed blacks in Jamaica were the product of "interculturation, cultures influencing each other to form . . . new entities".[12] Michael Craton supports the theory of creolization, arguing that, especially after the cessation of the British slave trade in 1807, generational removal from African traditions strengthened the tendency towards a blending of European normative systems with African retentions. This, Craton contends, resulted in the emergence of "an integrated society: not European or African (or even plural) but creole".[13]

Undoubtedly, the tendency towards creolization of black familial forms and traditions was enhanced by the passage of time and by the increasing ratio of creole to African-born blacks in the Jamaican population, both during the period of enslavement and thereafter. In this respect, the issue of generational removal from the cultural locus of West Africa becomes crucial to any discussion of the impact of West African traditions on the black family. Especially after the ending of the British slave trade in 1807, the numbers of African-born blacks in Jamaica continued to reflect a decline, with a concurrent increase in the numbers of creole blacks. Thus, in 1817, there were 126,903 Africans, representing 37 per cent of the total enslaved population of Jamaica. By 1844, there were 33,519 Africans, constituting 11.4 per cent of the total free black population of 293,128 in Jamaica, while by 1861, of the total black population of 346,374, only 10,501, or 3 per cent, were African-born.[14] While it is logical to acknowledge the acceleration of creolization within this framework of a declining African population after 1807, this did not signal the disappearance of West African cultural links. Bush affirms that "the influence of African-derived values remained strong" for the duration of enslavement.[15] This analysis posits the view that blacks in post-slavery nineteenth-century Jamaica created and embraced a creolized family-based culture of their own, and that the familial culture of some black Jamaicans continued to reflect West African–derived traditions up to the end of the period investigated in this work.

Familial forms and values of blacks in the period under analysis were also influenced by factors external to West African traditions. Evolving socio-economic pressures, especially low wages, insecurity of tenure and out-migration of family members, no doubt contributed to increased reports of neglect and destitution of family members, especially the elderly, and to cases of deserted women and children. Such cases do not necessarily reflect the absence of African cultural influences in black familial interactions; rather, they should be recognized for what they represented: a breakdown in relationships within the family in response to socio-economic factors. This is discussed further in chapter 6. Of significance, too, are the pervasive efforts made by religious bodies and by the colonial authorities to inculcate European norms and values in the freed population with a view to achieving cultural compliance. It is clear that some members of the black population had strategically accepted or internalized aspects of these Euro-cultural family values, such as the equating of Christian, legal forms of marriage with "respectable" and acceptable social behaviours. As the nineteenth century wore on, the social class differences among black Jamaicans became more complex, and this held implications for an evolving black familial culture. As Patrick Bryan has indicated, the post-slavery nineteenth century witnessed the emergence of a black middle class of professionals, successful small farmers, master craftsmen and constables, among others.[16] Although this middle class remained a very small minority among the black population, they were more likely, as Brian L. Moore and Michele A. Johnson have argued, to consciously absorb and represent Euro-cultural norms and values in their quest for social validation.[17]

In assessing the impact of West African traditions on black family life in post-slavery Jamaica, it becomes crucial to clarify this concept of a traditional West African familial culture and to determine whether this concept is valid. Of significance in this respect is the reality of the diverse origins of the enslaved and, by extension, the freed black populations. Shula Marks and Richard Rathbone emphasize that the "cultural and linguistic pluralism of West Africa" could pose problems for the historian of the family.[18] In elucidating some of these potential problems, Higman identifies the issue of ascertaining the ethnic and regional origins of enslaved Africans as well as the challenges of "establishing the social and cultural patterns" which existed in Africa at the height of the Atlantic slave trade.[19] In his quantitative analysis of the origins of Africans brought into Jamaica between 1655 and 1807, Philip Curtin assesses the main sources of captives, in order of numerical significance, as the Bight of Biafra, the Gold Coast, West Central Africa, the Bight of Benin, Sierra Leone and Senegambia.[20] From these areas, the ethnic groups represented in the greatest numbers in Jamaica's enslaved population were the Coromantyn, the Ashanti-Fanti and the Ibo or Igbo.[21] Since the majority of the enslaved population came from the Bight of Biafra, the Ibo or Igbo arrivants were predominant.[22] Against this diverse background, it is clear that there would have been some variation in the West African traditions and values which influenced black familial culture in Jamaica.

Despite linguistic and socio-cultural diversity, however, there were commonalities evident which legitimate the concept of a West African familial culture. Bush emphasizes the existence of many cultural similarities, especially in marriage and kinship patterns, and underscores the enduring nature of these commonalities when they were transferred to the Caribbean.[23] Higman also concedes that the "amount of genuine variation in family structure between the different regional groups was not great".[24] This view is supported by Sudarkasa, who affirms that among the peoples of West Africa, there had been a prolonged history of culture contact, and extensive similarities existed in familial structure and in familial norms and values. Examples of these similarities include the emphasis placed on large co-resident extended families and polygynous marriages, the importance attached to consanguinity (blood ties), commitment to collective responsibility in child-rearing and life crises, and generational attachment to ancestors, which often found expression in reverence for seniority.[25] For the purposes of this analysis of the black family in freedom, it is mainly at the level of familial forms, values and traditions that the legacy of this West African link will be explored.

Exploring the West African Connection

This section examines some aspects of West African familial forms and values which may have exerted a formative influence, albeit with modification, on black family life during the period of enslavement and the post-slavery period to 1882 in Jamaica. Central to the examination of family life in indigenous pre-colonial West African societies is the necessity of doing so within a conceptual framework which is not derived from Western paradigms. Indeed, the pervasive weakness of ethnocentrically based assessments has been the evaluation of West African family forms and African-influenced derivatives which emerged in the Caribbean within a Western framework which posits the nuclear co-residential family, united by bonds of Euro-legal, Christian marriage, as the norm. At best, this has led to a miscomprehension of West African familial culture and to the stereotypical designation of Caribbean variants as dysfunctional, chaotic and unstable.

In conceptualizing the family in pre-colonial West Africa, an essential challenge is presented by what Marks and Rathbone identify as "an acute problem of definition . . . [as the] very term 'family' is problematic in pre-modern Africa". In elucidating this conceptual hurdle, David Sabean underscores the fact that in many African societies, "there is no equivalent to the English . . . word 'family' at all".[26] This dilemma stems partly from the preoccupation on the part of Western scholars with using the nuclear family and the principle of conjugality (marital ties) as the cultural benchmarks with which to assess familial organization, irrespective of ethnological divergence. Once such conceptual barriers are removed, then it becomes possible to comprehend the parameters of kinship in pre-colonial state societies of West Africa such as the Yoruba and the Ashanti, and in pre-colonial stateless societies such as the Igbo.

In these societies, the predominant type of domestic group was the extended family, the foundations of which were usually laid by two or more adult siblings of the same sex. The founding members were thus bound together in kinship based on biological relationships or blood ties. These ties of consanguinity also brought into the extended family a wider array of blood relatives of the founding core members, such as siblings, parents, grandparents, aunts and uncles. This core group of the extended family was also expanded through kinship ties based on conjugality (ties established through marriage) to include the in-marrying spouses and children of the founding siblings. Importantly, ties of consanguinity usually assumed precedence over conjugal ties, and children were socialized to this value system. Typically, the traditional extended family was also co-resident – that is, members lived together in a group of adjacent or adjoining dwellings in one geographical locale referred to as a compound. Co-residence was reinforced by the fact that the in-marrying spouse customarily joined the compound in which the extended family of the other spouse was resident.[27]

Evidence exists to support the argument that there was continuity of West African–derived forms of the extended family network in Jamaica during slavery and in the post-slavery period as well. On Montpelier estate, for example, although most Africans arrived without kin and therefore initially tended to establish nuclear family households, with the passage of time, as Higman points out, "ramifications of creole kinship and generational depth made possible more frequent involvement in extended family networks". There is evidence, too, of continuity of the West African custom of extended family residence in adjacent dwellings within the compound during and after slavery. Higman's research findings on Montpelier and Shettlewood indicate that members of extended families tended to live in dwellings contiguous to each other, which was suggestive of yard formation similar to the West African compound.[28] Bush underscores the importance of these African-derived, extended, co-residential family networks among the enslaved in the Caribbean and also emphasizes the existence of non-co-residential extended networks, separated, no doubt, by the geographical and legal restrictions of enslavement.[29] This work shows that varieties of extended family networks continued to exist, especially on larger plantations, during the apprenticeship period and that these were characterized by generational depth and co-residence, although trans-residential networks (separated across estate boundaries) also existed. As late as 1866, too, testimony by survivors of the aftermath of the events at Morant Bay indicated the continuance of extended family networks (both co-residential and non-co-residential) as well as the continued practice among some of these extended families to establish contiguous or adjacent homes. These cases will be discussed in chapters 2 and 5.[30]

Certainly, one of the significant features of West African indigenous familial culture was the prominence of ties of consanguinity over those of conjugality. In West Africa, this principle was reflected among the patrilineal Igbo, who, as seen earlier in this chapter, were shown by Curtin to be of numerical significance in Jamaica's enslaved population. Among the Igbo, marriage was patrilocal, which meant that the in-marrying spouse established residence within the compound of the husband's kin. For the matrilineal Ashanti, another group shown by Curtin to be numerically significant among the enslaved population, marriage systems were matrilocal, with the in-marrying spouse coming to live in the compound of the wife's kin. This emphasis on bonds of consanguinity, especially in relation to residence, may very well have exerted a formative influence on the emergence of family groupings built around "two- or three-generational clusters of 'blood relatives' (such as a woman and her adult daughters and their children)", as Sudarkasa suggests.[31] This type of family formation, which was not restricted to female relatives, was very much in evidence in the strife-torn tenancy landscape of post-slavery Jamaica and in the aftermath of Morant Bay; sources from that time make fairly frequent references to family units comprised of grandfathers or grandmothers residing with their adult children and their grandchildren.[32] Such family formations may also have been explicable within the context of socio-economic necessity or may have been the expression of preferential positions which had nothing to do with a West African cultural legacy. Nevertheless, ties of consanguinity served to bond family members otherwise separated across estates (trans-residential networks) and in many instances proved, as they had in West Africa, to be vital networks of mutual support. The strength of these bonds of consanguinity as well as conjugality was demonstrated by the increased stipendiary reports of family visits beyond estate boundaries during the apprenticeship, by efforts to reconstitute families separated by enslavement and by the impressive record of black family advocacy in general, which permeated the entire period under review.

Bush emphasizes that "polygynous marriage among slaves", that is, the practice of men having several wives at the same time, "was essentially a direct cultural inheritance from Africa".[33] John Mbiti notes that polygyny, a widespread though not universal feature of West African familial culture, was an index of social status and productivity, both in a biological and economic context, as well as a link to immortality.[34] Studies of the enslaved population of Jamaica, done mainly by Higman, have pointed to the relatively rare transfer of polygyny from West African cultures to Jamaica, a situation which Higman attributes to a multiplicity of factors, including the demographic selectivity of the slave trade and limitations placed upon the re-creation of African family forms by the exigencies of enslavement and by the process of creolization itself. Nevertheless, wherever there were polygynous unions among the enslaved population, as on Montpelier plantation, these may have reflected the influence of West African traditions, as the husband and co-wives were sometimes from the same ethnic background and there was sometimes evidence of the West African practice of residential separation of mates.[35] In the post-slavery period, the continued impact of generational separation from Africa and the twin influences of creolization and the Christianizing mission no doubt contributed to the further diminution of the formal polygynous model. Significantly, too, as will be discussed in chapter 6, the extension of anti-bigamy laws to the freed population contributed to the virtual disappearance of formal polygyny in the later post-slavery period.

The encompassing force in traditional West African societies was the profound devotion to kinship, that is, affinity derived through blood ties or through conjugal bonds. The kinship system not only established connectivity horizontally to everyone in any local group, as Mbiti indicates, but it also extended vertically to "include the departed and those yet to be born".[36] Thus, the kinship system reinforced the West African reverence for ancestors and the significance attached to the birth of children as the vital channel for the perpetuation of the community. This centrality of kinship ties, although not unique to West African societies, was perhaps the most widespread and durable cultural transfer from West Africa to the Caribbean. Despite the fact that most West Africans who were subjected to forced migration came to this region without members of their families, the importance of kinship as a socially cementing force led not only to the re-creation of biological affinity networks over time, but also to the adoption of "fictive kin" by the enslaved and by the freed. This process of integrating persons not known to be biological relatives into the wider group or community allowed for the emergence of vital support groups among the enslaved and freed black communities.[37]

A related principle which characterized West African familial culture and which proved to be an enduring practice among black families in freedom was what Sudarkasa refers to as the "notion of commitment to the collectivity".[38] In pre-colonial West Africa, this precept was centred in the extended family, which was the medium of support for the entire community during crises as well as on an ongoing basis. An important example of collective responsibility enacted was the involvement of the extended family, and indeed the entire compound, in the socialization of the young.[39] Transferred to the Caribbean, "commitment to the collectivity" found continued expression in networks of familial support and family advocacy; in collective activism by communities of parents on issues such as education, health and welfare of children; and in the continued involvement of the extended family and the entire community in the upbringing of children.

While respect for elders was certainly not unique to West African societies, this was an intrinsic feature of the traditional West African world view, especially as advanced age was an index of imminent entry into the honoured world of the ancestral spirits.[40] This reverence for the elderly was sustained during the period of enslavement, and, as will be demonstrated by this assessment, freed blacks continued to express respect for and extend familial care to their elders. However, this work also takes into consideration the increased reports by the 1840s of neglect of elderly family members and the complaints by some parents, especially by the 1860s, of their inability to control their children. These issues are discussed further in chapter 6.

Given the West African emphasis on the vertical links of kinship, which include those as yet unborn, great significance was consequently attached to childbirth and children as the essential means by which the life force was continued. This value was reflected in the bond which emerged not only between biological parents and their children, but also between the entire community and the children within it, who became, as discussed before, the collective responsibility of the compound. Importantly, too, the bond between mother and child was extremely close, and the custom, widespread in West Africa, of delayed weaning reflected the desire to maintain this bond. Using contemporary descriptions of family-related traditions in eighteenth-century West Africa, Herbert Klein and Stanley Engerman conclude that this practice of prolonged breastfeeding was characteristic of many traditional, pre-colonial West African societies and that the period of lactation was generally extended for two to three years. Klein and Engerman point to the conviction among women that delayed weaning facilitated the child's welfare, stemming from a belief that nursing reduced the chances of conception. They also indicate the existence of strong sexual taboos which encouraged abstinence during the period of lactation, thereby reinforcing the argument that women delayed weaning to allow for maximum care of the young child.[41] Both Bush and Higman emphasize the continuance under slavery of the mother-child bond, the persistence of delayed weaning and communal responsibility for the welfare of children.[42]

As evidenced in this analysis, the close ties between mother and child were embodied in maternal advocacy, especially but not exclusively during the apprenticeship, and the welfare of children continued as the paramount feature of parental activism during the entire period under review. Thus, while not a uniquely West African familial trait, the primacy of children's well-being and the profound parent-child bond persisted as post-slavery familial values. It should not be concluded, however, that parental devotion was universal among blacks, and the increasing reports of child neglect, especially after the 1840s, may have been more explicable within the context of socio-economic conditions than as a commentary on the presence, or lack thereof, of African derivatives.

Given the dominance of consanguinity over conjugality in West Africa, marriage there was characterized by the affinity of both spouses to their respective extended families and by the residence of extended kin integrated into the compound. As Joyce Ladner notes, marriage was regarded as a "ritual that occurred not between two individuals alone, but between all the members of the two extended families".[43] Moreover, as Mbiti points out, marriage in West Africa was seen as an ongoing process which was only complete after the first child was born or after the marriage presents were paid or, in some cases, after the first children were married. Societies such as the Ashanti-Fanti allowed trial marriages provided that both sets of parents approved, and premarital sex was permitted within this setting. Mutual consent was the basis for termination of trial marriages.[44]

In spite of an initial upsurge in Christian marriage among freed blacks, the general trend during the period under review was a style of family organization that differed from the European norm of Christian legal marriage. Given the foundational influence of West African traditions, it is quite possible that when blacks lived in unions not formalized by Christian, legal ties, this may have represented, for some, a continuation of the tradition of culturally derived trial marriages discussed earlier.

Additionally, longevity of marital unions was a prominent feature of traditional West African familial culture. As Sudarkasa indicates, marital unions in matrilineal societies were usually terminated only by spousal death, in spite of the facility with which divorces were obtainable in those societies. In patrilineal societies, the tradition of "returning bride-wealth payments upon dissolution of marriage" was a major inhibiting factor against termination.[45] Irrespective of whether blacks in post-slavery Jamaica organized their families according to Euro-Christian norms or not, the evidence suggests that many unions, as late as 1882, continued to reflect this quality of endurance, as they had in West Africa. However, whether this was a function of African retentions or simply a reflection of individuals' commitment remains difficult to ascertain.

Generally, the relative ease with which divorce could be obtained in most traditional West African societies stood in significant contrast to European familial conventions, in which divorce was an extremely rare occurrence. In most West African societies, both men and women had equal access to divorce on grounds such as failure to provide sexual satisfaction, infertility, especially on the part of the wife, and cruelty on the part of the husband.[46] In the British Caribbean, given the Euro-Christian endorsement of the permanency of marriage without universal recourse to divorce (at least before the Divorce Law of 1879), it was hardly surprising that Christian, legal marriage was viewed by some blacks in the post-slavery period as a deprivation of their freedom and was widely resisted as a medium for the formation of conjugal unions.[47]

In West Africa, the priority accorded to consanguinity was reflected in the fact that it was the consanguineous core group which owned or had the right of usufruct over the land. Generally, spouses were not allowed to inherit land from each other.[48] The principle of inheritance of land through the consanguineous line bore similarity to what Jean Besson identifies as the tradition of "family land" in post-slavery Jamaica, a practice which she has shown to persist into the twentieth century. As defined by Besson, this tradition originated when the freed people decreed, both by custom and oral tradition, that freehold land which they had originally acquired by purchase should be preserved for the usage of all descendants of the kin group in perpetuity. Succeeding generations of the kin group had rights to cultivate and harvest the produce of the land, and each generation was entrusted with the responsibility of maintaining the land for use by their descendants. Besson challenges Edith Clarke's thesis that family land was derived from African cultural heritage, specifically an Ashanti tradition, and argues instead that this was a Caribbean creation, explained by the desires of the freed people to "protect their descendants against the constraints of post-emancipation Jamaican agrarian relations, and to provide them with an everlasting symbol of freedom . . . and personhood".[49]

These two interpretations of the origins of family land are decidedly not mutually exclusive. The strategy of family land, developed by the freed people to claim autonomy and ensure the future well-being of the extended kinship group, may very well have been culturally connected to their societies of origin. Issues of Ashanti derivation aside, the origins of family land as posited by Besson present indubitable evidence of the continuance of a crucial feature of West African familial culture: the primacy of kinship ties. This is seen in the freed

Figure 2. *Hut on the Summit, Blue Mountain Peak.* Cousins Hereward Postcard Collection, reprinted courtesy of the University of the West Indies Library, Mona.

people's motivation to preserve access to family land for future generations of kin in perpetuity. The West African influence seems all the more evident in view of the fact that in Jamaica, as in West Africa, family land was not subject to spousal inheritance but was made accessible to succeeding generations of consanguineous kin. It is also clear that this primacy of kinship ties found lasting expression in the deep sense of attachment among the enslaved to the grounds around their huts, which they regarded not only as "the common property of the extended family", but also as the burial places of their kin. Post-slavery family land continued to be the burial location for extended kin members, representing, therefore, a culturally derived tradition of reverence for and connectivity to the ancestors. As such, these lands became symbols of "family unity and continuity".[50] This cultural and economic significance of land, whether it was family land or individually owned, persisted for the entire period under investigation and was exemplified in the anguished testimony of so many who suffered loss of property during the targeted suppression of blacks in the aftermath of the Morant Bay uprising.

Conceptualizing the Black Family

Making valid conclusions about the black Jamaican family in the period under review rests predominantly on utilizing a conceptual framework whose parameters are not derived solely from a Western point of reference. Indeed, to analyse the family lives of people of African descent through a lens that perceives a co-resident nuclear union bound by Euro-Christian legal marriage as the norm results, at best, in a misconception of black family culture. As seen in the introduction to this book, the use of such a limited perspective in analysing black families (by contemporary observers and by some historians and sociologists) has led to a dismissive stereotyping of other methods of familial organization as dysfunctional, abnormal and unstable.

For the purposes of this work on the black family in freedom, a more inclusive conceptual framework has been adopted. Therefore, the nuclear family form bound by Christian, legal marriage as well as the nuclear family form bound by mutual consent and commitment (the informal nuclear form) are both important in conceptualizing the family. The perseverance over time of the informal nuclear form indicates that from the perspective of many blacks, this form was legitimated both by custom and by mutual assent and, as seen earlier, may even have been for some a symbol of African-derived cultural representation. Persistent Euro-Christian opposition to the informal nuclear union detracted neither from its importance to family members nor from the degree of commitment which they exhibited. Whereas sociological assessment in particular viewed informal nuclear families as fragmentary and chaotic,[51] more recent historical evaluation has endorsed the commitment which blacks displayed to this family form. Thus, Patrick Bryan categorizes unions outside of Christian, legal marriage as "the pragmatic functional marriage . . . widely practiced among the black and coloured classes of Jamaica" and argues that these unions displayed "commitment to permanence" as well as "commitment to family".[52]

Higman's study of the enslaved population also revealed another feature which is crucial to the conceptualization of the family. Some of the family units, he notes, were non-co-residential, or "visiting"; that is, the members did not live together in the same residence and were usually separated across estates by the exigencies of enslavement.[53] More often than not, these were couples who either were married (by Nonconformist missionaries, for the most part) or were partners in a relationship outside of Christian marriage but considered themselves married in terms of their commitment to each other. Visiting unions may have been interpreted by writers such as Frazier and Henriques as illustrative of the "disorganized" nature of slave unions, but when enslaved family members risked the harsh consequences of venturing off their estate for purposes of visiting their loved ones, this surely reflected their belief in the strength of their family ties despite the separation that enforced non-co-residence imposed upon them. In a more expansive conceptualization of the meaning of the term "family", these non-co-residential unions would indeed be included. Beginning in 1834, efforts by apprenticed couples and other family members who had been domiciled on separate estates to reunite and consolidate their families also indicated a recognition on their part that co-residence was crucial to the strengthening of their family ties.

Especially in the context of the foregoing discussion on African-derived family forms, any attempt at clarifying the concept of the black family must take into account the variety of extended families which existed during enslavement and which were sustained throughout the period under consideration. In this regard, both Sidney Mintz and Bush have emphasized the need to separate the concept of household – that is, the occupants of a house – from the concept of family.[54] Not all occupants of a house were family and not all members of a family resided in the same household, as demonstrated by the extended family networks which were separated by residence. Importantly, therefore, for purposes of conceptualization, a family may include consanguineous kin or blood relatives residing in separate houses (trans-residential or non-co-residential), whether in proximity or not; these comprised what Bush termed "the true extended family which forms a complex non-co-residential kinship network".[55]

Also important to the concept of family is what Bush outlines as "the extended . . . co-residential family unit". Given the African-derived importance of consanguineous ties over those of conjugality, this arrangement did not require the presence of a conjugal couple for validation as a family unit. Rather, the members were usually related across generations and lived in one household, as in Bush's example of a grandmother, mother and child comprising a family unit.[56] Sometimes there were variations on this model, and, especially in the strife-torn environment of post-slavery tenancy disputes, this extended co-residential family unit at times included a couple (legally married or not) along with their children and grandchildren.[57]

Higman indicates that the existence during slavery of single-parent families was observed mainly among female coloured house slaves who bore children for whites, but who themselves hardly ever formed stable relationships with black or coloured slaves.[58] Within the post-slavery context, single-parent units persisted, most often consisting of mothers and their children, the absent parent being accounted for by a variety of factors such as spousal death, desertion or out-migration. These single-parent units, described by Higman as "truncated nuclear families",[59] were an important component of an inclusive conceptualization of the meaning of family. The practice of adopting "fictive kin", noted earlier, was evident not only during the period of enslavement but also in the post-slavery period, in the responses of some black Jamaicans to a perceived need to extend a hand of kindness. By developing a support system of "relatives", black Jamaicans, in freedom as in slavery, signified that they accepted a broader concept of family, not bound by biological or conjugal ties but by force of circumstance. In the post-slavery context, this practice may well have found expression in the sense of community responsibility or commitment to the collective interest which allowed some blacks to promote the well-being of persons, especially children, who seemed in need of help. Witnesses testifying before the Commission of Inquiry upon the Condition of the Juvenile Population of Jamaica in 1877 (hereafter, Commission on the Juvenile Population) emphasized that blacks living in the same yard routinely looked after each other's children, when in need.[60]

Relational Issues within the Black Family in the Post-Slavery Period

REPRESENTATIONS OF BLACK PARENTHOOD: PERCEPTIONS VERSUS REALITY

Characteristic of the racist, elitist literature of Edward Long and Mrs A.C. Carmichael, among others, were their negative representations of the parental capabilities of black men and women. In seeking to demonstrate his view that people of African descent were intrinsically inferior and, by contrast with European parents, ineffectual, Long declared that black parents displayed an animal-like barbarity towards their children and represented them as characteristically neglectful.[61] In a similar vein, Carmichael stereotyped enslaved mothers as "cruelly harsh" to their children and neglectful of their maternal responsibilities.[62] Similar sentiments were expressed by Bryan Edwards, who categorized enslaved mothers in particular as derelict in parental responsibilities and lacking in "maternal affection towards children".[63] As detailed fully in chapter 2, the termination of slavery as of 1 August 1834 provided the legal context in which apprenticed mothers could strengthen their activism on behalf of their children. Although these mothers were no longer enslaved, their roles as nurturers and caregivers were endangered by the withdrawal of customary indulgences and by the labour maximization policies of estate management. In clear contradiction of the contemporary perceptions outlined earlier, they aggressively agitated against these infringements on their ability to care for their children.

Nigel Bolland notes that slavery entailed "the loss of control by the labourer not only over his labour but also over his person, and even his (and her) children".[64] Much of the advocacy in which black parents engaged during this period was explicable by their desire to reassert and confirm dominion over their children's lives and welfare, an objective which these parents viewed as integral to their realization of personhood within the context of freedom. In introducing the theme of black parental activism, this work has deliberately aggregated the concept of parents, precisely because the evidence from the period supports the argument that both mothers and fathers were instrumental in pursuing the well-being of their children. The various forms of evidence of parental advocacy – among them, the virtually universal refusal of apprenticed parents in Jamaica to agree to estate management's demands to apprentice their free children, the persistent efforts of parents to ensure optimal conditions in education and health care for their children (the subject of detailed discussion in chapter 2) and their refusal to support schemes for confining their children to industrial education (discussed in chapter 4) – all negate the stereotypical assertions of black parental indifference.[65] According to Eric Foner, similar initiatives on the part of black parents in the post-slavery American South reflected the conviction that "liberating their families from the authority of whites was an indispensable element of freedom".[66]

The "Marginalization of the Black Male" in the Family

Within the wider historiographical context, Errol Miller's marginalization thesis has been applied to the historical period under examination. Miller argues that the process of enslavement relegated both men and women to a position of insignificance or marginalization in the minds of the enslavers. He further posits that within the context of dominant white patriarchy activated under slavery and continued during apprenticeship and thereafter, black men were perceived by whites as a bigger threat than black women and were therefore subjected to a greater degree of suppression and marginalization. Black men were thus rendered ineffectual and inconsequential, especially as fathers within their families.[67] The marginalization thesis was reflected in assessments such as Patterson's, which states that under enslavement, "the male could not assert his authority as a husband or as a father. . . . The net result of all this was the complete demoralization of the Negro male. . . . It is no wonder that the male slave came to lose all pretensions to masculine pride and to develop the irresponsible parental . . . attitudes that are to be found even today."[68] This view of the black male as marginal in the context of the family became thematic in the historical discourse. Thus, Ladner posits that under conditions of enslavement and domination, "men were denied the right to fulfil the long-standing tradition of patriarch . . . and women, in effect, became the backbone of the family".[69] Emancipation, according to this perspective, did not signal the end of the black male's insignificance within the family, and what had originated as a marginal- ization imposed by the condition of enslavement became, for some observers, a behavioural characteristic of black males. Within this perspective, analyses of the familial role of the black male emanating from the contemporaneous literature were similar in message, though transmitted within the confines of a racist, elitist ideology. Thus, James Anthony Froude, while alleging the "natural indolence" of blacks, cast the male in a marginal role with respect to both labour output and familial commitment. Froude argued that the women were left to care for the children, "the men disclaiming all responsibilities on that score, after the babies have been once brought into the world".[70]

Twentieth- and twenty-first-century assessments of household structure, emphasizing the dominance of female-headed households, have supported the view of the negligible role of the male in the family, both in historical and socio-contemporary settings. Erna Brodber describes this diminished role in her remarks on Edith Clarke's book about family life in Jamaica, *My Mother Who Fathered Me*: "By its very title . . . [it] announced that the Jamaican black male is indeed . . . invisible and . . . worthless".[71] In seeking to explain the seeming marginality of the black male in the enslaved family, both Bush and Higman caution that the custom among British Caribbean slave owners of omitting enslaved fathers' names from plantation lists would very well have obscured the real significance of the enslaved man within the family.[72] Certainly, this practice was part of a wider philosophy on the part of slaveholders; because they had no vested interest in emphasizing black fatherhood, they had little to say about it. In this respect, white patriarchy helped to marginalize black fathers. Since the status of enslaved children was determined by masters, black enslaved men were relegated to a legal position of unimportance in the equation. Consequently, as Hilary Beckles concludes, "Slavery, as a socio-legal status, completely marginalized and alienated fatherhood, and focused its attention upon motherhood."[73]

Significantly, this raises the issue of the "invisibility" of the black male in family contexts in sources which comment on slavery, apprenticeship and the post-slavery period. Compared to the black woman, the black man in the family was indeed rendered marginal and largely invisible in sources from the periods of enslavement and apprenticeship, which were generated from a plantocratic perspective; far less was said about black men as husbands, partners and fathers than was said about black women as wives, partners and mothers. This may have been the reflection of white patriarchy's designation of black men as unimportant in the context of the family. However, as the apprenticeship wore on into "full free", the Euro-missionary agenda of promulgating a new gender order in which the black male would assume his "rightful place" as patriarch of the family had important implications for the visibility of the black man in familial contexts. As he communicated his views mainly to missionaries and stipendiary magistrates on his roles as husband, partner, son, father and grandfather and within other familial contexts, the black male as a family man increasingly found his way into the sources. However, because historians have written more about the black female than the black male in the familial environment during both the apprenticeship and post-slavery periods, the black male has also been subjected, as Beckles suggests, to a historiography of neglect in this context, hence reinforcing his apparent marginalization within the family in this period.[74]

It is therefore of importance to the historiography to unearth and assess evidence which may address this imbalance and which may indeed bring greater visibility to the black male within familial contexts during the period under review. Christine Barrow presents, albeit within a twentieth-century setting, a conceptual paradigm which facilitates such an undertaking. Barrow rejected the structural functional concept of family as the "co-resident unit of mother, father and children" and instead explored "extended family relations . . . such as that between an adult son and his mother, or between adult siblings, in which men are anything but marginal". With this approach, rather than uncovering more suggestions of male marginality, Barrow found that masculinity was "valorized . . . in familial roles of conjugal partner, son, grandfather, brother".[75] Having utilized a similar conceptual paradigm for exploring familial interactions among blacks within the period 1834–82, this work presents abundant evidence that the black male was anything but the ineffectual and inconsequential family member that he was alleged to be.

Thus, this undertaking seeks to do, in the historical setting of the apprenticeship and post-slavery periods, what scholars like Barrow and Brodber have done in their showcasing of a more modern-day male activism within the family setting. Indeed, George Beckford's introduction to Brodber's twenty-first-century study of the Jamaican male, *Standing Tall*, appropriately captured the essence

Figure 3. *Native Wedding Party, Jamaica, W.I.* Cousins Hereward Postcard Collection, reprinted courtesy of the University of the West Indies Library, Mona.

of black male initiatives on behalf of family, not only in today's Jamaica, but in the Jamaica of over a century and a half ago: "What comes out of the evidence . . . is a commitment to family . . . that is . . . strong empirical negation of the traditional view of the Jamaican (and West Indian) man in the family – of black men being irresponsible, lazy, shiftless. . . . There is no evidence of laziness; they go out and hustle, work where they can, work hard and save . . . make their own little family and look about their children."[76] What is particularly instructive is that the Jamaican black men whom Brodber interviewed for this work, who were born between 1883 and 1911, were the descendants of enslaved African arrivants, and as such, their continued demonstration of commitment to their families' welfare is a testament to the endurance over time of this familial value that was transmitted to the Caribbean by their ancestors.

Black over White: Black Attitudes towards Family Organization

In general, the plantocratic emphasis on labour extraction during slavery had contributed to elite (white) society's disregard for the importance of the family to blacks. Indeed, the adoption of pro-natalist policies by property managers after 1807 was more a reflection of the latter's interest in increasing the enslaved population than an expression of concern about the welfare of the enslaved family. However, slaveholders' impending loss of control over their slaves, and the "inevitable descent into barbarism" which white society feared would result from blacks' departure from the "civilizing" milieu of the estates and livestock farms after emancipation, prompted an upsurge of reforming interest in the family life of blacks. From the perspective of the colonial authorities, religious bodies and white elites in general, the adoption of European family forms and values by newly freed people was essential to the maintenance of hegemony and social order. Indeed, as emphasized by Henrice Altink, the concern on the part of the Colonial Office and the governor regarding the challenges posed to apprenticed couples by planters' policies was prompted more by a desire to maintain socio-economic stability and productivity under the apprenticeship system than by a genuine interest in the family lives of the apprentices.[77] These planter-generated obstacles to family life are discussed in chapter 2 of this work.

Maintenance of social order therefore relied on the adoption by the formerly enslaved of "civilized habits", especially with respect to their family lives. As Verene Shepherd points out, the emphasis in the post-slavery period was on missionary dissuasion of black family forms, which were perceived as conducive to "immoral" living, and on the promotion of the Victorian idealized family based on Christian marriage, which was conversely seen as the disseminator of "civilized" habits.[78] Importantly, this missionary quest to inculcate Euro-Christian norms was based on a cultural foundation which, as Catherine Hall suggests, refused "to recognize an existing black culture".[79] In the immediate post-slavery years, although the colonial government relied heavily on the missionaries' activities as a medium for the spread of Eurocentric family values, this effort was gradually reinforced by legislative measures designed to facilitate the adoption, by blacks in particular, of these idealized patterns and values. As the century wore on, the colonial authorities, confronted both by the growing "scourge of illegitimacy" and by the waning European missionary influence, resorted to greater reliance on legislation designed to proliferate Eurocentric family norms. Despite the many elitist efforts to transform their familial culture, most blacks continued to adhere to their own family forms and values, some of which, as discussed earlier, reflected a cultural derivation from West Africa. Moore and Johnson underscore the significance of the effort by the colonial authorities to influence the family organization of blacks, arguing that "sex, marriage and family . . . represented a powerful and resilient expression of cultural self-determination".[80]

From the late 1860s onwards, the comparative plethora of family legislation was directed predominantly at the "constituency of blacks". This group constituted the mass of the population and was still perceived by elite society and colonial officials as being in need of cultural reformation. Bryan notes that by the late nineteenth century, they were no longer merely "former slaves" but "the 'subject people' to be systematically 'civilized' ".[81] Irrespective of white society's continued efforts to fashion the black family to the parameters of Victorian Christian morality, however, blacks had well-defined ideas of how they should organize their family units and of the principles by which they should guide their families. Throughout the period under consideration, most blacks demonstrated a proclivity for informal nuclear unions, those based upon mutual consent rather than on Christian, legal marriage or, after 1879, on civil forms of legal marriage.[82] Reasons given by blacks for their preference included the ease with which their own unions could be terminated in the virtual absence of legal divorce before 1879.[83] A related explanation, and one which was frequently given by black women during slavery and as late as the 1870s, was their concern that legal marriage may have given the man "license to ill-treat or beat" them.[84] In this respect, Bush's observation that the African-derived marriage forms adopted by some blacks gave the women "more independence of action and equality in status, especially with respect to divorce"[85] underlines an idea that seems to have held great sway during this period.

Blacks placed great emphasis on the importance of their attachments and on the durability of their unions. Elite society's designation of their family arrangements as "faithful concubinage" unwittingly underscored their familial devotion and longevity. Some black couples voiced the view that having lived together for many years and having produced many children, they saw "no difference" between their unions and legal marriage,[86] thereby, in their eyes, legitimizing their unions. It could also be argued that many black Jamaicans who lived in these informal unions did not deem it necessary to gain legitimation from white society and so did not feel a sense of urgency to obtain the "legitimacy" that the middle and upper classes craved. From missionary and stipendiary reports of the upsurge in Christian marriages in the immediate post-slavery period, however, it is clear that some among the black population needed this legitimation by white society, as they had internalized the dominant European norm. Yet for some, economic concerns – particularly costs associated with weddings, including the governor's licence, the fee charged by the marriage officer and a body of expenses attached to dress and entertainment of the wedding guests – acted as a deterrent to the formal wedding ceremony. As indicated by Moore and Johnson, contemporary commentary on the issue from writers like William Livingstone concluded that many blacks refrained from formal marriage or postponed the ceremony because they simply could not afford the extravagant weddings put on by white society, and they did not wish to experience the social embarrassment which Livingstone assumed would result from "a poor man's wedding".[87] The idea that legal marriage invested the parties involved with "an air of respectability" was in evidence among some blacks during the period under analysis. This perspective was represented by some female apprentices, who, while defending their right to be treated as persons of dignity, objected to being deprived of the level of respect which they believed was due to married women.[88] The fact that by the 1870s, older blacks sometimes complained about the failure of some members of the younger generation to follow the example set by their elders and marry in the Christian, legal sense indicates that, at least for some members of this older generation, the passage of time and the process of creolization had resulted in the internalization of European-derived norms.[89]

Conclusion

Efforts by the colonial state, the church and missionary bodies to influence the forms by which blacks chose to organize their families clearly proved successful with some blacks over the years, as those who chose to do so within the parameters of Euro-Christian legal marriage had apparently accepted the culturally dominant norm which associated "the married state" with respectability and social acceptance. There were, however, some who remained unaffected by white society's mission to impose cultural conformity upon them for several reasons, as noted here, largely of a socio-cultural nature.

Regardless of the familial forms they chose, the fact remains that blacks of this period were exercising what to their minds was an important attribute of freedom: the right to choose their respective paths. Also irrespective of family form, they exhibited an enduring interest in familial goals and principles, many of which represented both the legacy of and the link with their societies of cultural origin in West Africa. As seen in the foregoing discussion, they prioritized plans to reconstruct their families and to pursue courses of action consonant with their well-being. They also expressed their intent to ensure the material welfare of their elderly and infirm relatives, a value system in keeping with the West African respect for seniority. In 1837, in response to a query by visiting anti-slavery writers James Thome and J. Horace Kimball as to how they expected to treat the old and infirm after full freedom, a male apprentice from St Thomas-in-the-East informed them that "we will support dem – as how dey brought us up when we was pickaninny, and now we come trong, must care for dem".[90] As discussed earlier, however, increased reports during the 1860s and 1870s of neglect of the elderly by relatives indicate that the reality was not always in keeping with the intent, and worsening economic circumstances no doubt contributed to this.[91] Yet conclusions made by other social observers – such as Methodist minister Reverend William Griffiths, who commented that after prolonged "interaction with the poor", he had seen "a good deal that is very commendable in the disposition of the Black people to help their fathers and mothers", and also noted the tendency of blacks who had migrated to Limon, Port-au-Prince and Navy Bay to support "their old people" in Jamaica – show that attachment to kin and willingness to honour familial commitments remained strong in spite of hard times and cases of neglect.[92] There is considerable evidence, too, that blacks accorded this "hand of care" to others within their extended families, their communities and indeed to those whom they regarded as their "wider family".[93]

Chapter 2

Black Activation of Freedom through Family Advocacy, 1834–1882

> Mr Barrett ordered busha to break our house . . . they broke part of the house in which my mother, Rosy Shaw lives. . . . I and my mother and husband were sitting in the house. . . . [They] only left the wall.
>
> *– Extract from deposition by Euphemia Smith, former slave, in an action of trespass brought against Schawfield Estate personnel by the Smith family, 1838*[1]

IN HER COMPARATIVE STUDY OF post-slavery societies, Rebecca Scott highlighted one of the most dynamic features of recent historical scholarship on the period: namely, that "monolithic portraits of . . . marginalization are superseded by accounts that emphasize negotiation, initiative and choice".[2] Indeed, the works of historians Nigel Bolland, Bridget Brereton, Woodville Marshall, Rebecca Scott and Swithin Wilmot,[3] among others, have provided invaluable assessments of the active roles of the freed peoples of the Caribbean in shaping the legacy of emancipation. An intrinsic component of this black activation of freedom was the phenomenon of family advocacy. For the purposes of this analysis, the term "family advocacy" denotes two salient features of black family strategy evident in the post-slavery period. First, in contexts external to the judicial system, family members constantly voiced their convictions, acted and struggled, with varying outcomes, in an attempt to prioritize and ensure the well-being of their families. In this way, the freed people acted as advocates for their family members. Second, with the avenue of judicial recourse having been opened to the formerly enslaved as of 1 August 1834, freed blacks began to advance the welfare of their families within the arena of the courts. In so doing, they developed and utilized what Scott described as "a new set of relationships to legal persons and to the legal process", thereby constructing a new sense of "legal personhood".[4]

Black forms of striving for attainment of family concerns did not originate after 1 August 1834, and indeed, as argued in chapter 1, black family activism both before and after 1834 was a significant indicator of the primacy of kinship ties as part of an enduring cultural legacy. The enslavers had sought to deprive blacks of autonomy over their personal lives, but in spite of this, as seen in the work of Barbara Bush and others, they were able to implement a variety of strategies to facilitate the welfare of their kin, such as delayed weaning and escaping the plantation to meet family members.[5] Because of the severe limitations imposed by plantation hegemony, and by virtue of being chattel, the enslaved were never the ultimate arbiters of their families' fate. However, the abolition of slavery in 1834 provided blacks with a more liberal legal framework within which they could attempt to secure their families' well-being. Section 49 of the Jamaica Abolition Act specified the judicial avenues through which apprentices could do so. Thus, they were entitled to lodge complaints against the parties entitled to their services, before one or more special justices. The same act also established the right of apprentices to proceed in the Supreme Court or assize courts, the courts of quarter sessions or the courts of common pleas. The predominant judicial medium used by apprentices to ensure family interests was the appeal to the special magistrates (also referred to as stipendiary magistrates and special justices) and the courts of these special magistrates. Although apprentices could themselves take their cases to the higher courts, special magistrates were usually the facilitators in this respect, reporting cases of a more serious nature (requiring a penalty in excess of five pounds or five days' imprisonment) to the governor, who sometimes advised the attorney general to seek an indictment to further pursue the case. However, the likelihood was great that the planter-affiliated juries of these higher courts would, as William Burn suggests, return a verdict more in accordance with "their political convictions than with the evidence".[6] Some black family members during the apprenticeship also undertook group visits to solicitors' offices to pursue their causes, although the evidence shows that this was not a commonly utilized strategy.

Appeals to stipendiary magistrates, despite the fact that they were not all sympathetic to the causes of black families, continued to be a focal point for family advocacy in the post-apprenticeship period. However, both a drastic reduction in their numbers over time and a decreased dependence on stipendiary reports by the British government contributed to the abatement of this medium by the late 1850s and early 1860s. In the post-slavery period, the assize courts, the courts of quarter sessions, the courts of appeal (1841), the Supreme Court, the later circuit courts (1855) and the district courts (1867) provided alternative judicial channels for black families. However, the expense and tedium involved in using these courts and the dominance of planter-affiliated judges contributed to the elusive nature of justice for blacks and their families. The fact that they persevered in their efforts to be the beneficiaries of the judicial system, and that they were at times successful in championing the rights of their families through this medium, underscores the extent of blacks' commitment to self, family and community.

Evidence of non-judicial striving by ex-slaves on behalf of their families is abundant during the entire period of 1834–82, and this was most frequently implemented through the channels of civil disobedience, petitions and visits to the governor as well as other forms of protest action and cooperative efforts. Indeed, the hallmark of black family advocacy for this period was the prominence of self-help schemes among individual family members and cooperative ventures by groups of families working in tandem to achieve their best interest. Families, for example, collaborated in building schools, organized group visits to stipendiary magistrates and gave group endorsements to numerous petitions intended to address issues affecting their families, such as the absence of health-care facilities. This display of group family advocacy demonstrated the "commitment to the collective" that was characteristic of the West African tradition, as discussed in chapter 1. Indeed, the significant amount of evidence of family-related activism during this period may well be explained by Scott's observation that the freed people had prioritized family and community welfare over individual concerns.[7] At the same time, the search for family welfare and the attempt to establish individual interests were clearly interrelated; when families took action, whether separately or in groups, they no doubt realized that they were indeed ensuring individual security.

Family members also advanced their welfare and that of their relatives by testifying before commissions of inquiry, the outstanding examples being the commission convened at Brown's Town in 1837 and the Jamaica Royal Commission of 1866. Although judicial and non-judicial forms of family advocacy have been discussed as separate channels in this section, it is clear that the symbiotic relationship between the two sometimes resulted in legal action emanating from non-judicial family initiatives.

Explanations from this period of black engagement with the judicial system centred on the stereotypical representation of the freed blacks as exhibiting a childlike fascination with attendance at court, from which much entertainment was supposed to be derived. This was illustrated by the comments of stipendiary magistrate Thomas Dillon, who described the Jamaican peasant as the "most litigious" in the world and offered this as the explanation for the abundance of cases brought by freed people before the courts of petty sessions. Similar sentiments were expressed by stipendiary magistrate Charles Lake in 1854 when he argued that blacks displayed an excessive fondness for litigation. This elitist misreading of the motivating force behind the use of judicial advocacy by freed blacks continued to find expression in the work of William Burn in the 1930s. In attempting to explain the "litigiousness" of the blacks, he trivialized their reasons for taking an interest in the justice system, dismissing them as being motivated by the search for a "spectator sport" or the desire for a day off from work. However, when blacks confronted the justice system in an effort to improve the lot of their families, they did so not out of a love for litigation, but out of a recognition that access to justice was their due by virtue of being free persons. Blacks had a vision of what freedom should mean for them and for their families, and as Marshall observes, "they recognized that access to justice was an attribute of citizenship".[8]

External to the system of justice available through the official courts were the alternative "people's courts", most notably in St Thomas-in-the-East in the 1860s. Undoubtedly, the expense and difficulty experienced by blacks in pursuit of justice through the official courts influenced their recourse to these alternative courts. It seems highly likely that, as argued by Diana Paton, use of this medium may also have been influenced by the tradition of resolution of community disputes by enslaved headmen. In such a scenario, there may very well have been a cultural connection with the West African tradition of dispensing justice through the compound council of village elders.[9] Thus, within and without the justice system, from 1834 to 1882 freed blacks chose to be advocates for their families.

The Search for Dignity and Honour: Reclaiming Personhood through Family Advocacy, 1834–1838

A crucial issue facing the black family during the apprenticeship was the need to strengthen and reaffirm the dignity, honour and self-worth of individual members of the family, especially since they were no longer defined as "legal things". In essence, they were engaged in a mission to reclaim personhood. This issue applied especially, though not exclusively, to female members of the family, who during slavery and apprenticeship had been forced to bear the brunt of attacks upon the person, ranging from physical assault to sexual harassment and rape. Illustrative of this is Thomas Thistlewood's virtually uninterrupted history of sexual exploitation of enslaved women during his tenure as overseer of Egypt estate and owner of Breadnut Island Pen, respectively, in the second half of the eighteenth century.[10] There is abundant evidence that during the transitional period of apprenticeship, intended as it was to prepare the formerly enslaved to live as free persons (and, by extension, persons of dignity), black family members engaged in constant advocacy to challenge and overcome perceptions that they were lacking in dignity and honour, as they had been perceived while enslaved. The activism by black men and women in this respect demonstrated not only their commitment to their self-worth as family members, but also their conviction that as persons soon to be fully free, they had every right to seek redress for attacks upon themselves and their families. In particular, the fact that men, as partners, husbands and sons, sought to uphold the dignity of their female relatives was an indication that they certainly did not view themselves as marginal within their families, even in the system of semi-slavery that followed emancipation. Black men's agency on behalf of their women may also have indicated their adoption of the ideals of patriarchy, as they were in a sense initiating the process of reclaiming authority over the females in their families as they prepared for full freedom.

The case brought before the court of special magistrate C. Brown in October 1834 by Jane Robertson, a married apprentice attached to Moreland estate in Vere, is illustrative of this type of advocacy. In her complaint brought against Robert George Bruce, a medical practitioner on Moreland estate, she deposed that witnesses had informed her that while she was unconscious from a fainting spell in the hot house (a place on the estate where sick workers were taken for treatment), Dr Bruce had "thrown up her petticoats" and invited other men "to make use of her", promising them "half a dollar in return". Jane emphasized that she was a married woman, thereby indicating that she had been inculcated with the value system that equated dignity with the Christian married state, and declared that "everyone had seen her nakedness and that her feelings were hurt". In her testimony, she stated that "it was the doctor's duty to take her into a room and examine her privately and not to turn up her petticoats before everybody".[11] Clearly, Jane was asserting her claim to be treated with dignity and respect as a woman and as a wife. Although she had her husband's support in this, the fact that she had initiated this action of advocacy by herself, reporting the matter to the stipendiary magistrate, was an interesting departure from the patriarchal norm in which the male served as protector and spokesman for the woman. Brown, having determined that this "was a case of great importance to the state of society", suspended judgment on the issue and made a full report to Governor Sligo, who instructed the attorney general to bring an indictment against Dr Bruce for his treatment of Jane Robertson. Although the planter-affiliated grand jury of the Supreme Court of Judicature, St Jago de la Vega, returned a verdict of *Ignoramus*, signifying their rejection of the bill of indictment,[12] the fact that Jane Robertson's advocacy had resulted in her case being brought to the governor's attention was in itself an accomplishment.

Black family advocacy of this sort had a significant, albeit unacknowledged, impact on colonial government reaction, in Jane Robertson's case as well as in others discussed in this chapter: namely, the eventual dismissal from office of the offending party. It is clear that Sligo's decision in 1835 to strip Dr Bruce of his commission as a local magistrate "for highly indecent exposure of a female while in a state of insensibility" and for his "offers of reward to any person who would violate her while in that state" would not have occurred without the efforts of Jane Robertson to gain redress.[13] Both Special Magistrate Brown's and Governor Sligo's handling of the case indicated a degree of acceptance, at the official level, of the right of apprenticed family members to be treated with dignity. Sligo's actions here may also have reflected his desire to oversee the smooth unfolding of the "Great Experiment" of emancipation.

Brereton emphasized the significance of issues of physical abuse and sexual harassment to black families emerging from slavery when she noted that from their perspective, freedom, especially for women, signalled the right to assert autonomy over their bodies in contexts free of abuse and physical assault.[14] The experiences of one apprenticed couple illustrate this expectation which was held by many on the eve of full freedom. Larchim Bucknor, a black constable on Montrose estate, and his wife, Margaret Bucknor, a non-praedial apprentice attached to Rock River estate – both in St Mary – were, in 1835, especially concerned about the continuous sexual harassment and physical abuse of Margaret by Thornhill, the overseer of Rock River. Their case exemplifies the multifaceted nature of some black families' struggles to establish the well-being of their members, the perseverance which many exhibited in the face of daunting obstacles and the efforts of many apprenticed men (as well as women) to not only affirm the dignity and honour of family members, but also to reunite dispersed members of their family units.

Larchim Bucknor's initial strategy was to complain constantly to McNeil, the overseer on Montrose, about Thornhill's sexual harassment and physical abuse of Margaret and to ceaselessly appeal to McNeil to intercede on his wife's behalf with the abusive overseer of Rock River. Although McNeil made no effort at intercession, Larchim's persistent complaints eventually led to his being given a letter of appeal to Stipendiary Magistrate Marlton in Port Maria, but only after three months of disappointment. Prior to that point, aware of their rights under the law, husband and wife had both separately and jointly made several requests of Special Justice Jackson, under whose jurisdiction the case fell, to value Margaret Bucknor as a prelude to her husband's purchase of her full freedom. Larchim later testified that he had made repeated trips to see Jackson in this regard, only to be informed by the magistrate that he could not purchase his wife's freedom without first writing to the governor.

That Larchim and Margaret did not cease their efforts after receiving this information was indicative of both their recognition of their rights on this issue and their mutual commitment to a unified family, free from abuse. This second channel of advocacy resulted not only in Jackson's refusal to value Margaret, but also in his committing her to lengthy stays in the dungeon – on the first occasion, "for being a nuisance", and on the second, because her first stay "had not done her any good" (that is, her eight days' confinement had not encouraged her to cease her advocacy). In spite of these punitive measures, including having had all her hair cut off on Jackson's orders, Margaret and her husband tried a third avenue, that of appealing to Special Justices Lloyd and Thomas, both in St Mary, but were turned down on jurisdictional grounds.

Their final appeal to Marlton at Port Maria resulted in the latter reporting the case to Sligo, who ordered Marlton to hold an urgent hearing into the matter.

This rather prolonged struggle by the Bucknors, lasting several months in total, ultimately proved successful on multiple levels. Upon receipt of Marlton's report that Special Justice Jackson had not only failed to protect Margaret from her abuser but had also himself perpetuated the cycle of cruelty, Governor Sligo dismissed Jackson from the magistracy, a result directly linked to the advocacy of both husband and wife.[15] The couple's activism was also successful on a personal level, enabling the eventual valuation of Margaret by Marlton, the purchase of her full freedom, her removal from Rock River and a permanent reunion with her husband. Finally, in October 1835, Governor Sligo had Thornhill removed from his position as overseer of Rock River on the basis of the couple's testimony that he had threatened to place every obstacle in the path of Margaret's manumission.[16]

Outside of the stipendiary courts, apprentices acted to uphold their own dignity and that of their families by adopting principled positions, often at their own peril. Edward Fearon, adult son of Amaryllis Gale, both apprenticed to Dunbarton estate in St Ann, protested the undignified treatment of his mother by estate constables; he declared that his mother was a married woman and that "busha" had ordered her confined to the dungeon, but that they had no right to "turn up her clothes in that manner". Fearon was subsequently committed to the workhouse.[17] Similarly, Amelia Lawrence, married mother of four and apprentice at Penshurst in St Ann, consistently acted as her own advocate in the face of constant sexual harassment by the boatswain at the St Ann workhouse in 1837. Though she "felt much hurt about it as she was a married woman", she refused to submit to his requests, preferring to endure the additional punitive measures. In this affirmation of dignity, it is clear that many apprentices had imbibed the view that the married state (Christian marriage, in Amelia's case) entitled persons to additional regard and was an indication of some level of adaptation to the dominant norm. As discussed in chapter 1, blacks often displayed commitment to the collective welfare and to a sense of kinship ties, values transferred from West African communities, which led them to prioritize the well-being of "fictive" as well as biological kin. This was clear in Amelia Lawrence's commitment to upholding dignity and self-respect not just for herself, but for others who apparently had no one to advocate on their behalf. Thus, when one of the estate workers wished to have "improper connexion" with a young girl named Catherine, Amelia pretended that Catherine was her daughter in order to protect her from his unwelcomed advances.[18]

It is evident from these examples that in the transitional period of the apprenticeship, some estate personnel continued to perceive the apprentices as lacking in both dignity and honour. It is equally clear, however, that apprenticed family members were operating from a different perspective, one in which they identified themselves as individuals of worth and, by a variety of strategies, acted to uphold this vision of self and family.

Their Free Children Above All Else: Parental Advocacy, 1834–1838

Black devotion to the importance and centrality of family was epitomized by parental advocacy during the period of apprenticeship. The care and nurturing of children has perennially been regarded as essential to the development of a strong family life, and this perspective characterized much of black parental advocacy during this period. A polarity of views, by estate management on the one hand and apprenticed parents on the other, relating to three main issues – attempts to apprentice free children, exclusion of free children from estate medical care and the withdrawal of traditional privileges from pregnant women, nursing mothers and mothers of six or more children – provided the staging ground for parental advocacy during the apprenticeship period. The Imperial Act of Abolition, in legislating the immediate freedom of children under six years of age as of 1 August 1834, and in providing for the apprenticeship until twenty-one years of age of any child not "properly supported" by his or her parents, highlighted the issue of the free children. Estate management, driven by labour maximization policies and by a perception that apprenticed parents were bringing up their free children "in idleness", adopted measures aimed at forcing parents to apprentice their free children or at setting them to work on the estates. Parents, on the other hand, clung tenaciously to the freedom of their children and consistently upheld their cause as a priority over estate needs.

Evidence of apprenticed parents' advocacy for their children's freedom rests undeniably in what they did and said during this period. Virtually every quarterly report by stipendiary magistrates in Jamaica during the apprenticeship indicated the refusal of parents to allow their free children to be apprenticed or to work on the estates. Indeed, Sir Lionel Smith reported immediately after the cessation of apprenticeship that only nine children had been apprenticed under the terms of the abolition law for the entire period.[19] The commitment of these parents to their children's freedom was maintained even in the face of threats by estate management to remove the children from the property if their parents refused to apprentice them. Parents in some cases also utilized the option of sending their free children to live with relatives or friends in the towns, so as to safeguard their freedom. This practice of "child-shifting", generated during the apprenticeship period, reflected the significance of the extended family networks which had developed across the island and the role of extended families as support systems which facilitated the survival and welfare of free children. In the post-apprenticeship period, this practice of child-shifting continued and remained a feature of black family life in Jamaica. Ironically, this culturally derived strategy was interpreted by elite society as another example of the "disjointed" and "dysfunctional" black family. Reverend Stephen H. Cooke, rector of the parish of St Thomas-in-the-East, reporting on this tendency among apprenticed parents in St Thomas-in-the-East, noted that on one estate which had had fifty free children at the start of apprenticeship, there remained only fifteen or sixteen by March 1836. The rest had been placed with relatives or friends in Morant Bay.[20]

In some cases, disputes arose over the exact age of the child who was being defended, but parents were prepared to suffer punishment rather than allow estate personnel to deprive their children of their freedom. This is illustrated by the case of Janette Saunders, apprentice to Orange Valley estate in St Ann, who repeatedly declined to obey the overseer's and Stipendiary Magistrate Dillon's orders to send her son, Archibald Forbes, to work with the apprentices on the basis of the estate's claim that he had already turned six years old on 1 August 1834. Estate records and parental memory often differed in such cases, and Janette Saunders adamantly insisted that her son was free, "being under six years of age when the new law came in". She was subsequently sentenced to the St Ann's workhouse and punished on the treadmill.[21]

Not many people were prepared to credit black parents for their support of their children's freedom; rather, many stipendiary magistrates and estate management personnel chided them for doing so. In fact, the paternalistic missionary perspective rejoiced that their warning "to all parents and guardians of negro youth against permitting . . . their children to be apprenticed" was "so faithfully followed".[22] However, Special Justice Chamberlaine accurately captured the essence of parental advocacy when he remarked that parents should be credited, not blamed, for their reluctance to apprentice their children, as this was "characteristic of their foresight and incontestably proves that they are inferior to none in the value and importance which they attach to freedom".[23]

Constant as they were in their refusal to allow their children to be apprenticed, parents displayed a similar persistence in rejecting estate schemes to get their free children to work on the estates. While recognizing the difference between the two strategies, parents regarded sending their children to work for "busha" as a step which could lead to the apprenticing of their children. As apprenticed parents from the Plantain Garden River Valley explained to Thome and Kimball in 1837, allowing the estate to command their children's labour "would be the same as acknowledging that they . . . were not able to take care of them themselves. The busha would then send word to the governor that the people had given up their children, not being able to support them, and the governor would have the children bound to the busha, '*and then*', said they, '*we might whistle for our children!*' "[24]

The expression "then we might whistle for our children" symbolized the parents' recognition that the forcible reapprenticing of their free children to the planter would signify loss of their parental control over their children's fate. They were not prepared to countenance that possibility. Parents generally held the conviction that the freedom of their children and work on the plantation were simply not compatible. As Stipendiary Magistrate Bell reported, a frequent response of parents to requests to allow their children to work on estates was, "Who ever heard of free work a field?" Special Justice Fishbourne indicated that apprenticed parents appeared to consider it disgraceful for their free children to work like apprentices.[25]

Estate management, having been released from their legal obligation to the free children by the Imperial Act of Abolition, generally excluded these children from gaining access to plantation medical care. Many parents, however, implemented strategies to ensure the continued health care of their children, and the quarterly reports by stipendiary magistrates for the duration of apprenticeship included several references to collective as well as individual parental advocacy on behalf of their children's health. Thus, Stipendiary Magistrate Marlton reported in 1837 that on some estates in St Mary, the parents (both mothers and fathers) had agreed to forego the alternate half-Fridays out of crop in exchange for medical attention and allowances for their free children. Similarly, John Davy, manager of several estates in Manchester, reported that on most of the properties under his supervision, the parents had agreed to either give their labour free of charge or to pay cash on an annual basis in exchange for medical treatment for their children. Group parental support for this purpose was also in evidence on Steelfield estate in Stipendiary Magistrate Hawkins's district, where the mothers had agreed with the overseer to work four days of their free time during the year in return for medical attention for their free children.[26] Although apprenticed parents were willing to undertake these types of initiatives, estate personnel were more interested in schemes to persuade them to apprentice their children. The consistent and widespread refusal of parents to agree to such schemes meant that they were often criticized and blamed by estate management as well as many stipendiary magistrates and colonial officials for the illnesses and deaths of free children. Neither metropolitan nor colonial authorities were prepared to accept responsibility for the mortality and sickness of free children whose lives had been ransomed by managerial and governmental decisions to exclude them from health care.

The apprentices' visions for their children's futures included access to schools where their children would be educated. Black parents were persistently opposed throughout the period under review to any form of industrial or agricultural education, as they perceived these as schemes to resubmit their children to servile status. However, the view of many whites, including some stipendiary magistrates, was that the refusal of the apprentices to set their children to work at estate tasks was indicative of a lack of interest in their children's welfare, and black parents were accused of bringing up their children in idleness and of not doing anything to contribute to their education. There is ample evidence, however, indicating that for black parents at the time, their children's education was not only a priority, but it also provided the motivation for many examples of group parental advocacy. In St Andrew in 1835, Special Justice Bourne indicated that he had just built a schoolroom and that "many negroes have given a part of their hire to reduce it"; apprentices had worked in their free time to help build the school. Special justice Henry Walsh, in reporting on Magistrate Marlton's district, spoke of advocacy by apprenticed mothers and fathers on Bailey's estates in St Mary, who had offered the estates' attorney, Charles Stewart, three dollars for the education of each free child and requested that a school be built to educate their children. Similarly, Special Justice Grant reported on the efforts of a rather large group of parents, predominantly fathers, to build a school on land donated to the Moravians at Adam's Valley in Manchester: "To this place do the apprentices repair in their own time to labour voluntarily. . . . One Saturday, about a hundred men engaged in preparing timbers . . . and in clearing the ground . . . the only benefit they wish to derive is that of having their children educated."[27]

The apprenticed parents' collective activism through the contribution of their labour is even more noteworthy in light of the fact that their free time was a scarce commodity, to be utilized only in what they perceived as worthwhile endeavours. This evidence of agency on the part of apprenticed parents challenged the stereotypical representations of blacks as lacking in parental love and values, articulated by Edward Long, Mrs A.C. Carmichael, Bryan Edwards and others, that were common at the time.[28] Such evidence clearly indicated the positioning of black apprentices' parental priorities on the eve of "full free". Additionally, the active involvement of apprenticed fathers in enterprises on behalf of their children contradicted commonly held notions of marginal fathers,[29] even as these men sought to affirm their responsibilities in their unfolding vision for their families in freedom.

Not only did apprenticed parents support their children's right to education, but they also, in some cases, insisted that their children have a proper learning environment. On Hall's Prospect plantation, Stipendiary Magistrate Bourne had informed the parents that the master would give them the "old lock-up house" as a schoolroom if they would assist in preparing the building. Having discussed the matter, one of the men informed Bourne of the apprentices' collective perspective: "They did not want the school to be held in the 'old lock-up house'. It was not a good place for their 'pickaninnies' to go to. They had much rather have some other building."[30] Their rejection of a site of punishment as a site for the education of their children indicates the vision of freedom which these apprentices had for their children's future.

Labour maximization policies, enforced during the apprenticeship, resulted in pregnant women working close to their confinement, the denial of special breaks to nursing mothers during the workday and the cessation of the services of infant nurses who, along with mothers of six or more children, found themselves pressed into field labour. Apprenticed mothers, in continuously objecting to these restrictions, may have been exploiting what Mimi Sheller termed "Christian morality, with its rhetoric of domestic motherhood and the mother's duty to protect her children".[31] More significantly, they were upholding and implementing their perspective on an essential meaning of freedom: to be able to nurture their families in optimum conditions.

Individual acts of initiative and civil disobedience were often the first avenue of choice used by mothers to promote their causes, and the quarterly reports of stipendiary magistrates are replete with examples of the struggles of these women to uphold their family concerns. Reports by stipendiary magistrates Ralph Cocking and Thomas Davies in 1835 for St James and Trelawny, respectively, conveyed the activism of mothers like Sarah of Orange Valley in Trelawny, who simply declined to work in the great gang as ordered within six to eight weeks of her confinement and was consequently sentenced to the treadmill and penal gang. Expectant mothers Caroline Watson, Milly Ord and Lydia Watson of Bellfield estate, St James, and Frances Neil of Spring Mount, also in St James, all took similar action and were all ordered punished by Cocking. Additionally, several mothers of six or more children on Orange Valley estate refused to work in the yard as ordered because they believed that as mothers of large families, they were entitled to appropriate consideration. Among these women was Maggy Lewis, otherwise called Ann Palmer, whose multigenerational extended family was resident at Orange Valley. An old woman, the mother of ten children, twenty-eight grandchildren and one great-grandchild, Lewis justifiably believed that she was entitled to some form of labour exemption, in keeping with the practice under slavery of exempting mothers of six or more children from heavy labour. Bellfield estate was also the scene of civil disobedience by several mothers of six or more children. On Latinum estate, Newman Hall and Logan estate – all in St James – nursing mothers adopted the strategy of delayed weaning in the face of orders to the contrary from estate personnel, and were punished by Cocking by being made to work "in and out of the cell" for an average of fourteen days.

Several of these women from St James and Trelawny were connected to the church of Reverend George Blyth, a Presbyterian minister. Undeterred by the punitive outcomes of their initial efforts, they reported their cases to Reverend Blyth, who communicated the substance of their situations to Governor Sligo. In this respect, collective action by these mothers resulted in further publicity at the governmental level, both metropolitan and colonial, on the issue of apprentices' maternal rights, even if Governor Sligo was less than impressed with Reverend Blyth's empathy with the mothers and with the criticism of

Davies and Cocking.[32] Moreover, these initiatives, along with other instances of family advocacy, provided material which eventually helped to mobilize British humanitarian and political opinion against the inequitable system of apprenticeship.

Apprenticed mothers clearly preferred group advocacy as a strategy in support of their young, having realized that effectiveness resided more in collective agency than in individual attempts. Indeed, group advocacy had proven so threatening to the powers that be that as early as December 1834, the Jamaican Assembly had included in the Second Act in Aid of the Abolition Act a clause which prohibited apprentices from proceeding in a body of five or more to seek interviews with special magistrates.[33] Had the act not been disallowed, a serious limitation would have been placed on group family advocacy. In 1835, Rosannah, Amy, Jane Clark and Juba, all mothers of young children and apprenticed to Old England plantation in St George, collectively appealed to Stipendiary Magistrate Kent about the absence of any special consideration which would allow them to properly nurse their children. Similarly, several mothers from Trafalgar plantation in St George appealed to Special Justice Palmer for redress in 1835 when they were deprived of time and nurses to care for their babies and after their initial request to Simpson, the attorney for Trafalgar, had not been met. Milley Thomas, the spokeswoman for the group, in her deposition before Dr Palmer's court, explained the earlier and unproductive group initiative: "We mothers complained to him that it was too straining to work with child on back, and begged him to give nurse same as at Mount Hybla and Hopewell." Here was an interesting indication of the networking done among the apprentices, most likely at the weekend market, which allowed them to be informed of family-related policies elsewhere and which encouraged them to agitate for similar treatment. Similarly, a group of mothers from Lower Lucky Valley also appealed to Dr Palmer in 1835 because two of their number had been placed in the dungeon after they had attempted to "mind their children" in the absence of a nurse. The efforts of these groups of mothers from Trafalgar and Lower Lucky Valley resulted in a supportive position on the part of Dr Palmer, who reprimanded and in some cases fined the offending estate personnel.[34]

In February 1836, the measures taken by several mothers from Mount Pleasant estate in St Thomas-in-the-East reflected collective planning and implementation in pursuit of their children's welfare. These women, most of them nursing mothers, were particularly concerned that upon their refusal to put their older free children to work on the estate, their master, Nockells, had withdrawn all medical attention and nurses and had refused them time to suckle their children. Their initial appeal had been made to Stipendiary Magistrate Ewart, to whom jurisdiction over Mount Pleasant had been transferred from fellow magistrate Lyon. Having evidently conferred on the matter, the mothers had determined that their cause would be doubly served by making a group visit to Morant Bay to visit Lyon, with whom they had had a "good relationship". That they made the journey on a Saturday, market day, indicates the urgency with which they viewed this mission on behalf of their children. This group endeavour proved successful, as Nockells was informed by Magistrate Ewart that "no woman could be prevented, much less punished, for affording her infant the only sustenance upon which the preservation of its health depends".[35]

The ultimate indicator of the significance of black maternal advocacy was its impact on a British public already sensitized by Victorian ideals to the rights of motherhood, as well as its effects on the debate in the House of Lords on the ending of apprenticeship – a discussion which focused on (among other issues) the loss of traditional indulgences by mothers of young children. The activism of apprenticed mothers forcefully brought to the centre of this debate the inhumane aspect of the apprenticeship and the need for its termination. This persistent demonstration of maternal advocacy was a reflection, too, of the continuity of the close bonds between mothers and their children, and in particular the desire to delay weaning. As seen in chapter 1, this bond was a prominent feature of family life in West Africa. Clearly, the primacy accorded by both fathers and mothers to the welfare of their children was in keeping with the West African emphasis on the importance of children to the perpetuation of kinship networks and the life force itself.[36]

Apprenticed Family Advocates: Three Case Studies

THE CASE OF TABITHA HEWITT

The struggle on the part of Tabitha Hewitt's family to gain justice at various levels of the judicial system between 1834 and 1837 epitomized the perseverance shown by apprenticed family members in spite of being placed at a disadvantage by a frequently partisan legal system. Tabitha's daughter, Sarah Williams, her son, John Nunes, and her granddaughter, Evelina Smith, all apprenticed to Content Hall Pen in St Elizabeth, sought to gain legal redress for her death, which they argued was caused by neglect on the part of her master, Thomas Mason, also of Content Hall Pen. The family argued in their depositions that Tabitha, aged between seventy and eighty years at the time, although seriously ill and incapable of helping herself, was given neither medical attention nor any other form of assistance by Mason. Moreover, they stated in their affidavits that all members of the family who were capable of caring for her were prevented from so doing on Mason's orders and that her death in late August 1834 was the result of a chain of neglect endorsed by Mason.[37]

The family's first channel of advocacy was Stipendiary Magistrate Oldrey's court in September 1834, and the testimony given there by both Tabitha's immediate family and "the wider family" of apprentices from Content Hall Pen resulted in Mason being sentenced by Oldrey to pay a fine of five pounds. On receiving the substance of the family's testimony from Oldrey, Governor Sligo ordered a further investigation by Stipendiary Magistrates Ramsay and Clinch. Again, on the basis of the family's depositions that "their mother had died from want of medical attendance, medicine, nourishment and someone to take care of her",[38] Mason was judged guilty of neglect of a "most cruel and atrocious nature", and on Governor Sligo's recommendation to the attorney general, he was indicted "for killing and slaying Tabitha Hewitt". However, the indictment was thrown out by the Cornwall grand jury in March 1835 on the basis of being "improperly drawn up".[39] Nevertheless, the family of Tabitha Hewitt persevered, and with new affidavits submitted by them, attorney W. Henry Anderson applied for and was granted a new trial, to be held at the Middlesex grand court in June 1837. Although the sources are not definitive on this matter, it may be surmised that the family was able to retain Anderson through the pooling of funds saved from working during their free time and from the sale of market provisions.

In that case, *King v. Mason*, Advocate General Panton argued on behalf of Tabitha's family that Mason had acted contrary to the Abolition Act (4 Wm. 4, c. 41 & 5 Wm. 4, c. 7), section 16, which stated that the person entitled to the apprentice's services was required to supply him or her with food, clothing, lodging, medicine and medical attendance, and that Hewitt died as a result of his neglect. At this final trial, several members of Hewitt's family testified that although Mason knew of her illness, he "never sent her a dose of physic nor gave her any attendance . . . neither black nor white doctor" and that her son had, in vain, asked Mason for medicine for his mother. The defence argued, however, that the prosecution, using the family as witnesses, had failed to prove that Mason had "unlawfully, maliciously and wickedly neglected" Tabitha Hewitt, and that "medicine was no cure for old age".[40] Although the jury returned a verdict of not guilty, thus depriving the family of judicial redress on this occasion, the publicity given to the issue of estate management's obligations to ailing and elderly apprentices no doubt contributed to the criticism of the apprenticeship system that was mounting by 1837.

FAMILY ADVOCATES FROM RECESS PLANTATION: COMMITMENT TO COLLECTIVE FAMILY WELFARE

In September 1836, nineteen apprentices, including members of several families attached to Recess plantation in St Thomas-in-the-Vale, embarked on a twenty-one-mile collective quest to ensure security for themselves and their families in the face of threats to their lives and property by their master, Nicholas Gyles. Included among this group of nineteen were husband and wife James and Eliza Byfield; Susan Finlay and her mother, Eliza Gyles; Ann Johnston, mother of a twelve-month-old baby; and sisters Ann Lea and Mary Ann Reid. This case has been highlighted here because it exemplifies the principle of "commitment to the collectivity"[41] that was embraced by apprenticed family advocates and because the group's visit to a solicitor's office to pursue their cause, albeit atypical of strategy employed by such advocates, proved extremely consequential.

Initially, the Recess plantation families and the other apprentices had approached Dr Palmer, one of the two stipendiary magistrates for St Thomas-in-the-Vale, to seek redress for their grievances but had ascertained that neither Palmer nor Stipendiary Magistrate Harris was able to assist them, as they were embroiled in a conflict with the local justices of the parish.[42] The apprentices concluded that "there was no special magistrate in their parish" who could help them, so they effected a collective decision to proceed to Spanish Town, accompanied by Dr Palmer, in order to "seek protection from the authorities . . . protection against Massa and . . . [for the purpose of] having him bound over to keep the peace".[43] Once in Spanish Town, the apprentices proceeded first to the house of special justice Richard Hill, where they encountered solicitor and attorney of the Supreme Court Charles Harvey, who agreed to be their legal adviser and consented to prepare affidavits on their circumstances.

An examination of these affidavits reveals the apprentices' preoccupation with family concerns: the implications of Gyles's threatening behaviour for the safety of family members; the destruction wreaked by Gyles on growing provisions and livestock, the sources of their families' livelihood; and cruelty to pregnant women and children. James Byfield and his wife Eliza were very concerned about their safety after their objections to the shooting of their hogs by Gyles were met by threats on James's life. Gyles had declared that if he had had his cutlass in hand, he "would have had deponent's head off his body". Ann Johnston complained that because she had refused to leave her twelve-month-old baby in the "negro houses" where there was no one to care for it, on Gyles's orders, the child was each day removed from her side in the field and "put in same place in the road". Gyles further informed her that he did not care if the child died and that she "might take the child and cram it into the Magistrate's ***" (sic). Sisters Ann Lea and Mary Ann Reid were concerned about Gyles's physical violence to Mary Ann, which had resulted in her miscarriage, while Eliza Gyles and her daughter Susan Finlay both objected to Gyles's repeated destruction of their garden fence, which had resulted in "massa's horses and apprentices' hogs damaging their corn, cassava and plantation suckers".[44]

The fact that the group set out from Recess plantation on a Wednesday morning (7 September 1836), the middle of the workweek, on a twenty-one-mile journey, indicated their commitment to the collective safety of themselves and their families, even if this meant risking the further ire of their master. Their actions also demonstrated their awareness of their rights under the law, as they opted first to appeal to Palmer regarding their plight (as provided for under section 49 of the local Abolition Act) and when this option failed to satisfy, they turned to other legal personnel and expressed their confidence in the "authorities in Spanish Town" to guarantee their safety. They were aware, too, of the role which they had to play to facilitate justice; thus, they gave detailed affidavits which they hoped would convey to "the authorities" the full extent of the danger which they and their families faced at the behest of Gyles. They were also cognizant of the fact that no action could be taken to restrain Gyles from threatening them unless they took oaths to the truth of their testimony. When Harvey tried to persuade the apprentices to return to Recess on the following day, 8 September, because he was unable to find someone to administer the oaths, the people "would not be induced to their homes until assured that their master was bound to keep the peace towards them".[45] When the affidavits were sworn "at a late hour" on Monday, 12 September, the apprentices returned to Recess, having been assured that their master was now legally restrained from endangering them and their families.

At a subsequent hearing pertaining to a charge brought by Gyles against Charles Harvey for harbouring his apprentices, the four sitting justices of the peace dismissed as "intolerable" that "apprentices should resort to Spanish Town to professional men . . . that these persons, pauper persons should apply to them". The justices, betraying a persistent perspective which designated apprentices as devoid of rights even after 1 August 1834, further declared that it was "monstrous and ridiculous in the extreme that during the existence of slavery, they should have any such right".[46] It is therefore both illuminating and significant that these apprenticed family members, contrary to the justices' view of what behaviour was within their rights, had collectively demonstrated their belief that, as persons soon to be fully free, they had every right to pursue such an avenue of advocacy, and that their combined efforts indeed resulted in legal restraint against their master.

ADVOCACY THROUGH APPEALS TO THE GOVERNOR: THE CASE OF CATHERINE PINDAR

Governors' despatches and quarterly reports by stipendiary magistrates indicate that personal appeals to the governor were periodically, though not extensively, used by apprentices to advance family concerns.[47] The case of Catherine Pindar is detailed here because, although initiated in the last days of slavery, it was the first case of family advocacy of this sort reported in the apprenticeship period and thus spanned the transitional divide between slavery and abolition. Her case also demonstrates that appeals to the governor by enslaved family members were not unknown, even if reports of their occurrence were rare.

Catherine Pindar, mother of a six-month-old baby and an enslaved person belonging to John Coates of Montego Bay, was severely beaten on the back and breasts by her owner a few days before 30 July 1834, because she had misplaced a letter pertaining to the christening of her child. Having been ordered to accompany Coates's servant into Kingston, Catherine used the opportunity to present her case to Governor Sligo on the Thursday before 30 July. Her primary concern, expressed to Sligo, was that the beating had made it virtually impossible to breastfeed her baby.[48]

The subsequent hearing ordered by Sligo into Catherine's charge of cruelty against Coates could not be concluded before 1 August 1834, by which time she was legally an apprentice. Her efforts to advance her case before the governor resulted in Sligo's decision to purchase her full freedom for thirty-five pounds, and on Coates's admission of the charge of cruelty, Sligo also deprived him of his commission as a magistrate.[49] Thus, advocacy by an enslaved mother turned apprentice had resulted in the ultimate prize of freedom. Significantly, this was the first in a number of reported cases of black family advocacy which was to result in the dismissal of the offending party from public office.

The Significance of Black Family Advocacy at the Brown's Town Commission of Inquiry, 1837

In 1837, in response to secretary of state Lord Glenelg's instructions to governor Sir Lionel Smith, two sittings of a commission were convened at Brown's Town to inquire into the veracity of two sets of allegations: first, reports of abuses outlined in James Williams's *Narrative of Events* and, second, complaints by various missionaries of acts of cruelty allegedly perpetrated towards apprentices in St Ann. James Williams was the eighteen-year-old apprentice attached to Penshurst in St Ann. His *Narrative of Events* reflected the publication of his accounts of abusive treatment of apprentices at the St Ann workhouse as told to visiting abolitionists, Joseph Sturge and Thomas Harvey. By 13 November 1837, the report and minutes of proceedings from both sessions had been conveyed to the Colonial Office, confirming that the allegations were generally true and that "every material fact has been supported and corroborated by an almost unbroken chain of convincing testimony".[50] In providing this "convincing testimony", the apprentices epitomized family advocacy in two respects. First, a great deal of their evidence was centred on family concerns, such as the treatment of pregnant women, nursing mothers and elderly family members. Second, of the 117 apprenticed witnesses who appeared before both sittings of the commission, 57 were adjudged, on an evidential basis,[51] to be family members themselves, and through their testimony they were advancing their own cause as well as that of the wider "family" of apprentices across Jamaica. This example of black family advocacy proved both multifaceted and far-reaching in its repercussions.

Evidence presented by the fifty-seven family members included accounts of treatment inimical to both the lives and well-being of the family. These details came from young mothers like Mary-Ann Bell of Penshurst, forced to work the treadmill twice a day while five months pregnant; Susan White of Dunbarton, also five months pregnant, who was worked and flogged on the treadmill and who suffered a miscarriage two months after falling off the apparatus; and Bella Richards, apprentice to Hiattsfield estate, who, in spite of informing the authorities that she was three months pregnant, was whipped and forced to work the treadmill and miscarried shortly after leaving the workhouse: "I was three months in the family way. . . . I told Mr Woolfrys that I was breeding . . . he said he could not help it; my back gave way when I was on the mill . . . after I went out of the workhouse . . . I had a mischance."

Several family members testified before the second session of the commission regarding the death of expectant mother Eliza Christie of Cave Valley estate, who died shortly after being kicked by one of the bookkeepers. Older family members, taking charge of improving their own predicament, spoke out on the flogging of the elderly and the very weak on the treadmill. An example of this type of advocacy was the testimony of Mary James, approximately sixty years of age, very weak and infirm, yet forced to work the treadmill and whipped every day for six days.[52]

These cases were only a microcosm of the larger body of damning testimony by the fifty-seven apprenticed family members, and indeed by all the apprenticed witnesses, before the two sittings of the commission. Their efforts contributed significantly to the mobilization of British humanitarian and public opinion and were, as Mimi Sheller points out, "important signifiers of the immorality of this 'experiment' in half freedom. Public debate kept returning to the unacceptability of physical punishment of women, especially mothers."[53] In a very real and immediate way, these witnesses' advocacy exposed the horrors which the apprentices in a large part of St Ann had endured, mainly under the stewardship of Stipendiary Magistrate Rawlinson, who was the first casualty of black family advocacy before the Brown's Town commission. On 13 November 1837, Sir Lionel Smith informed Lord Glenelg of his suspension of Rawlinson, not only for his conduct towards James Williams, but also for abuses of other apprentices in St Ann. Smith's instructions to the attorney general to bring to justice parties who may have been perpetrators of the various offences exposed by the investigation[54] conveyed his perception that it was the commissioners, John Daughtrey and George Gordon, who should be credited with unearthing the abuses. The fact remains that none of these offences would have been so explicitly brought to public attention without the testimony of the 117 apprenticed witnesses, including the 57 family members. Bills of indictment, brought by the attorney general of Jamaica against Rawlinson and Senior, the proprietor of Penshurst, where many of the abuses had been perpetrated, were later ignored, not surprisingly, by a planter-affiliated grand jury.[55]

Nevertheless, black family testimony had a crucial impact on amendments to the Jamaica Abolition Act, most notably playing a key role in the emergence of treadmill legislation by early 1838. Prior to June 1837, when Glenelg requested the convening of the commission of inquiry, Sir Lionel Smith had circulated a set of regulations governing treadmill punishment, but as late as November of that year, he had been unable to convince the assembly to pass these regulations into a general law.[56] In reality, Smith was waging a losing battle with the assembly on this issue. In March 1838, when Glenelg, tiring of the assembly's tactics of delay and non-cooperation, requested that Parliament amend the Jamaica Abolition Act directly, his decision appears to have been influenced by a number of factors, one of which was the governor's failure to make progress with the assembly. More significantly, the findings of the Brown's Town commission, based on black family testimonials, had made it undeniably clear to British political and humanitarian opinion makers by December 1837 that the allegations of abuse against apprentices described by James Williams in his *Narrative* had indeed been substantiated. No doubt, Glenelg's decision was also influenced by the strengthening of British abolitionist sentiment after the publication of Sturge and Harvey's *The West Indies in 1837*, an investigation into the lives of formerly enslaved peoples (which was itself based on black family testimony), and Lord Sligo's *Jamaica under the Apprenticeship*. Importantly, however, neither of these publications had appeared until January 1838, by which time the validation of James Williams's *Narrative* by black family testimony before the Brown's Town commission had left its indelible imprint upon British humanitarian and political opinion.

Lord Glenelg's bill, introduced into Parliament on 19 March 1838, became the Act to Amend the Act for the Abolition of Slavery in the British Colonies (1 & 2 Vict., c. 19), effectively becoming law on 11 April 1838. This law directly

Figure 4. *"Home! Sweet Home", Jamaica, W.I.* Cousins Hereward Postcard Collection, reprinted courtesy of the University of the West Indies Library, Mona.

prohibited placing women on the workhouse treadmills or in penal gangs, flogging women or cutting their hair,[57] all subjects of painful testimony by apprentices at Brown's Town. Black advocacy, and in particular black family advocacy, had succeeded where the colonial governor had failed. Within the next few months, the impact of Williams's *Narrative* and the testimony before the Brown's Town commission would also contribute to the British government's decision to terminate the apprenticeship system.

Family Advocacy in Full Freedom, 1838–1882

Shelter: A Case for Family Advocacy

The issue of shelter was central to the survival of family units. One of the greatest challenges to the welfare of freed families in the decade after full freedom was the insecurity of tenure resulting from coercive rental polices aimed at compelling all members of the family to supply labour to the plantation. Indeed, families suffered the brunt of discriminatory rental practices, such as the charging of per capita rent for each member of the family residing in one house, the punitive deductions from a husband's pay when his wife remained ill at home or, as reported in St Mary, the deduction of ten pence for each child sent to school instead of to the field.[58] Wilmot, in his instructive assessment of the post-slavery labour and tenancy landscape, has emphasized a variety of initiatives on the part of freed blacks, ranging from refusal to pay rent to violent resistance against attempts to levy on goods. Likewise, Douglas Hall, Woodville Marshall and Veront Satchell, among others, have examined the phenomenal rise of the peasantry, not only in response to labour and rental conflicts, but also as an enactment of the freed peoples' visions for social and economic self-determination.[59] The purpose of this section is to expand the discussion on the responses of freed peoples to rental conflicts into the arena of family-based activism, ranging from collective confrontation by family members to judicial advocacy by families through the medium of the stipendiary magistrates' courts as well as the higher courts of the land.

The efforts of different families to lend support to each other in the face of coercion and intimidation were exemplified by the actions of families on Beckford's Retreat estate in August 1838. In attempting to serve notices to quit to the people of Beckford's Retreat, the bookkeeper, William Scott, reported that he had been "greatly abused and assaulted" by several women, including Elizabeth Taylor and Selena Benlay. A subsequent effort by constables to execute arrest warrants for these women was foiled by "a multitude" of supporters, including Elizabeth's husband, Robert Taylor, who insisted that he would not allow his wife to be taken to Chapelton. Members of other families in the crowd included Christiana Dinout and her husband John, who, according to the constables, was even more vociferous than Robert in his insistence that Elizabeth should not be taken to Chapelton. Apparently, the demonstration of collective action by these family members and others was influenced by their belief that the man who had signed the arrest warrants was no longer a magistrate. John and Robert expressed their desire to visit the king's house to ascertain the legality of the warrants, and the crowd emphatically declared that "they would not be served with notices to quit their houses and grounds and that they were free". A second, highly reinforced attempt to execute the warrants resulted in the arrest and charge of Elizabeth Taylor for assault, her husband for attempting to rescue her and the sentencing of both to one month's hard labour.[60]

Newly freed peoples advocated on behalf of themselves and their families by making constant complaints to the stipendiary magistrates about inequitable practices such as charging separate rental fees for each member of a family resident in the same house. Within this context, both male and female family members emphasized the importance of security of tenure to familial well-being. It is instructive, too, that in the earliest days of "full free", the black male in the role of partner or husband, father and provider was anything but invisible, unheard or marginal. Thus, for example, Henry Burgess, protesting the weekly rental charge of six shillings and eight pence for himself and five shillings for his "common law wife", complained to stipendiary magistrates Edward Fishbourne and William Hewitt in 1839 that he thought eleven shillings and eight pence a week too much, adding that "we must quit Cherry Hill". Thomas King complained to the same magistrates of the injustice of paying fifteen shillings per week for himself and his two children, each under nine years of age, while Gaumett of Lovely Grove argued that he did not think that his wife, Seraphine, with whom he had lived for "a long time", should also be charged five shillings a week. Upholding his position before Fishbourne and Hewitt, he explained, "I cannot pay two rents; Governor told us to pay 1s. 8d. I am willing to pay that sum. Free is no good to we if we must pay all we work for."[61]

An examination of such tenancy disputes also indicates the continuity, as in West Africa, of extended family networks, many of which were co-resident and comprised of three-generational clusters. On Lovely Grove plantation, for example, Michael Lafitte, known as Gailey, lived with Madeline, whom he considered his wife because they had lived together for so long; three of their adult daughters, Nano, Tonsan and Mary Jane; an adult son, Michael; and Nano's one-year-old child. The case of Henry Burgess, discussed earlier in this section, reflects a more complex extended network. Burgess resided with his father, Charles Williams, his father's wife and two of Burgess's siblings. Additionally, Burgess's wife, so designated by him because they had lived "so long together", and four of their six children also lived in the same house.[62] While these familial networks reflected some characteristics of the West African extended family, especially in their integration of spouses into the core household, as shown in chapter 1, the extent to which such residential arrangements in the post-slavery period were motivated by affinity to culturally derived traditions remains difficult to determine. Economic considerations may well have influenced some of these living arrangements, although given the pervasiveness of per capita rentals across Jamaica at the time, these co-resident networks could prove to be more expensive, as each member of the family was charged a separate rental fee. However, the very fact that, faced with the extra expense of per capita rentals, these co-resident extended family networks persisted may have been an index of a more deep-seated affinity to kin, a bond which proved an enduring link with West Africa.

Parents were also powerful advocates on behalf of their children when confronted with unfair housing practices, such as the jailing of children for failure to pay rental fees already paid by their parents. This can be seen in the activism of three separate families on Peter's Rock plantation in St Andrew in May 1839. Henry Whittle, father of sixteen-year-old Priscilla Henry, took his family's predicament to Stipendiary Magistrate Daly after his daughter had been in jail for five days for refusal to pay rent. In his deposition, Whittle argued that Priscilla lived with him and that he paid three shillings and four pence for house and ground, but because she had neither house nor ground allotted to her, she was unlawfully being charged rent. Molly Robertson's mother also informed Daly that her daughter lived with her and was supported by her, challenging the demand for a separate rental fee from her daughter. The mother of teenaged Diana Johnson supported her daughter's case on the additional grounds that she was crippled from childhood and unable to work, again questioning the right to demand rent from her daughter, who lived with her. She felt particularly aggrieved since she was informed that infirm persons were exempted from paying rent until 1 June 1839, by the sixth clause of the Act of Abolition of Apprenticeship. Advocacy by these parents from Peter's Rock proved successful to the extent that Daly was able to secure the release of the three girls from jail upon pointing out the illegality of their detention to Fowles, the proprietor of Peter's Rock.[63]

Very old and infirm family members, exempted by law from paying rent for house and grounds until 1 June 1839 but subjected nevertheless to rental demands, also brought their plight before the special magistrates. Richard Parchment, an "infirm old man", father of Isabella Richards and resident of Corby Castle plantation, St Elizabeth, complained to Stipendiary Magistrate Gurley not only of having to pay rent, but of having his fees increased to three shillings and four pence per week as of 1 November 1838. John Berlin, also old and infirm, grandfather of two girls and resident at Corby Castle, lodged a similar complaint to Gurley.[64] The clear illegality of exacting rental fees from elderly persons before June 1839 placed these older family advocates in a comparatively favourable position because, although estate management frequently brought suits against the elderly for non-payment of rent, such suits were more often than not thrown out by the magistrates' courts.[65]

Interestingly, married women did not always rely on their husbands to plead their cases but sometimes acted as their own advocates before the special magistrates. Perhaps this was a reflection of their non-acceptance of European gender constructs, which emphasized dependence on males in issues such as shelter. This was demonstrated by the visit to Stipendiary Magistrate Lyon in September 1838 by several married women from Gibraltar estate in Trelawny, who were protesting notices to quit given to them because they "had devoted their attention to their husbands and families". Lyon assured the women of every legal protection which he was empowered to provide.[66] However, for many blacks who placed their plight before the special magistrates, the consequence was ejection by plantation management and being driven from the estate. Families' continuing efforts at advocacy in light of this possibility accentuated their commitment to the priorities of kinship and community.

Freed families advocating against discriminatory rental practices were equally active in seeking to repudiate claims made by Colonial Office officials in April 1839 that blacks believed that they had a right to occupy their houses and grounds rent-free. At meetings held in Baptist chapels at Spanish Town, Mount Carey, Montego Bay, Shortwood, Bethel Hill and Salter's Hill, apprentices, predominantly male, declared their intent to assume responsibility for the material needs of their families, thus signalling that they had accepted the roles assigned them by patriarchy and that, in their minds, their familial place would be anything but marginal. Thus, "headmen and late apprentices . . . members of the peasantry" upheld their commitment to "the payment of a fair and just rent". However, when these rental demands became prejudicial to their families' interests, they would adopt a principled opposition; they stated in their resolutions that refusal on their part to pay rental fees only occurred when "exorbitant and unreasonable demands of rent" were made, especially when these extended to each member of their families, "though residing in one house".[67]

The expense entailed in seeking judicial redress on matters of rental disputes as well as obstructive planter tactics militated against successful outcomes of this type of advocacy. Stipendiary magistrate Henry Walsh reported in 1839 that in St Mary, when freed family members, especially married women, took out summonses against their employers, the strategy used by the employer was to enter an objection, which usually resulted in the postponement of the case. In such a scenario, the ex-slave had to pay the two shillings and sixpence necessary to have a summons issued and served on two separate occasions. This no doubt had a discouraging effect on potential complainants.[68] Moreover, as stipendiary reports for this period indicated, blacks who spoke out against the injustices of rental practices were usually ejected outright, and indeed they were more often on the receiving end of summonses over rental disputes. Many of these cases ended up in the court of common pleas, where pro-planter juries did not usually dispense verdicts favourable to black families. In light of such discouraging conditions, it is therefore especially significant that freed families persevered in judicial advocacy on issues of fair housing practices. Their successes in this arena, though comparatively few, were a crucial endorsement of black family advocacy.

One such success related to the action of trespass brought against personnel of Schawfield estate in Trelawny in 1838, at the instance of Charles Smith and his wife Euphemia, labourers resident on the estate. In the case, which was tried before the court of Special Magistrates Lyon and Kelly, the Smith family charged the two estate constables and the bookkeeper with pulling off the roof of a house which had been allocated by the estate to Rosie Shaw, Charles Smith's mother-in-law. Both Charles Smith and his wife were at work on the plantation and resided in Rosie Shaw's house, and they felt it a grave injustice for the proprietor, Samuel G. Barrett, to have given orders to estate personnel to break down the house on the very day that Barrett had ordered Smith to quit the estate. Charles Smith felt particularly aggrieved at the action as Barrett had refused to pay him the nine dollars owed to him for labour; Smith, in turn, had refused to quit the estate until he received his due. It was clear to Lyon and Kelly that the order to remove the roof had been given also because of Rosie Shaw's refusal to give labour to the estate – an issue central to many tenancy conflicts at the time. At the trial, Shaw testified that when she asked the bookkeeper, "Massa, what me do to make you pull down house in that manner?" he replied, "Well, it is because you do nothing." Lyon and Kelly, upon ascertaining the cost of putting a roof on a "negro house", convicted the three estate personnel of trespass and ordered each to pay the sum of five pounds with costs to Charles Smith, failing which they were ordered to be confined to the Falmouth jail.[69] Although the three were later released on the basis of a writ of habeas corpus obtained by Barrett,[70] the outcome of this advocacy at the level of the special magistrate's court against unjust destruction of a family's shelter indicated that freed families could and did litigate successfully against an unfair system of tenancy.

The patent injustice of charging rental fees of each member of a family resident in one house, and the inequitable pro-planter judgments emanating from the courts of the local magistracy, were successfully challenged in the Supreme Court in 1839 by black families of Richmond estate, St Ann, in the landmark case *Bernal v. Green*. In February of that year, Robert Green and his wife, Susannah, and William Jones and his wife, Caroline, along with three other labourers of Richmond estate, were summoned and convicted by local magistrate George Robinson for debt allegedly owed to Ralph Bernal, the estate's proprietor. Robert Green and William Jones were committed to prison for rents said to be owed by their wives, a committal which reflected the philosophy of Bernal's attorney, Charles Smith, that "if the wives did not work, he would make the husbands pay".[71] The other labourers, also summoned and convicted for rental debts due to Bernal, included Susan Hull, "weak and sickly", Amelia Dane, who lived in her elderly mother's house, and another labourer on the estate, William Tracy.

While confined to the common jail in St Ann, Robert Green, William Jones and the other Richmond labourers took steps, with the assistance of solicitor Charles Harvey, to have their case appealed before the Supreme Court. Harvey applied for writs of habeas corpus, by which the Richmond labourers were to be removed from the jail for the purpose of appearing before the court. Harvey also applied for writs of certiorari, by which transcripts of their cases could be transferred to the Supreme Court. In various depositions, Robert Green, the apparent spokesperson for the group, advocated his family's stance on the injustice of both the rental demands on his wife and the committal by Magistrate Robinson. Through Harvey, Green questioned the legality of the absence of the usual second magistrate, and the convening of the hearing outside of regular court hours, when "the sun had gone down and it was time for candlelight". Green further contended that the "trial" was a strategy used by Smith, the attorney for Richmond, to intimidate his wife into working on the estate, and also to punish him for failing to enforce Smith's expectations of his wife. William Jones argued similarly in his deposition. In their affidavits, both Green and Jones insisted that neither they nor their wives had entered into any agreement to pay rent, but had agreed to work on the property for reduced wages in lieu of rent. Both were emphatic that because their wives resided with them, they should not be charged for occupancy of their houses, as illustrated by William Jones's reply to Smith's demand that he pay rent for his wife's tenancy: "No, my wife live with me."

Bernal v. Green was decided on the fact that the warrants of committal did not state the amount of charges for which the labourers were imprisoned; this rendered their indefinite detention illegal. Consequently, the Supreme Court's decision in June 1839 quashed the entire proceedings of the local magistrate's court, declared the imprisonment of the Richmond labourers illegal and ordered their immediate release. The contentious issue of charging separate rental fees for husband and wife was of crucial significance to the judgment; the chief justice declared that not only was the summoning and convicting of Susannah Green and Caroline Jones "clearly illegal", but also that "the wife is not liable, nor can the husband be made to pay any extra rent because his wife or friends are permitted to reside with him".[72] Advocacy by the Richmond family members culminated in a subsequent suit against the estate's personnel, which resulted in their being awarded just over fifty pounds as compensation for their illegal committal to jail.[73]

Within the evolving experience of freedom, therefore, the struggles of many black families to obtain security of shelter proved instructive in several respects. Faced with numerous obstacles in the attainment of such security, family members, both male and female, indicated that commitment to kin remained an enduring feature of black familial culture as well as an integral part of their vision of a free community. The foregoing discussion also reveals a critical realization on their part that security of tenure was attainable not only through individualized agency, but through commitment to the collective well-being by way of group advocacy.

FAMILY WELL-BEING THROUGH COLLECTIVE ACTION

As emphasized earlier in this chapter, one of the prominent features of black family advocacy was its collaborative nature, a feature which reflected the principle of commitment to the collective welfare which was characteristic of pre-colonial West African familial culture. Under the legal and physical constraints of apprenticeship, group responses had been undertaken mainly among apprentices of a single estate at a time. Full freedom, by its removal of geographical barriers to easy movement and hence to communication, facilitated collaboration for purposes of advocacy, especially (though not solely) through the medium of public meetings and the resultant submission of petitions and resolutions. Public gatherings of "members of the labouring class", whether under denominational aegis or not, focused on issues central to the welfare of the black majority and reflected concerns such as deteriorating economic conditions, health and education, and the growing problem of praedial larceny. An analysis of the petitions and resolutions generated during this period indicates that aside from the general importance of whatever issue was under discussion, the participants constantly expressed their specific concerns with the issue's impact upon their families or on their continued ability to support them. Such gatherings were therefore clearly channels of collective family advocacy, as they represented, among other things, group decisions about common concerns related to their families. Although most of these collaborative efforts failed to influence policy direction, this did not diminish the significance of the exercise in group advocacy.

The passage in 1851 of the Act for the Establishment of an Orphan Asylum, and for Certain Other Destitute Children (hereafter, the Orphan Asylum Act) provided an occasion for group responses from parents who were members of Baptist congregations in some parishes of the island. Originally intended to provide care for those orphaned by the cholera epidemic, the act also empowered the chairman of quarter sessions to commit to the orphanage any child adjudged by him to be "vagrant and destitute". It is clear that the many meetings held at Baptist chapels in Kingston, St Ann and St James were sponsored by Baptist missionaries who were especially concerned that the children committed to these orphanages would be instructed in the tenets of the Church of England, and it is equally clear that the petitions were articulated by the respective ministers of the Baptist faith. Nevertheless, these petitions conveyed the collective spirit of objection by Baptist parents, many of them very poor, to the "forcible seizure of a child whose only offence is its apparent destitution". Representatives of the Baptist congregations certainly voiced the combined objections of black parenthood to the act when they criticized "the interference with the natural rights of parents who appear to be allowed no voice in such a disposal of their own children" and called for the disallowance of the act. However, Colonial Office officials, seeing no grounds for disallowance, concurred with Governor Grey's view that the act be left to its operation, with only slight amendments.[74]

The virtually universal adversity faced by blacks in the period preceding the events at Morant Bay provided ample opportunities for collective advocacy. In an effort to relay their concerns to the queen in early 1865, approximately 108 "poor people of Jamaica and parish of Saint Ann's" signed a petition that emphasized, among other problems, the vulnerability of their crops to unpredictable landlords and the impact of the loss of their growing provisions on their ability to sustain their families, "numbers of us having a large family of 11 or 12 children depending on the provisions for subsistence".75

In 1865, Edward Underhill, secretary of the Baptist Missionary Society of Great Britain, wrote a letter to the Colonial Office, underscoring the socioeconomic plight of the poor, in which he highlighted problems of unemployment, low wages, heavy taxation, drought and rising prices. Island-wide meetings in response to the difficulties detailed by Underhill's letter embodied a collective representation of the people's dilemma in caring for their families and outlined, in some cases, their search for solutions which would enable them to more successfully facilitate family welfare. Thus, for example, the fourth resolution of a public meeting at the Spanish Town Court House, on 16 May 1865, spoke not only of the adverse effects of unemployment on labourers' ability to support their families, but also of the implications that some solutions might have for the quality of their family life: "People have been compelled to leave their homes to seek employment in foreign climes, and many others are only deterred from doing so, because they do not know what is to become of their families in their absence."76

The self-described "poor people" of St Ann had also, in their letter to the queen, suggested a cooperative solution, reminiscent of the commitment to the collective interest discussed earlier, in order to ensure greater security in their efforts at farming for a living. Thus, they offered to form a company to administer operations from a community-based farming effort, which no doubt would have entailed collaboration between families, if the queen would allow them some land. They indicated their intent to pay for the land and to work it in order to support their families.77

Groups of families also collaborated to advocate improvements in health facilities for their family members and for their communities. Illustrative of this is the petition submitted to Governor Darling in 1861 by approximately 117 "mechanics and labourers" of St Joseph's District in St Andrew, concerning the absence of medical facilities in their community. The petitioners had evidently consulted with each other prior to the petition being drawn up, as they expressed knowledge of "several young, active and healthy persons" who had died, but whose lives "may have been spared to their families" had medical assistance been available in "a timely manner". They also indicated that because they had "large families to maintain" and received very low wages, they could not afford the high fees of the medical man who lived a great distance from their community. Suggesting to the governor that the island be divided into districts and that a "medical man" be appointed for each district, the petitioners indicated their willingness, as a group, to contribute a small sum towards the remuneration of the doctor. This, they felt, would guarantee improved medical care for their families and for their community. There is no evidence that there were any improvements to the medical facilities in St Joseph's District during this period. In fact, Governor Darling regarded this petition as a disrespectful indictment of his administration as far as meeting the health-care needs of the people was concerned, and he suspended Robert Osborn, who had delivered the petition on behalf of these family members, from his position as member of the Privy Council.[78]

Family members also demonstrated group advocacy in pursuit of the welfare of their loved ones without participating in formalized meetings or submitting petitions. In 1847, black parents in several parts of St Elizabeth became very agitated over reports arising from a Baptist meeting at Ruthven, to the effect that the governor had issued instructions to compel their children to work for a certain number of hours each week and to be taught for three hours. Interpreting this reference to industrial education as an attempt to re-enslave their children, parents of children attending the curate's school in Lacovia, having evidently discussed the issue, proceeded together to the school and withdrew their children on the grounds that "they would not consent to the children again being enslaved". Importantly, this reaction led both Governor Charles Grey and the Honourable John Salmon, member of the council, to recommend caution in any proposal to implement industrial education.[79]

Parents also collaborated to advocate their children's progress in education by providing the labour for school construction within their communities. The significance of these collective forms of family activism is heightened by the fact that after full freedom, blacks evidently did not view residence in different locations as an obstacle to group action on behalf of the family. Thus, in 1854, Thomas Witter Jackson commented that three Presbyterian schools had been built by parental labour in St Mary, St Thomas-in-the-Vale and Metcalfe, while in Phillipsburgh, he pointed to "a commodious and beautiful residence for the teacher . . . erected by [the parents'] own unaided efforts".[80] In 1873, inspector of schools John Savage also highlighted collective parental advocacy when he reported that on his "tour of the west" he visited two schools "which had been established by the people themselves without any assistance whatever from any societies or the government". These collaborative efforts did not stop with the physical structures, as the fathers had also formed their own school committees, complete with rules, and had agreed to pay certain fees towards their children's education, actions which were indicative of the men's central role in familial contexts. The quality of their efforts was enhanced by the fact that the parents were of "scanty means". Savage emphasized the calibre of this example of group parental advocacy when he stated that the parents, all of whom belonged to different religious groups, "had simply as neighbours combined together of their own accord for the good of their children . . . and this they had done independently without advice or assistance".[81]

CHALLENGES TO FAMILY WELFARE: THE OBSTACLE COURSE OF THE JUSTICE SYSTEM

Persistent reports emanating mainly from stipendiary magistrates during this period convey the pervasiveness of the dilemma of partisan judgments and prohibitive costs, both of which militated against black access to equal justice. The crippling effects of costs were acutely demonstrated especially in relation to families around the time of the cholera epidemic, in 1854. Stipendiary magistrate Charles Lake, reporting from Portland in that year, emphasized the plight of many "bereaved mothers and children from the labouring class" who were turned out of doors because the male heads of their families had died intestate and the surviving family members could not afford to settle disputed claims to their landed property,[82] the jurisdiction over which properly resided in the Supreme Court. The evidence indicates, however, that in spite of such obstacles of expense and partiality, freed blacks in this period became their own advocates, particularly when they or their family members were victims of corruption or malpractice by "the authorities", and particularly when such practices threatened the continuance of their family income or the safety of their family members and homes.

One facet of malpractice which certainly threatened the security of the homes and property of many black families was the problem of corrupt petty-debt collectors. As governor Sir John Peter Grant pointed out in 1868, many freed people and their families – already economically marginalized by burdensome taxation, drought-plagued yields, miniscule wages and a general economic slump – found themselves being defrauded by debt collectors. These corrupt officials sometimes failed to turn over to them sums collected in payment of judgments for petty debts which blacks had filed at great cost to themselves. In addition, as Governor Grant further noted, "very great hardships" had been "inflicted on the poorer classes" against whom petty-debt judgments had been made; after sacrificing to pay the debts, they found their homes and families' security endangered by distress warrants to levy on their goods and property, with a view to recovering payments which they had, in good faith, made to these fraudulent debt collectors.[83]

The options available to individuals and families thus aggrieved were severely restricted, as few could undertake the expense involved in bringing legal suits against the offending collectors. Nevertheless, mounting complaints to local magistrates and justices of the peace served as an effective avenue of advocacy. This no doubt contributed to the passing of the Petty Debt Act of 1856, which specified penalties for fraudulent collectors, ranging from repayment, with costs, of money extorted to fines, imprisonment in default of payment and mandatory discharge from office. Black activists, through their complaints to justices, contributed to the exposure and removal of dishonest collectors, such as Morris in St Ann and Silvera in St Mary, between 1867 and 1868.[84]

Two victims of this type of corruption, husband and wife William and Jane Peterkin of St Ann, pursued their quest for justice to the fullest extent. In 1867, in response to a judgment against William Peterkin in a suit brought by Abraham Harris, the petty-debt collector for St Ann, the Peterkins paid in full their debt of five pounds and nine pence to Joseph Wilson, one of the deputy debt collectors for the parish. Thus, when later that year Wilson and another deputy collector attempted to seize goods and a pig from the family's home for payment of the said debt, the Peterkins not only prevented the removal of their property, but they took further steps to support their struggle for a just resolution. In her sworn deposition before Justice Lowry at Liberty Hall, Jane Peterkin pointed to the illegality of the attempted seizure on the twin grounds of prior settlement of the debt in full and the absence of a distress warrant. She accused the deputy collectors of petty debt of conspiring with Harris to "extort this sum from herself and her husband". The family's advocacy culminated in successful criminal proceedings against Harris and the two deputy collectors, as a result of which Harris was fined, with the alternative of imprisonment for one month if he defaulted.[85]

Corrupt officials and inordinate and costly delays in trial hearings were among the impediments which brought the district courts across the island into disrepute, and in many instances rendered the search for justice by blacks futile. Notwithstanding, freed blacks continued to advance their causes through this medium, and their perseverance, regardless of outcome, was indicative of their commitment to advocacy on behalf of family and home. The case of James Henry, who resided near Annotto Bay, is illustrative of this struggle, despite hurdles which led justice W.D. Bruce to describe him as an "unfortunate black man".[86] In 1871, Henry's landlord, Hitchins, refused to give him a receipt for a payment which he had made on a small place which he rented from Hitchins at Job's Hill, and thus Henry informed the landlord of his intention to ascertain from a magistrate whether he was legally entitled to a receipt. On his return home, Henry found that Hitchins had confiscated all his goods, destroyed his provision ground and turned his wife and three children out "into the wilderness". Concerned that he and his family were homeless and that their livelihood had been destroyed, Henry brought a suit against Hitchins in the Annotto Bay district court in 1871.

Over an eighteen-month period, Henry's case was postponed three times by the presiding judge, Blair, as Hitchins "could not attend". This delay not only occasioned additional difficulties of bringing all of Henry's witnesses to court each time, but also signalled a postponement of justice for the family. The eventual award of twenty pounds' worth of damages against Hitchins, in addition to costs, was never paid, so Henry took his advocacy one step further by taking out an execution order against Hitchins's property in order to recover damages and costs. However, Hitchins's pre-emptive step of signing over all his property and furniture to his son, the assistant clerk of the Annotto Bay district court, meant that the bailiff could not levy on Hitchins's property. Henry persisted in seeking a just resolution and restitution for his family, however, and his final effort through the district court was to apply to Judge Bruce for a judgment summons against Hitchins. This request was granted but not implemented in time for the case to be tried, because both Hitchins's son and the clerk of the district court refused on three occasions to comply. Penniless, Henry appealed to Judge Bruce to present his case to the governor, as he "could not get justice from . . . the District Court at Annotto Bay". Henry's persistent advocacy resulted in the removal of Hitchins's son from his positions in the courts, but he was unable to recover damages and costs from Hitchins. Nonetheless, Henry's commitment to his family and home was evidenced by the fact that he had exhausted all his money against an adversary who had boasted that he "had plenty of money and would ruin [him]", and had patiently navigated the obstacle course of the district court.[87]

When determined advocacy through the district courts failed to produce equitable results, freed blacks sometimes utilized a medium which they believed held more possibility of impartiality, that of petitioning the governor. The comparative abundance of such petitions to Governor Musgrave in the late 1870s to early 1880s may be explained by both the mounting complaints about the quality of justice dispensed by the district courts and the people's perception that appeals to Governor Musgrave held greater promise of just outcomes.[88] Thus, Elizabeth Campbell, a poor black woman, petitioned Musgrave in 1880 after Judge Kerr of the central district court granted judgment of two pounds and ten shillings against her and her children for trespass. Campbell's grandmother had bequeathed land to her and all her children, but after her grandmother's death and without Campbell's knowledge, a relative had sold three acres of the property to a Mr Tracey in payment of a debt. Tracey brought an action of trespass against Campbell when he found her picking pimento on property which she regarded as hers.

In upholding her case to the governor, she pointed out that her husband, who had previously deserted her, had maliciously destroyed her grandmother's will and that after Judge Kerr's decision, her house and furniture had been levied on, leaving her and her children destitute and incapable of affording the costly appeal process. Although Campbell's advancement of her cause won the governor's attention to the issue, she was ultimately denied a just settlement as Judge Kerr, opposing as "impolitic" the "Governor's encouragement of petitions of this sort", respectfully declined to comply with Musgrave's request for further information on Elizabeth Campbell's case.[89]

Other representations from freed blacks to Governor Musgrave focused on illegal actions taken by bailiffs of the district court and the failure of judges to grant redress to the aggrieved persons. The case of Mrs Dacres, an elderly widow whose adult son lived with her, provides one example. A bailiff of Judge Kerr's court, who had been instructed to effect a judgment levy against one of Mrs Dacres's sons, ordered that her home be invaded and all her property sold, and threatened both her and her son with violence. In 1878, when she initially presented her plight to Judge Kerr, she was given a series of convoluted legal measures to take, which she could neither understand nor afford to seek legal advice on. Her subsequent petition to Governor Musgrave resulted in her case being brought before another judge, who ordered the offending bailiff to make restitution to Mrs Dacres.[90] The same year, another woman, Mrs Burke, had her donkey illegally seized by the additional bailiff of Judge Kerr's court, who was executing a judgment against a friend of her son's who was staying at the family's house. Concerned that her source of livelihood for herself and her children and her means of transporting her produce to market in Kingston had been illegally taken from her, Mrs Burke sued the additional bailiff for misconduct. However, Judge Kerr's acquittal of the bailiff and his recommendation that she seek a remedy in civil action, an alternative she could not afford, led Mrs Burke to redouble her efforts at advocacy and to petition Governor Musgrave.

Although she never received compensation for the loss of her donkey, Mrs Burke's representation of her plight to Governor Musgrave convinced him that she had been an obvious "victim of injustice". Significantly, the efforts of Mrs Dacres and Mrs Burke, who were both heads of their families, focused the attention of Governor Musgrave, attorney general Edward O'Malley and indeed the Colonial Office on the "miscarriage of justice" perpetrated by officers of the district courts. Moreover, by bringing the details of their cases to the governor, these two family advocates contributed to Musgrave's censure of Kerr for his failure to use the power conferred on all judges of district courts, by section 53 of Law 22 of 1874, to redress the wrongs inflicted on innocent persons by officers of the court.[91] Ultimately, these cases of family advocacy reveal the extent to which blacks were prepared to go to ensure that, even if its course was interrupted, justice would eventually prevail for them and for their families.

Conclusion

The stereotypically negative representations of blacks as parents which had permeated the literature of Long, Carmichael and others, as discussed in this analysis, proved characteristic of elitist views of blacks during the entire period under review. Later scholarship produced by some sociologists and anthropologists (see chapter 1) also categorized the black family in the Caribbean as disorganized, dysfunctional and generally chaotic. In 1854, Alexander Fyfe, stipendiary magistrate for St David, reflected this negative perspective in reacting to one family's dispute, representing all blacks as "almost indifferent to the ties of kindred".[92] A quarter of a century later, the Commission on the Juvenile Population assessed black parents as irresponsible: "The limit of parental care is to provide them with a shelter at night . . . they are turned out into the streets to pick up a living as best they may."[93] The evidence presented in this chapter clearly contradicts any generalized assertion of black people's nonchalance to family, of irresponsible parenthood among blacks or of the marginal role of the male in familial contexts. Under the most challenging of circumstances, many black men and women prioritized the welfare of their children, and indeed of all family members, as part of their unfolding vision of freedom. In this respect, they did not view themselves as peripheral to their family and community groups. The many examples of family-oriented advocacy from this period, of both an individual and collective nature, demonstrate that primacy of kin and the kinship networks continued to be an indispensable hallmark of black familial culture in post-slavery Jamaica, as it had been during slavery and in pre-colonial West Africa. Black families in freedom faced numerous challenges, and the inability of many people to overcome these no doubt contributed to the reported cases of spousal desertions, child neglect and juvenile delinquency of which the commissioners investigating the juvenile population spoke. However, the social ills facing the black family in this period did not eclipse the evidence of activism by so many in advancing the welfare of their own. Rather, such extensive examples of family advocacy despite hardships are a clear indication of the extent and endurance of their familial commitment.

Chapter 3

Affirmation of the Ties That Bind

REUNIFICATION OF FAMILIES IN THE AFTERMATH OF SLAVERY

> I wanted to live with my wife and children at Mount Hyblar, to which property
> I had been attached until I was removed to Trafalgar . . . I wished, when my time
> should come, to be nursed and buried by my wife and family.
>
> – *Samuel Barnett, apprentice, 1836* [1]

IN HIS COMPARATIVE ASSESSMENT OF emancipation in the British Caribbean and
the American South, Demetrius Eudell emphasized a commonality which was
characteristic of blacks' expectations of freedom. Essential to their shared vision
was the fact that they "insisted upon . . . the attainment of freedom on their
terms".[2] In pursuit of this, blacks across the Americas viewed as a priority the
significance of familial ties. As discussed in chapter 1, there was a foundational
link between pre-colonial West African familial traditions and black familial
norms and values in the post-emancipation Caribbean. A profound devotion
to kinship, although not unique to western Africa, had been a significant
force in traditional West African societies, and this proved a durable cultural
transfer to the Caribbean, and indeed to the Americas as a whole. For blacks
in the region, freedom enacted meant, among other things, the reaffirmation
of the importance of kindred, whether biological, conjugal or even fictive,
and this was embodied in their determined efforts to reunite family members

Figure 5. *Negro Girls.* Valdez Collection, reprinted courtesy of the National Library of Jamaica.

separated by enslavement and to thereby reaffirm the ties that bind. In his assessment of the hopes and expectations which British Caribbean blacks had of freedom, Woodville Marshall emphasized that one of the principal benefits they anticipated was the opportunity to strengthen their families through the "reconstitution of units that had suffered forced separation".[3] Freed persons in the post-war southern states of America had a similar priority to locate relatives and to reunify family units.[4] In Cuba, too, freedom brought opportunities for reconstitution of family units broken apart by the experience of enslavement.[5]

"Reconstitution" refers to the process whereby family members separated by enslavement or other disruptive forces tried to achieve reunification or strengthening of the family unit. Although essentially permanent by design, it was also at times embryonic. For the purposes of this analysis, "embryonic reconstitution" denotes reunification sustained over a period of short or temporary duration. This was in evidence in Jamaica mainly during the apprenticeship period when many family members were able to execute short visits to relatives on other estates for the purpose of short-term reunification. In this respect, the reunions were embryonic as they were in the preliminary stages and many apprentices expressed their hopes that when full freedom came, this reunifica-tion with family would be placed on a permanent footing. The phenomenon of reconstitution, although the subject of a considerable body of literature in the post-bellum American states and a point of interest for some British Caribbean historians,[6] has generally not been the object of much research, especially in the Jamaican context. Thus, for example, Bridget Brereton comments that the evidence of family reconstitution after emancipation in the British Caribbean is "rather thin" but that "there is no reason to doubt Marshall's conclusion that many ex-slaves did succeed in this goal".[7]

Brereton's observations about the relative paucity of data are valid, especially when applied to the immediate post-slavery period in Jamaica and viewed com-paratively with the post-bellum American South. This is explained partly by the plethora of sources on the American experience, which was in itself a more sizeable undertaking because of the greater expanse of territory involved. In this respect, the work of the Freedmen's Bureau in the United States contributed significantly to the data on the post-slavery experience of blacks there, while the reports of the stipendiary magistracy in Jamaica fulfilled a similar purpose. It is also apparent that both agencies rendered assistance to blacks in the task of re-establishing links with separated family members; the Freedmen's Bureau, in particular, acted as "a clearing house of information and [provided] free transportation in some cases". The American database was further enhanced by teachers' and missionaries' letters on behalf of ex-slaves and by advertisements in newly established black newspapers.[8]

As noted previously, blacks' efforts at reconstitution in Jamaica, especially in the apprenticeship period, were bolstered by the help of a few stipendiary magistrates as well as some missionaries and itinerant abolitionists, although on a significantly smaller scale than the assistance provided by the Freedmen's Bureau. Nevertheless, documentation of reconstitution efforts generated by stipendiary magistrates and others gave rise to a comparatively greater amount of data for the apprenticeship period than for the immediate years after 1838. However, the crucial explanation for the relative dearth of data on reconsti-tution immediately following 1838 rests in the fact that, unlike in the United States,[9] the foundation for black family reconstitution in Jamaica was firmly laid in the period preceding full emancipation – that is, in the apprentice-ship period. Having established embryonic reconstitution during this period and having been freed of legal and physical constraints after 1 August 1838, blacks went on to transform these preliminary and temporary reunions into permanently reconstituted family units. In this endeavour, freed blacks in Jamaica, operating on a smaller expanse of territory than their counterparts in the United States, needed and received comparatively less assistance from stipendiary magistrates and others in reuniting with loved ones. Most of the formerly enslaved must have acted on their own initiative to re-establish family ties and there may have been no data pertaining to these personal efforts. Thus, it is hardly surprising that the sources, mainly stipendiary reports, make only cursory and generalized references to efforts at black family reconstitution in the years immediately following 1838.

This analysis therefore seeks to contribute to the discussion on the reconstitution of black families by first establishing that far from being the purely post-1838 phenomenon that it is traditionally understood to be, the attempt at reconstitution was very much in evidence during the apprenticeship period in Jamaica. Further, it will seek to examine the evidence of the embryonic reconstitution that took place during apprenticeship. Apprenticeship, however, was not merely a staging ground for temporary reunification of families. Notwithstanding the significant obstacles placed in their path, some apprenticed family members were in fact able to achieve permanent reunions through the purchase of their full freedom before 1 August 1838. Such instances will also be examined. Finally, as the consolidation or strengthening of the family unit was complementary to the process of reconstitution, this analysis also examines the efforts of blacks to consolidate their family units during apprenticeship by purchasing the freedom of family members, especially those residing on the same plantation.

Although a limitation of the sources is the relatively sparse information available on specific cases of reconstitution in the years immediately following 1838, a further aim of this chapter is to discuss the documented cases of family reconstitution that do exist for the period right after "full free". Additionally, after the abolition of slavery, some black families in Jamaica once more faced the spectre of forced separation. This was largely, though not solely, the result of the abduction and sale of family members to the slave markets of Cuba and the American South. (While out-migration of family members to destinations such as Colon and Limon Bay, for example, no doubt also had a divisive impact on the lives of some families, this analysis does not emphasize such scenarios, focusing instead on enforced separation through either enslavement or kidnapping.) The database generated by the combined efforts of family members, colonial government officials and the British Foreign Office to effect reunification of members separated by kidnapping was considerable. Thus, a final objective of this analysis is to contribute another dimension to the theme of reuniting black families by examining case studies of the attempts to restore such persons to their families in Jamaica. Ultimately, this chapter demonstrates that for freed men and women, re-establishing and strengthening the bonds of kinship proved to be intrinsic to their interpretation of the meaning of freedom.

Towards the Reconstitution of Families during the Apprenticeship Period

During apprenticeship, blacks utilized a variety of strategies to effect the re-establishment and consolidation of family links disrupted by slavery. In efforts to achieve temporary or embryonic reconstitution, the most common approach was the execution of visits to family members who were resident on other properties. Additionally, although rarely reported, some apprentices also appealed for a transfer of status from "praedial attached" (doing field work on a designated property) to "praedial unattached" (working in jobbing gangs) so as to enhance opportunities to be with family members, even for a brief while. For some, however, temporary family reunions were not enough, and these apprentices were prepared to endure the obstacle course of valuation tribunals in order to achieve permanent reunions through the purchase of full freedom for themselves or their loved ones. In some cases, apprentices requested transfers to other estates where their loved ones were in order to facilitate permanent reconstitution of their families. In instances where apprenticed members of a family were already resident on the same estate, blacks sought to consolidate their family units through purchasing the freedom of as many members as possible. Such strategies, whether conducive to temporary or permanent reconstitution and consolidation of families, signalled that in a transitional period designed to prepare them for full freedom, blacks were, in a very significant sense, preparing to put their families first.

The Imperial Act of Abolition, by affording apprentices some measure of autonomy over their time as well as a degree of mobility, provided opportunities for blacks to begin to undertake temporary reunions with relatives residing elsewhere. Although not universal, the adoption of the nine-hour workday, which allowed apprentices Friday afternoons or alternate Fridays off, certainly facilitated family visits. Indeed, special justice Watkins Jones in St Thomas-in-the-Vale stated that one of the reasons why apprentices favoured the nine-hour workday was that it enabled them to have more time towards the end of the week "for the purpose of seeing their paramours", even though this sometimes meant that they had to travel "an immense distance from the property to which they were attached".[10] Weekend reunions, especially when executed over considerable distances, raised the prospect of punishment for late returns to estates on Mondays, but this was a price which many family members were prepared to pay. On Hall's Prospect estate, for example, a female apprentice charged with being late on Monday morning explained that she "had gone to an estate some miles distant to spend the Sabbath with her husband".[11]

Although many weekend excursions to see separated family members were sporadic, some were characterized by regularity and frequency; naturally, this was most common for families whose properties were located within the same parish or within relative proximity to each other. This is illustrated by the case of Hamilton Brown, who was apprenticed to Culloden in St Ann, and Jane Carter, apprenticed to Alexandria, also in St Ann, about five miles from Culloden. Alexandria estate utilized the nine-hour system, so every weekend, Jane Carter went to visit with her partner, who was a mule man on Culloden. Apparently, the frequency of the effort could not be reciprocal; Hamilton explained that as a mule man he was constantly employed "in carrying grass". Jane's commitment to these weekly reunions earned her the reputation of being very late every Monday, resulting in frequent punishment. Unfortunately for this couple, Jane died before any permanence could be established, apparently from an infected wound aggravated by a stay in the workhouse and, reportedly, by her constant travels to and from Culloden.[12] Jane Carter's case is illustrative of the high price which some blacks ultimately paid in their quest to maintain family ties.

Some apprentices, if they lived on estates fairly near to those of their loved ones, were able to visit family on a much more frequent basis than on weekends only. This was the reality for an apprentice living on St Catherine's Hall estate in St James whose wife, an apprentice attached to nearby Fairfield, visited him each night "to lodge" with him. This case adds another dimension to the analysis of black efforts at reconstitution. In this case, as no doubt in some others, attempts to reunite and consolidate family bonds may have been underway prior to 1 August 1834. The husband's statement in 1837 that his wife had borne him seven children would seem to support this.[13] Of course, it is also possible that they were resident on the same property during slavery and were subsequently separated.

Similarly, Peter William Atkinson, apprenticed to Penshurst estate, and his wife, apprenticed to nearby Knapdale, both in St Ann, established a regular schedule of overnight visits during their time on separate estates. Devoted Baptists, the couple got together for prayer meetings every Monday, Wednesday and Friday night, after which Peter's wife slept at his house before returning early the next morning to Knapdale. On the other nights, Peter slept at his wife's house at Knapdale. It is clear that before the proprietor of Penshurst ordered Peter's house destroyed "on account of the prayer meetings", he and his wife had regarded this house as the focal point for their family activities. Thus, Peter "kept everything in it that he was worth", ate meals there with his wife and two children, prayed, socialized with friends and had regular conjugal visits there.[14]

Attempts to reunite on weekends and after hours, apart from the possibility of late returns on Mondays, did not usually result in conflict with estate management, as these options were exercised in the apprentices' free time. However, some blacks who were unable to achieve permanent reunions during apprenticeship were clearly not satisfied with the short-term, temporary substitutes of weekend or overnight visits. Thus, some family members opted for prolonged visits during the workweek, while others engaged in extended reunions, sometimes of several months' duration. Because they were in contravention of managers' expectations of their workforce, such actions brought family members into direct conflict with estate authorities. Susan Reid, attached to Epsom settlement in St James but characterized by Stipendiary Magistrate Cocking as a known runaway, utilized this option on more than one occasion. Her case offers an interesting example of "running to family", which departed from the norm of running away to escape slavery or, in this case, apprenticeship. Between late 1834 and early 1835, Susan spent approximately three months with her husband, Percy Reid, an apprentice at Friendship estate, also in St James. Cocking sentenced Percy, who had acknowledged his "defiance" in "harbouring his wife", to be worked in and out of the cell until his wife returned to Epsom.

Upon her return shortly thereafter, she also was punished, by being sent to the workhouse.[15]

Endeavours such as these, while signalling apprentices' commitment to maintaining family ties, also raised the wider issue of whether apprentices had the right to visit family members attached to other estates, especially during the workweek. Legal bases on which to punish apprentices so engaged certainly existed in the body of legislation enacted by the Jamaican Assembly during this period. Clauses 22 and 26 of the local Abolition Act labelled as a vagabond any apprentice found to be absent from the plantation for three or more days, and prescribed maximum punishment of fourteen days' hard labour or thirty-nine lashes. Conversely, under clause 20 of the first Act in Aid of the Abolition Act, apprenticed family members who received relatives from other estates could be charged and punished for "harbouring [and] concealing any apprentice absent without leave".[16]

This issue of apprentices' rights to visit family members on other estates was highlighted by the case of Jane White, brought to the governor's attention shortly after the start of apprenticeship in 1834. Jane, a female apprentice attached to Carey's property in Montego Bay, was reported to Special Magistrates Norcott and Hill for absenting herself from the estate for four consecutive workdays to be with her "reputed husband", Sam Beckford, who was attached to another property, Purling Stream estate. Jane White's son, Billy, had been instructed by his mother to inform Carey that "she intended to take a few days".[17]

Acting on the basis of laws such as the local Abolition Act (clauses 22 and 26), Carey felt quite within his right to regard Jane White as a vagabond and to send a special constable to Sam Beckford's house on Purling Stream estate. Jane was subsequently locked up and Carey brought the case before Norcott and Hill, charging Beckford "for harbouring the said Jane White". Carey, dissatisfied with Norcott's seemingly lenient punishment of Jane (he directed her to repay the time lost) and his refusal to punish Sam Beckford for harbouring her, lodged official complaints against these special justices for St James. More significantly, the responses of Norcott and the attorney general, Dowell O'Reilly, on the issue indicated the perceptions which both men had regarding the right of an apprentice to visit family members on other properties. Norcott's explanation for his refusal to punish Sam Beckford for harbouring an apprentice conveyed some degree of accommodation to black family forms:

"Sam Beckford was Jane White's reputed husband and that was as sufficient
. . . as if they had been married by the Archbishop of Canterbury and that
man and wife could not be separated and . . . [he] desired Sam Beckford to go
home, refusing to take further notice of the case".[18]

The attorney general's response also appeared to endorse the right of apprentices to undertake conjugal visits on separate properties and reflected official
awareness of the extensiveness of black family forms: "I do not think it improper
in Jane White to have been at night at her husband's or sweetheart's house
. . . the law seems to recognize the connexion as it says, clause 25, 4 Will. 4,
cap. 41, 'no apprenticed labourer shall . . . be subject to be separated from his
or her wife . . . or persons reported to have any such relation to him or her'."[19]
Similarly, Colonial Office official Thomas Spring Rice supported the right of
apprentices to visit their spouses or paramours on other properties. Although
he acknowledged that under the law, constables could arrest any apprentice
found loitering on an estate to which he or she was not attached, Spring Rice
was adamant that those terms certainly could not apply "to the case of a
woman engaged in her ordinary duties or pursuits under the roof of her real
or supposed husband".[20] In light of the frequent reports of apprentices being
punished for visiting their partners or spouses, these comments were, at least
in theory, a comparatively liberal affirmation of the legal right of the apprentice
to execute such visits.

In giving reasons for disallowing the second act in aid, passed by the
Jamaican Assembly in December 1834, the secretary of state for the colonies
further confirmed the right of apprentices, married or not, to visit each other
on separate estates without sanctions being applied. Clause 13 of the disallowed
act had provided for the arrest of any apprentice who was found on another
plantation but who was not legally married to the partner in whose dwelling
the visiting apprentice was staying. The secretary of state's response indicated
that given the reality of so many apprentices having formed unions outside
of marriage, the act, if allowed, would have infringed on the rights of many
apprentices to execute visits with their partners living elsewhere.[21] Such reactions lent support, at least theoretically, to apprentices' efforts to undertake
temporary reunions with family members.

This apparent official endorsement of the rights of apprentices to visit their
family members elsewhere was, however, in contradiction to the labour maximization concerns of estate management. Thus, the harassment and punishment

of apprenticed family members for attempting to re-establish and consolidate family links continued unabated. Indeed, by 1837, special justice E.D. Baynes reported that one of the main reasons for dissatisfaction among the apprentices was "the difficulty too often thrown in the way of apprentices who cohabit together as man and wife . . . living with, or visiting each other, when accidentally attached to different properties".[22] The fact that apprentices made this issue a subject of frequent complaints to the special magistrates confirmed their awareness that the ending of slavery on 1 August 1834 had conferred on them the right to embark on the re-establishment of family ties. That they persisted in effecting these visits in the face of continued opposition signals their abiding commitment to the ties of kinship.

The threat of punishments and sanctions inspired some apprentices to undertake alternative strategies in order to reunite with family, such as appealing to magistrates to arrange transfers to other properties. In 1831, Samuel Barnett, like so many other apprentices, had been separated from his wife and children when he was removed from their shared place of residence, Mount Hyblar, to Trafalgar estate while they were left behind. Thus, in 1836 he appealed to special justice Dr A.L. Palmer to arrange for his transfer to Mount Hyblar or, if this could not be done, to assist him in getting valued so that he could purchase his freedom and return there. Samuel Barnett's description of this event conveys the profound sense of family ties, real or desired, which inspired apprentices to persevere in their quest for reunification: "I went [to Dr Palmer] . . . to be removed from Trafalgar to Mount Hyblar, or if this could not be done, to buy my freedom . . . I wanted to live with my wife and children at Mount Hyblar . . . I wished when my time should come, to be nursed and buried by my wife and family . . . if I could only return to Mount Hyblar to live."[23]

There is no evidence to suggest that Barnett was successful in his attempt either to be transferred or to purchase his freedom, but the depth of his commitment to this quest, communicated by this testimony, is instructive of the stance which some black males, positioned in the transitional dilemma of neo-slavery, had adopted towards their family lives.

In 1837, another apprentice, Joseph Bowen Morris, made a similar attempt to reunite with his family. Formerly resident with his wife on Rome estate, Morris, a praedial apprentice, was removed to another estate, Saxham, along with several other Rome apprentices shortly after the start of the apprenticeship period. Thus separated from his wife, who was forced to remain on Rome,

Morris appealed to Special Justice Hulme to determine whether his removal
was legal and whether he could be restored to Rome plantation and to his wife.
However, Governor Sligo informed Dr Hulme that as a praedial unattached
apprentice (jobber), Joseph Morris was, by law, liable to be removed.[24] Almost
ten months later, Dr Hulme informed Sligo's successor, Governor Smith, that of
the twenty-three apprentices originally transferred from Rome to Saxham, ten
non-praedials and five praedials unattached had purchased their freedom. Of
the remaining eight, three had run away and the five who were still at Saxham
did not desire a return to Rome, as they were comfortable there. Although no
specific reference to Joseph Morris's fate was ever located, it seems quite probable that he was among those praedials unattached who had purchased their
freedom or perhaps among the three listed as runaways.[25] In any event, given
the initiative Morris took to accomplish his return to Rome and to his wife, it
is hardly likely that he was one of those who had opted to remain on Saxham.

More often than not, the status of praedial unattached, referring to apprentices working in jobbing gangs, was detrimental to the maintenance of close
family ties, as these apprentices could be hired out over great distances, and so
could be far from home for unpredictable durations. In unusual circumstances,
however, the status of jobbing apprentice could facilitate the reunification of
family members dispersed over several plantations, albeit temporarily. The James
family was one such case. During slavery, Eliza James belonged to Valley Minor
and Robert James, her husband, belonged to Mount Pleasant, fairly close by.
Together, they had five children. However, at the start of apprenticeship, Eliza
and one of her children, John, were transferred from Valley Minor to Owen
estate by Mr Utten, the owner of both properties. Eliza was concerned that
no one had ever asked her whether she wished to remove to Owen and, more
significantly, that the twenty-three miles separating Valley Minor from Owen
meant that she would hardly ever see her husband on Mount Pleasant or her
other children left behind on Valley Minor. She ascertained that Mr Utten's
jobbing apprentices were hired out only to his three properties, Valley Minor,
Owen and Castleton, and usually the duration of their stay at each property
was about a week. Therefore, in an effort to see all the members of her dispersed
family on a regular basis, Eliza successfully petitioned Utten to allow her to
hire herself out as a jobbing apprentice to his properties. Although her twelve-
year-old son, who was apprenticed to Owen, had an aunt and uncle on that
property, he regularly ran away to Valley Minor whenever he thought that his

mother might be there.[26] These actions on the part of both Eliza and her son were a significant indicator of the strength of family ties and the lengths to which apprentices were prepared to go to maintain or re-establish these bonds. Through a combination of strategies, members of the James family were able to conduct temporary but regular reunions with each other.

Many apprentices, wishing to establish permanent reunions with family members under conditions of "full free", sought valuation and purchase before the end of apprenticeship. The fact that many men, in pursuit of this goal, acted to prioritize the purchase of full freedom for their family members even before their own[27] indicates the premium which they placed on the well-being of their families and clearly demonstrates their intention to fulfil central, not peripheral, roles in their families once they had achieved freedom. Indeed, within the transitional parameters of the apprenticeship period, the cases of Samuel Barnett, Joseph Bowen Morris, Peter Atkinson and Larchim Bucknor, among others discussed in this chapter, all provide evidence which challenges the view that the black male was marginal within familial contexts and that he was indifferent to his family's welfare. Providing further evidence is the case of James Finlayson, a former apprentice on Penshurst in St Ann who was able to achieve permanent reconstitution of his rather large family through purchase in the latter half of 1834. Although the sources do not tell us much about Finlayson's wife, it is clear that while he was an apprentice on Penshurst, she was not living with him. Having purchased his freedom for £73 6s. 8d., he also bought his wife's freedom, and between them, they were able to buy the freedom of his wife's five children before marriage and that of five of his own, whom he had also "got before marriage". To support his large but reconstituted and free family, Finlayson bought a small plot of land, and he was able to make what he described as a comfortable living by 1837. Even before "full free", therefore, Finlayson had clearly put a great deal of effort into securing the freedom and consolidation of his very large family, a fact which endorses the idea that primacy of the family was on the agenda of many apprenticed males. Indeed, a devout Baptist and "always ready to help a fellow-creature who is in want of assistance", Finlayson was doing well enough to lend money to other apprentices when they, too, wished to purchase their freedom.[28]

Peter Atkinson, whose attempts to maintain regular visits with his wife were discussed earlier in this chapter, was among those who received assistance from Finlayson to purchase his full freedom. Atkinson and Finlayson had been good friends while apprentices on Penshurst, and Atkinson had allowed Finlayson to live at his house before the latter had been able to reconstitute his family and relocate. Thus, when Senior, the Penshurst proprietor, ordered Atkinson's home destroyed, Finlayson loaned Atkinson the thirty pounds and five shillings, which enabled him to purchase his full freedom and eventually achieve permanent reunification with his wife and two children.[29] Significantly, the examples of outreach displayed by both Finlayson and Atkinson were also reflective of their awareness of the need to contribute to their community. This sense of commitment to the collective welfare, characteristic of traditional West African cultures, continued to serve as a vital network of support in the quest for full freedom and consolidation of families.

Details of the struggle of Larchim Bucknor and his wife Margaret to obtain her valuation as a prelude to purchasing her freedom were highlighted in chapter 2. Their experience represents one of the most well documented and outstanding efforts of blacks to achieve permanent reconstitution of their families during the apprenticeship period. Married but separated by location on different estates in St Mary – Larchim on Montrose estate and Margaret on Rock River – this couple had been involved in a long-distance relationship from the period of slavery. Their desire to achieve permanent reunification was strengthened by the abusive treatment and sexual harassment of Margaret by the overseer of Rock River. Despite several failed attempts by both Margaret and her husband to obtain her valuation, and in spite of repeated threats by the overseer to obstruct her release from apprenticeship, the couple was finally able to get Margaret valued at thirty-five pounds and to purchase her release from apprenticeship in 1835. Thus, the Bucknors, by dint of their own perseverance, realized their goal of permanently reuniting as a family before the arrival of "full free". Margaret relocated to Montrose estate, where she lived with her husband and worked as a washerwoman.[30]

The efforts of apprentices to have themselves and their family members valued and to purchase their complete freedom were no doubt influenced by a variety of motives. Notwithstanding Governor Sligo's rationalization that many sought valuation either out of curiosity or out of a desire to experience a change in masters,[31] the large numbers of apprentices who chose this path were in fact a reflection of a widespread desire to experience the benefits of full freedom. Significantly, "depth of familial love and emotional attachment"[32] inspired many to seek family reunification through the purchase of remaining terms of apprenticeship. As noted previously, male apprentices, especially when faced with excessive valuations, prioritized the purchase of their partners or wives as well as their children as the first step towards reunifying and consolidating their families.[33]

However, many apprentices, in trying to rebuild their families, were ultimately frustrated by inequitable assessments from valuation tribunals. Although clause 8 of the Imperial Abolition Act made mandatory the release from apprenticeship of any person upon the payment of their assessed value, the composition of the valuation tribunals militated against fair appraisals. The two local justices, who were usually owners of apprentices, often inflated the apprentice's value over that suggested by the special justice. In 1836, Special Justice Hawkins from Trelawny complained to Governor Sligo about the consistently excessive valuations given in certain cases by Local Justices Lemonius and Samuels. For example, Eleanor Barnett of Arcadia estate was unable to afford the assessed value either for herself or for her eleven-year-old daughter, Francis Christie, even after a second valuation was requested by Hawkins. Similarly, Susanna Johnson of Craig Elleckie wished to purchase the freedom of her older sister, Cecelia Richards, from the same property, but was unable to afford the valuation of £46 6s. 8d. which Governor Sligo himself described as excessive, in view of her poor health and the fact that she had borne five children.[34]

It is clear that many enslaved families had not experienced the trauma of separation through sale or transfer; these families had entered the apprenticeship period with their immediate family members and, in some cases, their extended family located on the same property. Indeed, Barry Higman points to the predominance of these simple family households on Montpelier estate, many of them of the nuclear type, with "husband", "wife" and children sharing a common household.[35] Thus, many apprentices, already having their family members in the same locale as themselves, sought to consolidate their family units by purchasing, wherever possible, the complete freedom of their family members.

Sometimes, financial constraints forced apprentices to prioritize in selecting members of their families for purchase, and as previously indicated, the tendency was for the men to first purchase the freedom of their wives or partners and their children. In 1836, John Wilson, apprentice at a Kingston estate, opted to remain in apprenticeship while securing the release of his nineteen-year-old son, who was valued at thirty-six pounds.[36] As part of the general trend of mothers and children being released, Helen Kenlock and her two children from a Portland estate were released for a total sum of sixty pounds, while in St Andrew, Amelia Moody and her two children, Cecelia and Richard, had the rest of their terms purchased. Similarly, Eliza Henlen and her two children, of Trelawny; Jesse Campbell and her son, from Retrieve Old Works, Hanover; Margaret Roughly and her grown daughter, Jeannette Rissock of Pembroke Hall, St Mary; and Elizabeth Thomson and her son, of Oxford estate, also in St Mary, were among those who received full freedom through purchase.

Where resources permitted, many members of a single family purchased their release from apprenticeship together. For example, on Blenheim estate in St Ann, Margaret and Thomas Ingram, both non-praedial, as well as Eliza, Peter, Charlotte, Alexander and David Ingram, categorized as one family in the returns of Stipendiary Magistrates Connor and Chamberlaine, were all purchased at the same time.[37] Five members of the Sicard family, all attached to York Castle in St Ann and all non-praedials, were required to pay very different sums, based on assessed value according to age. Thus, Mary was the "most valuable", being assessed at thirty pounds, Ellen was valued at twelve pounds, Isaac at ten, Rachel at six and Maria at two. The total sum was paid to Stipendiary Magistrate Laidlaw, and these members of the family were released from apprenticeship at the same time.[38]

Intentions to free all members of a family at the same time, however, could not always be fulfilled in light of the total sum required. For example, when four adult members of the McKie family from Lyssons, all non-praedial, were each valued at £27 13s. 4d. each, requiring a total payment of £110 13s. 4d. to the stipendiary magistrate, this was too hefty a sum for the family. By June 1835, only Eliza and Ann McKie had had their valuation sums paid, while the freedom of John and Susan McKie had been deferred.[39] No doubt, painful decisions had to be made regarding whose freedom should be prioritized. Jane Warder, a non-praedial mother attached to Great Pond estate and valued at £40 11s. 3d., and one of her daughters, Eliza McCole, also a non-praedial attached to the same estate and valued at £20 5s. 5d., had their full freedom purchased in 1835. However, another of Jane's daughters, Ann Sterling, also of Great Pond, a non-praedial and valued at £20 5s. 5d., had seen her full freedom delayed because of limited funds.[40]

Clearly, then, the processes of valuation and purchase of full freedom held mixed fortunes for blacks hoping to reconstitute and consolidate their families before the termination of apprenticeship. Given the obstacles to obtaining fair valuations, it is especially significant that between 1 August 1834 and 31 May 1836, 998 apprentices obtained their full freedom through purchase. However, in the same period, for 624 apprentices, inability to pay the assessed value postponed "full free", with all its attendant benefits for families.[41]

Further, for many apprentices who were able to overcome the hurdles of unfair valuations, the reconstitution of their family units was still far from assured. Perhaps in an attempt to enforce the payment of rentals by freed family members, estate management tried to enforce separation of families by preventing persons freed by manumission or purchase from residing with family members who remained apprenticed. To achieve this, they used strategies including the serving of notices on the freed person to quit the premises, which he or she had occupied while an apprentice, or declaring the freed persons tenants and charging exorbitant rents.

Stipendiary magistrate E.B. Lyon detailed numerous cases of families afflicted by these coercive policies. Lyon noted that on Mount Vernon estate, owned by McPherson, two female apprentices had their remaining terms purchased by their husbands, but were subsequently ordered off the estate and prohibited from entering their husbands' houses, unless they paid a weekly sum. The fact that McPherson threatened to use the Trespass Act to remove these two women would suggest that in this case, the families refused to acquiesce to the payment of rent. At Island Head plantation in Mr Lyon's district, Robert Graham, having purchased the rest of his term, was immediately ordered off the property and forbidden to enter his wife's house. Graham persevered, however, and continued to visit his wife, with some assistance from Lyon.[42]

Similarly, in 1836, Elizabeth Brown, who was apprenticed to Tulloch plantation, St Thomas-in-the-Vale, encountered great difficulty in effecting the permanent family reconstitution which she had envisioned. Abraham Gordon Anthony, a free man "to whom she was married" but who resided elsewhere, had been denied the right of access to her residence. Special justice James Harris, in bringing the case to the attention of Governor Smith, pointed to the rights of Elizabeth, as an apprentice, to the free use of her house and grounds and to the reception of her "husband" or any of her friends there. Moreover, as Harris pointed out, the fact that Anthony was arrested twice for being with his "wife" was in direct contravention of the principles enunciated by the secretary of state for the colonies when, in late 1835, he had defended the disallowance of the second act in aid.[43] Apprentices, legally married or not, had every right to reunite with their spouses or partners without fear of sanctions.

Brereton speculates that in light of the obstructive tactics pursued by estate management, and given the apprentices' dedication to re-establishing family ties, these experiences must have "brought home to the ex-slaves . . . the precariousness of family life for people who were fully dependent on the estates for survival and . . . must have made many women – and, no doubt, many of their male relatives – determined to withdraw from full-time estate labour once 'full free' came".[44]

By extension of Brereton's point, such experiences, stumbling blocks to reconstitution, must also have strengthened the resolve of family members to establish themselves as soon as possible in independent freeholds where their families could truly be consolidated. Ultimately, the experience of apprenticeship had provided far more than a warning to blacks of the uncertainty of family life under the aegis of estate management. Fully aware that 1 August 1834 heralded the road to "full free", black men and women had used every opportunity and resource available to them in the quest to re-establish links, whether temporary or permanent, with family members separated from them by slavery. In large measure, they had succeeded in establishing a foundation which would enable them to move forward into full freedom with their families.

Reconstitution of Families after 1838

The arrival of "full free" on 1 August 1838 removed all remaining barriers to the ongoing processes of reconstitution and consolidation of families. Liberated from the restrictive deadlines of apprenticeship and invested with unfettered mobility and the ability to determine residence and employment, freed blacks were able to transform short-term visits into permanent reunions with relatives and spouses. In this respect, the Jamaican experience paralleled that of some American states, where, according to Litwack, "after emancipation, husbands and wives who had lived in this manner [short-term visits] . . . quickly seized the opportunity to spend more than weekends together and settled down, usually, on one or the other place".[45]

Clearly, the genesis of reconstituted families rested in the depth of blacks' familial attachments and ancestral devotion to kin. Not crediting blacks for this nor sharing in this perspective, paternalistic colonial administrators, missionaries and others sought to extend to blacks on the eve of full emancipation a set of Euro-cultural guidelines for the reconstitution of their families. At a public meeting held at the Baptist chapel at Falmouth on 12 July 1838, Special Justice Lyon advised the apprentices, soon to be fully freed, that "husbands and wives must live together. . . . During your state of slavery, separation was at times unavoidable . . . and [with full freedom] you must . . . determine which will be preferable; to choose the residence in which the husband may be fixed, or the estate on which the wife may be domiciled."

Not only was Lyon failing to acknowledge black initiative in the reunification and consolidation of their families, but he was also promoting the Euro-cultural norm of Christian marriage as the status quo for reconstituted families. Possibly in reference to the separation of some children from their parents during slavery, Lyon went on to advocate that "the younger branches of the family must reside under the same roof until they become married and form separate families".[46]

Once "full free" had been attained, the internal migration patterns of former apprentices give some indication of the efforts they made to reconstitute their families. Such migration could be explained by economic factors as well, including the desire to gain access to optimum working conditions and to benefit from differentials in compensation. In particular, the urban attractions of a greater variety of employment opportunities coupled with higher wages, especially for skilled and semi-skilled labour, prompted many rural-to-urban migrations. However, the movement of freed blacks around the island was, undoubtedly, also a reflection of their efforts to permanently reunite with their families, many of whom would have experienced some degree of embryonic reconstitution during apprenticeship. Brereton highlights a corresponding motivation for population movements in Trinidad, where "in the weeks after 1st August the freed people were moving around the island, migrating to different areas to resume 'family connexions'. At Orange Grove Estate, for instance, people were reported to have left and 'attached themselves to friends and family elsewhere'."[47]

In Jamaica in 1839, stipendiary magistrates Edward Fishbourne and William Hewitt sought to explain why the effective labour force of St George had been reduced by approximately four thousand persons. They reported that about five hundred persons had left the estates to which they had been attached during apprenticeship, having "returned to the southside or to other parishes from which they were removed before the Apprenticeship".[48] Although they gave no further details, this was a clear reference to the migration of former apprentices to other parishes in order to permanently re-establish familial links broken by the separation of enslavement. Similarly, stipendiary magistrate J. Daughtrey, reporting from St Elizabeth in September 1838, referred to efforts by "two tradesmen" to relocate to the estate on which their wives were resident. During apprenticeship, these two men, attached to other estates in St Elizabeth, had arranged temporary reunions with their wives, having visited the estates where they were located and "worked the ground there". Shortly after 1 August 1838, "being willing themselves to settle there", the men bargained with the proprietor of the estate where their wives lived and offered two days of their labour as rent. Although their proposition was rejected, it demonstrated the seriousness of their intentions to relocate in order to achieve permanent reconstitution of their family life.[49]

After 1 August 1838, population movements on coffee plantations owned by Hinton Spalding also indicated similar desires on the part of freed family members. On Platfield plantation in St Mary, Spalding noted that the labouring population had increased because "they returned from the locality where I had placed them, to their old locality of Platfield from which I had removed them; but the consequence is that I had a great diminution in labourers at the Hermitage [another of Spalding's coffee plantations, located partly in St George and partly in St Andrew]".

Some proprietors, including Spalding, who gave evidence before the 1842 House of Commons Select Committee on the West India Colonies were predominantly concerned with the problem of labour which confronted them. As such, Spalding may not have grasped the full significance of what had occurred on his properties. However, it is quite clear that during apprenticeship, Spalding had transferred quite a few of his workers from Platfield to Hermitage, a change which had evidently disrupted familial links among the affected apprentices. Thus, with "full free", these workers opted to leave Hermitage and return to their former location at Platfield so as to permanently re-establish their family lives.[50]

On another of Spalding's properties, Grove coffee plantation in Manchester, there was also a noticeable increase in the labouring population after 1 August 1838. Prior to this time, the female working population on Grove had outnumbered their male counterparts by three to one. Spalding attributed the subsequent increase in the male population to migration onto the property: "The husbands of some of the women were induced to settle there and join their wives instead of carrying them from the property." Spalding suggested that these removals were primarily due to the availability of rent-free houses and grounds at Grove. However, these were clear evidence of family strategies to reconstitute family units through relocation. As such, the tenancy incentives at Grove would have facilitated the decision regarding which property they would choose as the site for relocation.[51]

Although the empirical base is relatively restricted, there is little doubt that relocation for the purpose of reconstituting families would have contributed to fluctuations in the labour force on other coffee and sugar properties as well as on livestock pens. The withdrawal of some women and children from the workforce of these properties, often reflective of family-based decisions such as contribution to the labour needs of the family home and grounds, may also in some cases have been indicative of efforts at consolidating families. Thus, the attempt by some men to establish a common residence with their women and children from whom they had been previously separated would have contributed to the decline in the numbers of females and children at work on sugar, coffee and livestock properties.[52] In an unwitting reference to black male initiative, Stipendiary Magistrate Fishbourne, reporting from St George in 1839, commented that "many respectable people are now availing themselves of opportunities of purchasing or leasing small pieces of land where they are preparing to place their wives and children, and where they also will retire when they can quit the estates".[53] While this was no doubt a reference to the general effort at establishing family residence away from the estates, some of these relocations must have represented the endeavour to permanently reunite by instituting a common residence. Indeed, the significant accomplishment by blacks of establishing free villages and peasant holdings across the island was, as Swithin Wilmot points out, "a family enterprise" in which "they reconstituted their families and exercised options that came with freedom".[54]

Many blacks rejected the European ideal of Christian marriage as the only context in which to promote stable families and, much to the chagrin of missionaries and other representatives of "polite society", continued after 1838 to consolidate their family units outside of this idealized state. Others, however, had imbibed the value system which equated legal marriage with propriety, as

Figure 6. *The Poor Man's Heritage.* Reprinted courtesy of the National Library of Jamaica.

demonstrated by the spokesperson for a group of apprentices who had refused to attend service in a "temporary church" located on an estate residence: "No, minister, we can't go to you church – god no dere! . . . Busha livin wid woman in a house where minister preach widout dem married, and god can't come bless di word where . . . wickedness carry on."[55]

For those who accepted Christian marriage as the ideal, many were convinced that it provided opportunities to further reconstitute their families. Thus, even while they were still apprentices, as Stipendiary Magistrate Daughtrey reported, many men were preparing to marry women with whom they had children: "Multitudes are preparing to marry and in by far the greater number of instances, they unite themselves with the proper persons, the mothers of their children."[56]

Missionary and stipendiary reports between 1838 and 1842 indicated an upsurge in marriages among the freed population. James Phillippo, a Baptist missionary, reported that "out of a population of 420,000, not fewer than 14,840 marriages have taken place annually" since the passing of the Dissenters' Marriage Act in 1840, which legalized marriages performed by dissenting missionaries.[57] At least among those blacks influenced by missionary and denominational values, Christian marriage was perceived as a gateway to the "respectability" that elite society had assigned to that state. This report by Phillippo indicates that in the context of a non-marrying culture, the idea of Christian legal marriage must have held tremendous significance for the thousands of freed people who saw the formal marriage ceremony as an opportunity to solidify family ties which had been forged under slavery.

Efforts at Reuniting Families: Some Case Studies, 1834–1860

> In November 1842, a negro lad calling himself "Charles" presented himself to the Syndic procurador general at Puerto Principe and stated that he had been stolen from the beach near a town in Jamaica . . . but the name of the place he forgets . . . he was carried to . . . Santiago de Cuba, where he remained in slavery.[58]

For some black families in Jamaica, the spectre of forced separation from their loved ones was resurrected after 1834 by the continuance of slavery in places such as Cuba and the American South. From 1841 onwards, reports emanating from Jamaica, ultimately destined for the British Foreign Office, detailed incidents of the kidnapping of black children and juveniles, usually boys, from seaport towns such as Lucea or Montego Bay and their eventual sale into slavery either in Cuba or in the southern United States. According to Governor Charles Grey, by 1848, reports of such occurrences had been sufficiently frequent to alarm "the black population through the western parishes of Westmoreland, Hanover and St James", who feared that the "inhabitants of Cuba . . . would soon be coming upon the coast to seize them to carry them off into slavery".[59]

Especially in the 1840s and 1850s, the traffic of foreign vessels to Jamaica's seaport towns provided transient employment for juveniles and others, while presenting much fare for childhood curiosity. Such a scenario facilitated successful ventures by unscrupulous ships' captains who enticed youngsters on board for "a quick look" or with promises of lucrative jobs at sea for short periods. Some who disappeared in this way were never heard from again. The continuation of these episodes prompted Lord Grey in 1851 to request Governor Charles Grey to warn "the black and coloured inhabitants of Jamaica" about the dangers posed to their children in consenting to go aboard these vessels, whether out of curiosity or in response to some incentive.[60]

Efforts to reunite the victims of such kidnappings with their families in Jamaica proved a daunting task, and the outcomes were not always successful.

In the execution of these attempts, black family members sometimes played a crucial, though at times unacknowledged, role. Such cases indicate the strength of the ties that bound members of these families together, while revealing the depth of despair which resulted when reunion efforts proved futile. On some occasions, information about missing children was first brought to the governor's attention through the efforts of relatives who had contacted a trusted missionary or stipendiary or local magistrate. In some cases, family members who had themselves been enslaved in Cuba, for example, but who had been liberated and brought to Jamaica, petitioned the governor to assist them in their efforts to reunite with relatives still enslaved on that island. On other occasions, the victims themselves aided in the reunification process by alerting the authorities in the country of their captivity and by supplying, where possible, information about their families and homes in Jamaica.

Ultimately, however, the process of recovering kidnapped or otherwise enslaved family members from overseas could only be accomplished through the intercession of the British government, and more particularly the Foreign Office. The detention in slavery of blacks from Jamaica, who had become British citizens upon emancipation, prompted swift and thorough action by the British Foreign Office. This, however, was more likely the result of the British government's refusal to countenance a violation of its sovereignty rather than an index of its concern for its newest black citizens. Through diplomatic channels, Foreign Office officials sought to have the governments in question release victims from slavery or detention and undertook measures, where possible, to restore them to their families in Jamaica. This analysis therefore seeks to extend the discussion on the post-slavery reconstitution of black families by demonstrating the pivotal roles played by the Foreign Office and the colonial government as well as by family members in pursuing the return of those who had been kidnapped and enslaved to their loved ones in Jamaica.

Case Studies in the Reunification of Families

THE CASE OF THE KELSON/KELSALL FAMILY

Subsequent to the abolition of the slave trade in the British colonies and prompted by the amelioration movement, several planters in the Bahamas, fearing the loss of their slaves without adequate compensation, removed with their slaves to other territories such as Cuba. In 1822, the family of Cuffee Kelson – his wife, Eve; their two daughters, Harriet and Elizabeth; and Cuffee's brothers, Nat, Billy, Newton and John Kelson – were among a group of slaves removed by their owner, Forbes, from Nassau to Cuba.[61] Although such relocation of slaves was in contravention of clause 1 of the 1806 Foreign Slave Trade Abolition Act,[62] the entire Kelson/Kelsall family remained enslaved in Cuba for approximately twenty years. During this time, Cuffee and his wife went on to have eight more children: George, Maria, Edward, Robert, Amelia, Alexander, Eve and Adam.[63]

In 1842, the British government, acting through Joseph Crawford, the British consul general in Cuba, was able to release Cuffee and his four brothers from slavery. Given a choice as to residence, they chose Jamaica and, with the exception of Newton, who died in a Santiago hospital after being liberated, they were relocated to Kingston in 1844.[64] Unfortunately for Cuffee, his wife and their ten children were not freed at this time, thus remaining separated from him and enslaved in Cuba. A clear explanation as to why such an anomaly occurred was not given in communications between Crawford and the British foreign secretary, Aberdeen, regarding the brothers' liberation. It could be surmised that in 1842, these authorities were not aware of the existence of Eve and their ten children, nor of their relationship to Cuffee. This explanation would seem plausible based on the fact that although the British officials were aware from 1841 that the Bahamian planter, Forbes, had transferred his slaves to Cuba,[65] the sources do not indicate that Cuffee Kelson gave any detailed accounts of his family to the authorities until after his arrival in Jamaica in 1844. However, even if there is no evidential basis on which to prove that officials knew of her existence at the time of his liberation, it seems highly unlikely that, given a chance, Cuffee would have failed to communicate this vital information to them.

As will be discussed shortly, the Foreign Office, by 1845, had been given detailed information on Cuffee's wife and children. Thus, Aberdeen's comments in 1846 on the prospects of Eve and her children being liberated from slavery in Cuba offers another explanation as to why they had not been released in 1842 along with Cuffee and his brothers. Aberdeen argued that if documentation of Eve's freedom prior to being transferred to Cuba could be produced, Cuban authorities would agree to their release, "bearing in mind the principle laid down and acted upon by the authorities of Cuba in the cases of Cuffee and others of the Kelsall [*sic*] family".[66] This suggests that evidence had been presented to the Cuban authorities in 1842 of the prior freedom of Cuffee and his brothers, and that either such evidence was not available on Eve in 1842, or the authorities had no knowledge of her relationship to Cuffee.

By conveying information on his wife and children to the authorities after his arrival in Jamaica, Cuffee Kelson played an instrumental role in the subsequent quest to have Eve and their children freed from slavery and reunited with him. Almost as soon as they arrived in Jamaica, Cuffee and one of his brothers, Nat, gave sworn affidavits on Eve, the children and their location on a property in "the district of Candelaria", owned by the widow of Captain Ising, formerly of the British West India Regiment. These affidavits were brought, through Governor Elgin, to Lord Stanley's attention in 1845.[67] In a later petition, in 1847, directed to secretary of state Earl Grey and routed through Governor Charles Grey, Cuffee (with professional assistance) spoke of his unrelenting efforts to help in the recovery of his family. He had made "unwearied efforts but without success to establish a communication with his wife Eve and with his ten children".[68]

These early initiatives by Cuffee and his brother Nat set in motion a series of efforts on the part of the Foreign Office to have Cuffee's family liberated and restored to him. Crawford, the British consul general in Havana, initially "appealed to the humanity" of the authorities in Cuba to obtain the release of the family, but this was, as Crawford had anticipated, "in vain".[69] Evidently, the stance of the Spanish authorities as early as 1845 was the aforementioned condition that Eve and her children would be released only if documentation of Eve's free status before being transferred to Cuba could be provided.[70] Once again, in an unrelenting affirmation of the ties that bind, Cuffee tried to help, and in a sworn statement in 1845 to David Turnbull, the British commissary in Jamaica, he indicated that his wife had been a free person when removed from Nassau.[71]

In order to verify Cuffee's deposition on his wife's formerly free status, Consul General Crawford made repeated requests of the governor of the Bahamas to obtain and submit evidence of Eve's status at the time of the transfer. Aberdeen anticipated that once this was produced, Crawford "should not hesitate to demand her immediate and unconditional freedom together with that of her children". As mentioned earlier, Aberdeen felt that the precedent of releasing previously free persons, which had been set in the case of Cuffee and his brothers, would be honoured on a second occasion, if the requirements of the Cuban authorities were met.[72]

The governor of the Bahamas was unable to locate any evidence of Eve's free status prior to 1822. In light of this, Aberdeen closed the door on the possibility of the Foreign Office taking any further action. Issuing a stern reminder, he pointed out that the British government would not "claim from foreign governments as a . . . right, the restoration to liberty of . . . British subjects who while in the condition of slaves may have been removed from British colonies to foreign slave holding colonies . . . and may be held in slavery there".[73]

Having struggled to place the predicament of his wife and children before both colonial and metropolitan officials, Cuffee Kelson, undaunted by these disappointments, redoubled his efforts in 1847. The illiterate Cuffee obtained help to present to secretary of state Earl Grey a poignant but thorough account of his family's background, the circumstances of their transfer to Cuba and his subsequent efforts to help in their recovery. The account clearly conveyed the profound emotional ties between Cuffee and his family as well as his commitment to the task of reunification. Emphasizing that he would try everything in his power to achieve his goal, Cuffee spoke of his abiding sense of duty to his "unhappy relatives", and of the affection which he felt for his family. Thus, he petitioned the British government to intercede with the government of Spain so that his wife and children might be restored to him. Cuffee's untiring efforts in the face of daunting obstacles were the embodiment of that dedication to kin which was the dominant theme of the efforts at reuniting black families during this period. His persistent activism demonstrated that for him, the freedom and reconstitution of his family took precedence over all else and, as with other examples discussed so far, located the black male at the very centre of family reunification efforts. However, despite having fathered ten children with his wife of over thirty years and having become a grandfather in Cuba, Cuffee was never to experience reunion with his family, who remained enslaved in Cuba.[74] For Cuffee, his personal saga of enslavement, his forced migration from Nassau to Cuba, the pain of separation from his wife and children, and the final failure of diplomatic measures revealed an awful reality. The end of slavery did not always signal the end of family trauma.

The Case of George Wellington Crawford, "Wellington"

Shortly after the inception of apprenticeship in August 1834, George Wellington Crawford, referred to in the sources as "a negro boy named Wellington", was kidnapped from a beach in Montego Bay. His abductors, a Captain James and his wife, Hannah, took him to Cuba and sold him to a planter, a "bald-headed old man" named Garcia. Evidently, in kidnapping Wellington, Captain James utilized a strategy that had been employed in abducting other boys, which was to confine the child on deck after he had completed a chore for the captain.[75]

The steps by which news of Wellington's disappearance was conveyed to the authorities in Jamaica could not be ascertained from the sources. Although no reference to the identities of either his father or his mother was ever discovered, it is clear that he had family and close friends who missed him in Jamaica. In communications between Governor Elgin, the Colonial Office and the Foreign Office, several references were made to the authorities' anxiety to "restore him . . . as speedily as possible to . . . his kindred".[76] Moreover, as will be discussed shortly, two other boys, Francis Grant and William Mitchell, who were either relatives or close friends of Wellington, became involved in the effort to rescue him. It may be surmised that either a family member or a close friend must have reported his disappearance, perhaps to a stipendiary magistrate or a trusted missionary.

Prior to 1838, direct negotiations between Charles Clarke, the British pro-consul in Havana, and the Cuban authorities to obtain Wellington's release had proven unsuccessful. By late 1838, cognizant that only the intervention of the government at Madrid would guarantee Wellington's successful restoration, British foreign secretary Viscount Palmerston, through the Earl of Clarendon, Britain's consul in Madrid, communicated the circumstances of the boy's abduction and enslavement to the Spanish government, requesting its urgent intercession. By 31 January 1839, Madrid had ordered the captain general of Cuba to dispense justice in the matter and "cause the negro in question to be returned".[77]

Thus, under orders from Madrid, the previously uncooperative captain general acted swiftly to investigate and aid in Wellington's recovery. Garcia, Wellington's enslaver, was "arrested and placed in prison".[78] In a compelling demonstration of the strength of friendship and kinship, Francis Grant and William Mitchell – who were identified in the sources as "two other negro boys" and "witnesses to Wellington's identity", and who were possibly either relatives or close friends of his – provided critical assistance in the search effort. Dispatched to Cuba in late 1838 by the governor of Jamaica, the boys were placed under the official protection of the British consul there.[79] Although the exact circumstances were not given in the sources, it is clear that William Mitchell, in particular, provided the crucial identification of Wellington as the boy for whom the search had been launched. This is supported by Wellington's later declaration that he had been "found by William Mitchell".[80]

By August 1839, Wellington, Francis and William were turned over by the captain general to Charles Clarke at St Jago de la Cuba. Wellington's reunification with family and friends in Jamaica was delayed, however, because the Cuban authorities, desirous of retaining him as a witness in proceedings against Garcia and others involved in his purchase and enslavement, refused to expedite his passport. Consequently, Francis and William were sent back to Jamaica without Wellington.[81] Further appeals from the Foreign Office, through the British pro-consul in Cuba, to the captain general finally resulted in Wellington's passport being granted in September 1842. Wellington was placed on the Royal Mail Steam Packet Company's vessel *Tweed* on 1 October 1842 by Charles Clarke,[82] and he arrived in Jamaica two days later. Subsequent communications from Governor Elgin indicated that after a "lengthened detention in slavery in Cuba", Wellington had been reunited with friends and family.[83] Although the sources consulted revealed no details of the reaction of Wellington's family to his homecoming, Governor Elgin's remark, no doubt uttered from an official perspective, conveys something of what they must have felt: "Wellington is, I rejoice to say, safely landed in Jamaica."[84] It is significant that after his return home, Wellington provided, through his deposition, valuable insights into the cases of three other boys – Saulman, William and Charles – similarly kidnapped and enslaved in Cuba.[85] Thus, in his own way, he sought to assist others in their quests to be reunited with their families. Charles's experiences are examined in the following case study.

THE CASE OF CHARLES ROGERS

Wellington, as a former kidnapping victim who had been returned home, played a significant role in the effort to reunite another kidnapped boy, Charles Rogers, with his family in Jamaica, as did the abducted boy himself. The plight of Charles and two other boys, Saulman and William, was first brought to the attention of the colonial authorities in Jamaica by Wellington after his return home in 1842. In his deposition of November of that year, Wellington indicated that he had known the three boys while in Cuba and that he had encountered one of them, Saulman, in a town called St Jago about five months after he had been found by William Mitchell. Wellington, relaying information that he had received from the boys, indicated that all three had been apprenticed to properties in St James. Charles, "a black boy", had been attached to Tryall estate; Saulman, also "a black boy", to Latinum estate; and William, "a mulatto boy", to Ironshore estate.

According to Wellington's recount, approximately one month after his own abduction, Charles and the other two boys were taken from a beach in Montego Bay by the same Captain James and Hannah James, whom the boys emphasized "had stolen them". Subsequently, they encountered a fate similar to Wellington's, being delivered in Cuba to "the same bald-headed old man" and enslaved. Charles and the other boys were then taken "to the interior to Coffee mountain", and at the time of his deposition, Wellington believed that they were still at that location.[86]

Almost at the same time that Wellington gave his deposition in Jamaica, November 1842, Charles somehow found his way to Puerto Principe and related to the syndic procurador general details of his abduction and enslavement, which had occurred sometime in 1834. This account, together with his subsequent interview in 1843 with Joseph Crawford, the consul general in Cuba, allowed Charles to make a significant input into efforts to reunite him with his family in Jamaica. Although only about nine years old at the time of his kidnapping, he had, in most respects, a clear recall of the circumstances of his abduction and details of his family in Jamaica.

Charles indicated that the captain who "stole him" usually had his laundry done at his mother's house, and that when he delivered the captain's clothes to the ship on that day (as he usually did), he was kept on board the vessel until it sailed the next morning. Once in Cuba, Charles was enslaved, and he subsequently experienced several changes in owners. Described by Consul General Crawford in 1843 as "about eighteen years of age", Charles gave his full name as Charles Rogers; he said that father's name was George Rogers but that he sometimes went by the name Hodge, his father's mother's name. He recalled that his mother's name was Priscilla and that his only sister, Sukey, was much older than he was and consequently took care of him. Significantly, Charles did not give his mother's surname, nor did he confirm that his parents had been legally married, but this was presumed to be the case by Consul General Crawford.

Evidently affected by the trauma of both his abduction and his detention in slavery, as well as by the blurring of some childhood memories, Charles was unable to give the name of the town near to the beach from which he was taken. However, in seeking to assist the authorities in locating his family, he recalled that the clergyman who preached in his district was called Tolan and that he was always "so kind" to Charles. He recalled often walking with the clergyman from "the village" to the church and felt sure that he would know him if he saw him again.[87]

Early initiatives to find Charles's parents were centred on stipendiary magistrate W. Stainsby's suggestion that he might be the lost son of Mrs Eason of Lucea, Hanover. Her son had disappeared from home around the same time as Charles's kidnapping. More importantly, in Stainsby's view, Charles was reported to have identifying marks similar to those borne by Mrs Eason's son: a scar on his forehead, a pockmark beside his left eye and a slight defect of the left eyelid. However, she could not recall her son having a large scar under his chin, a scar which Charles insisted that he had received in Jamaica as the result of being kicked by a horse. Although Mrs Eason's husband and Charles's father were both named George, Charles was adamant that his mother's name was Priscilla and not Lavinia, as Mrs Eason was called. Before Consul General Crawford's interview with Charles, Governor Elgin had suggested that Wellington accompany the Easons to Cuba for the purpose of identifying Charles. However, the interview raised serious discrepancies which indicated that the Easons were not his parents.[88]

No further definitive references to success in finding Charles's family were ever found in the sources. However, in 1848, governor Charles Grey brought to the attention of the Colonial Office the refusal of the Spanish consul in Jamaica to give a passport to a "black woman", Priscilla Browning. According to Grey, "The woman is supposed to be the mother of a kidnapped boy detained in slavery in Cuba and her evidence is required to identify him."[89] The "kidnapped boy" in question was not named, but if this was a reference to Charles, Governor Grey may not have had much information on him, as the case had been highlighted during Elgin's administration. In any event, the sources indicate that only one "black boy" was awaiting identification in Cuba around this time, and that this most likely was Charles.[90] His parents may not have been married, or Priscilla, if this was Charles's mother, may have changed her name by a subsequent marriage.

Palmerston initially considered the use of coercion against the Spanish consul in Jamaica for his refusal to grant a passport to Priscilla. However, upon further investigation, it was discovered that the Spanish consul was merely acting on orders to deny passports to any "free persons of colour" wishing to enter Cuba after 1847. Moreover, cognizant of the repercussions on British commerce if relationships deteriorated between London and Madrid, Palmerston pursued the matter no further.[91] Governor Grey was advised to communicate with the governor of Cuba and to point out that "injustice of a serious character will be done in this case if the existing regulation cannot be waived a bit".[92] No evidence of Governor Grey's implementation of this advice was ever found in the sources, and the outcome of Charles's and Priscilla's cases remains undetermined. If Charles was eventually returned to Jamaica and reunited with his family, this was never recorded in the correspondence up to 1882.

By 1850, colonial authorities and family members alike expressed mounting concern about reports of boys abducted from Jamaica's seaport towns and taken aboard American vessels for the purpose of sale in the slave states of the South. The mayor of Kingston, Hector Mitchell, indicated that on numerous occasions, parents had appealed to him for advice and assistance in recovering their children who had disappeared in this manner. However, the American consul in Jamaica, Robert Harrison, viewed some black parents and their missing children as willing participants who had insisted on their "right to go with anyone who would be willing to take them from the starvation which they were here suffering". Whereas this explanation may have held true for some, many reports of genuine abductions continued to surface. Anthony Barclay, British consul to New York, reported in 1851 that these kidnappings were occurring "to a considerable extent", and that in that year, approximately fourteen boys from Jamaica were landed at Norfolk, Virginia, and it was feared that they had been sold into slavery.[93]

THE CASE OF ALEXANDER HENRIQUES AND WILLIAM EDWARDS

Alexander Henriques and William Edwards, described in the sources as "boys of colour" and "of African origin",[94] and both about twelve or thirteen years old, were certainly not willing participants in their own disappearance. Sometime between 1850 and 1851, both boys were abducted from the dock in Kingston by two passengers aboard the American steamer the *Illinois*. In keeping with the tendency of many boys in the seaport towns to gather at the dock out of curiosity or a desire to earn money, both Alexander and William were "idling about the spot". There, they were "accosted by two gentlemen" who gave them parcels to carry on board in return for promises of payment. In their subsequent recount of their experiences to the British consul general in New York, the boys told of being confined in the staterooms of the two passengers until the vessel set sail.

When the *Illinois* docked at New York, the boys were promised, in return for their silence, "that they should be made fine fellows of, be given a hundred dollars, fine clothes, and horses to ride". They were left at a "Negro boarding house" in New York by their captors, who instructed the keeper to "retain them until they were called for". As with other victims, Alexander and William were instrumental in getting assistance in their predicament. Suspicious of the ultimate motives of their abductors and anxious to return home, the boys informed the innkeeper of the saga of their kidnapping. The innkeeper's consequent summoning of the police set in motion the series of events which facilitated their reunions with their families.

Barclay, the British consul in New York, once informed by the police of the boys' presence at the boarding house, undertook immediate steps to ensure their safety. Efforts to capture the perpetrators proved futile and no action was taken against the captain of the *Illinois*, as his complicity in the abduction could not be proven. However, quick action by the boys and the innkeeper had spared them from what Barclay felt certain would have been the auctioneer's hammer.[95] Early in October 1851, with Barclay's assistance, Alexander and William were dispatched for Kingston on board the British brig *Nautilus* and were reunited with their parents.[96]

The Case of John Chisholm, William Raeburn and Jackey Vaughan

In 1860, three black youngsters – John Chisholm, aged ten years; William Raeburn, fourteen; and Jackey Vaughan, eighteen – were removed from Montego Bay by the captain of the *Alice Rogers* for the purpose of selling them into slavery in the United States. The circumstances surrounding their departure indicated that there was some degree of "willing participation", as described earlier in this chapter by the American consul in Jamaica, Robert Harrison. However, the actions of the British-born Captain Brayley, who deceived the boys and in some cases, their mothers, as to the ultimate purpose of their journey, were tantamount to kidnapping and were treated by the authorities as such. This case is noteworthy for the extent of involvement by the mothers in the effort to secure the boys' return and to bring the captain to justice. (No reference was made to their fathers in the sources, and thus no conclusions can be made about either their absence or presence.) Stipendiary magistrate Richard Chamberlaine was also instrumental in bringing the details of the case to the attention of colonial authorities.

Margaret Vassal Williams, the mother of William Raeburn, had been opposed to his sailing on the *Alice Rogers*, but she had acquiesced at the wharf when told by Mr Lindo, the consignee of the vessel, that Captain Brayley would employ her son for a brief journey aboard his ship. Although she could neither read nor write, William's mother had asked Lindo for some document to prove that her son was going away on the *Alice Rogers*, and she had no reason to suspect duplicity when Lindo provided her with a signed paper, witnessed by Samuel Payne. However, when she showed the paper to the customs officers in order to ensure that her son's departure was legal, "they laughed at it". In her deposition, Margaret stated that she became very alarmed when its contents were read to her because the paper stated, "I would either receive back my child in this world or in the world to come." By the time she confronted Lindo, obviously an accomplice of Captain Brayley, it was too late, as the *Alice Rogers* had sailed with William on board.[97]

Ten-year-old John Chisholm was also whisked away on that voyage of the *Alice Rogers* under similarly deceptive circumstances. In her deposition to Chamberlaine, Sarah Campbell, John's mother, indicated that she had gone to Lindo's wharf in Montego Bay in search of her son, having been told that he was working on the *Alice Rogers*. However, she strongly objected when Captain Brayley asked her to agree to his apprenticing John for seven years "to go to sea". Sarah eventually consented to Brayley's employing her son, on the understanding that the vessel would make a return voyage in three months and she would see her son then. Moreover, she fully trusted the judgment of William Burton, a stevedore working aboard the vessel, when he told her that "the captain was an English captain and there was no danger". When she requested papers from Mr Lindo to outline this agreement, Sarah was told that "there was no occasion for any papers".[98]

Also a resident of Montego Bay, Penelope Campbell described her son, Jackey Vaughan, as "a grown up young man". She was the only mother who was not present at the dock when the *Alice Rogers* set sail. Her son had informed her that he had obtained employment on that vessel as a cook. In May 1860, she informed Chamberlaine that she had neither seen nor heard from her son since the vessel had left Montego Bay in March of that year.[99]

Captain Brayley was arrested by Virginia police as he was about to sell two of the boys, Chisholm and Raeburn, to a "gentleman in Hampton" for the sum of nine hundred dollars. His spurious arguments in his defence indicated his ill intentions from the outset. Claiming that he had discovered that the boys' mothers were participants in a robbery of his vessel's goods in Montego Bay, Brayley told police that the mothers had "compromised by each giving him a boy to do as he pleased with". He argued that he therefore regarded the boys as his "bona fide property", and, realizing that he was in a slave state, he had decided to sell them before leaving Virginia. In an argument ironically reminiscent of eighteenth-century rationalizations of African enslavement, Brayley stated that "he was doing them good service, by taking them from a condition of nakedness and starvation like that of thousands of Jamaica negroes and providing them with good homes and kind masters".[100]

The mothers of the three boys, by acting on their suspicions of foul intent and by seeking the assistance of Chamberlaine, had contributed to the speedy reunion with their sons. Unlike in other cases of similarly motivated abductions, there was no need for an exhaustive search by colonial authorities in order to locate the missing family members. Moreover, the mothers' sworn depositions assisted in the punishment of Brayley, who after being handed over to the British authorities under the terms of the extradition treaty with Washington, was sentenced to imprisonment for three years and a fine of one thousand dollars. Chisholm, Raeburn and Vaughan were sent by the British vice consul in Norfolk to the British consul in New York, and from there shipped to Kingston on 17 May 1860. Shortly thereafter, they were returned to their homes in Montego Bay.[101]

Conclusion

These case studies represent only a few of the reported instances of children and adults, abducted or otherwise, who were separated from their homes in Jamaica and dispatched to overseas enslavement. Certainly, these experiences were not unique to Jamaica, as indicated by reports of similar abductions of boys in territories such as Antigua.[102] Incidents of enforced separation, whether engendered by the period of colonial enslavement or implemented by opportunists thereafter, occasioned disruption, disintegration and devastation for many black families.

This analysis has sought to demonstrate that blacks viewed the abolition of slavery as the opportunity to re-establish and strengthen familial links that had been interrupted or, in some cases, severed by enslavement, and that they perceived this activity as intrinsic to their evolving vision of freedom. The evidence presented here of blacks' efforts at family reconstitution during apprenticeship and thereafter challenges racist and elitist perceptions of black nonchalance to family and indeed indicates the persistence of the devotion to kindred which had been characteristic of traditional West African familial culture. This discussion has further shown that both men and women undertook initiatives to reconstitute their families on both temporary and permanent bases during the transitional period of apprenticeship, and that they did so within a context of serious limitations. Once blacks had achieved full freedom, these efforts found continued expression in population movements, fluctuations in the labour force and the drive to establish family freeholds. In particular, persistent activism on behalf of family consolidation by black males throughout the period under review indicates both the central role men played in their families as they emerged from enslavement and the importance with which they regarded their families.

This analysis has also demonstrated that when again confronted with enforced separation after 1834, some black family members, with crucial assistance from the colonial authorities, undertook measures to find and return their loved ones. However, the continuing efforts by freed blacks to reunite with family members thus separated were not always successful. As with the American experience in attempts at reconstitution, for many blacks in Jamaica, "such quests ended in failure, and others produced wrenching disappointment".[103] Nevertheless, the almost universal spirit of perseverance and dedication to the ties of family that were evident in these efforts remained a hallmark of many black families during and after the period of apprenticeship.

Chapter 4

Children of the Free

CONFLICTING VISIONS OF THEIR FREEDOM ROAD

> I think if parents won't look after their children and send them to school then the
> state should step in and take charge of them.
>   – *Reverend George Sargeant, 1877*[1]

> . . . a despotic and cruel interference with the natural rights of parents who appear
> to be allowed no voice in such a disposal of their own children . . .
>   – *Governor Charles Grey, 1851*[2]

GUIDED BY THEIR VISION OF freedom and their goals for enhancing family
welfare, blacks zealously guarded the continued freedom of their children
and insisted on the right to raise them under their own terms and conditions.
Accordingly, they viewed decision-making on issues such as their children's
education and their role in the domestic family economy as a parental prerogative. However, the ending of slavery entailed a different perspective on the part
of the colonial state, the church and other representatives of the ruling elites in
the colony. These institutions perceived a need to enhance mechanisms of social
control to forestall the anticipated danger of black retrogression into innate
barbarism. Essential to this design was the task of socializing the children to
Eurocentric norms and values and inculcating in them "habits of industry".
Indeed, as Brian Moore and Michele Johnson point out, "It was felt that
the real hope of civilizing Jamaica lay in the children." From the perspective

Figure 7. *Negro Children, Jamaica*. Cousins Hereward Postcard Collection, reprinted courtesy of the University of the West Indies Library, Mona.

of the British government, the colonial state, the church and elite society in general, schooling for black children was to be utilitarian in value, instilling a healthy dose of Christian, "civilized habits" while imparting basic literacy and numeracy. As Moore and Johnson indicate, education was "designed to transform [black children] into an intelligent class of agricultural workers" but not to "pull them away from the land".[3] This, the rationale suggested, was a crucial step in the attainment of elite society's goal of accomplishing what Demetrius Eudell has referred to as "cultural reconstruction" of freed blacks within the Americas.[4] Ultimately, then, attainment of socio-cultural control over freed children would promote social assimilation and economic equilibrium, and equip blacks to fulfil their "station in life".

Such a rationale was informed by white society's generalized perception of black parents as being largely debased and derelict in their child-rearing responsibilities. As discussed in chapter 1, this notion was given literary currency during the period of enslavement by the negative representations of the parental qualities of black men and women depicted in the works of Edward Long, Mrs A.C. Carmichael and Bryan Edwards.[5] The views that blacks abrogated their parental responsibilities and that they were morally reprehensible persisted for the entire period under examination and were reflected in the frequency of post-slavery complaints that freed blacks were raising their children to live in idleness. Reporting from Trelawny in 1854 on the failure of "negro parents" to pay three pence per week for their children's schooling, stipendiary magistrate R. Emery revealed the persistence of this stereotype in his complaint that "sixteen years of freedom has . . . proven to the world that the Negro spurns [education] for his children". This prevailing view that many societal ills resulted from parental indifference was mirrored by Governor Eyre's claim in 1865 that "the total absence of all parental control or proper training of the children [among the poor] . . . and the degraded and immoral social existence which they all but universally lead are quite sufficient to account for any poverty or crime which may exist amongst the peasantry of Jamaica".[6] It was, therefore, within this dual context of a need for cultural compliance and a perceived abrogation of parental responsibility that efforts were made to exert varying degrees of control over the children of freed blacks within this period.

The concept of control was multidimensional and included all attempts to influence children for desired outcomes, such as the regulation of children's labour and ideological assimilation. Outside of the parental domain, agencies of control during this period included estate management, the stipendiary magistracy, denominational and educational facilities, and, importantly, the state. For the purposes of this analysis, the state encompassed two arms of government in Jamaica during the period under review. First, there was the colonial state – that is, the governor, council and assembly up to 1865 and, thereafter, the governor and legislative council. Second, the state also included the imperial government, whose views on colonial matters were channelled through Colonial Office officials. Perspectives of the colonial and imperial states regarding policies on black children were not always convergent, but were at most times complementary.

In the quest to exert control over the children of blacks, the state played a crucial role in two respects: by encouraging discussions on policies intended to achieve desired outcomes for children and by implementing legislation to enforce such outcomes. Clearly, there existed a symbiotic relationship between the state and the other agents of control within Jamaican society at the time. Thus, the state's policies and laws designed to control black children were usually, though not always, a barometer of magisterial, missionary and plantocratic perspectives. Additionally, as Patrick Bryan points out, "The Jamaican oligarchy . . . was always sensitive to ideas coming from abroad."[7] Thus, the movement for reforming children and juveniles which was influential in Britain in the nineteenth century had repercussions for the formulation of state policy towards black children in Jamaica during this period. This attempt to exert state control over the children of freed blacks had its parallel in developments in the post-bellum United States, where apprenticeship laws enacted by a number of states gave arbitrary power to the courts to "bind out" children whose parents were deemed to be incapable of looking after them. As in Jamaica, black parents in the United States viewed this as an infringement of their rights, and they challenged the authorities for "custodial rights to their children".[8]

Issues of state involvement in efforts to exercise control over the children brought sharply into focus concerns of parental prerogative, as legislation to implement organs of jurisdiction, such as the apprenticeship of minors and industrial and reformatory education, held serious implications for parental domain. Black parents, lacking both the economic and political sway needed to block efforts by the state to infringe on their parental rights, nevertheless expressed opposition, either directly or through missionaries and other spokespersons, to such efforts. These parents believed that determining the parameters by which their children lived was their right and privilege, conferred on them by virtue of being parents, and free ones at that. Thus, the insistence by blacks on the re-establishment and maintenance of dominion over their children was an integral part of their quest for recognition of their personhood as fully freed parents. In affirmation of this stance, black parental initiatives were an indication of the persistence and strength of the parent-child bond and of parents' acknowledgement of their children's significance to the continuation of wider kinship networks. As demonstrated in chapter 1, the centrality of children to kinship networks was an integral feature of traditional West African familial culture. Given the foundational nature of the West African cultural links among blacks in Jamaica, it is hardly surprising that many black parents continued to assert their right to determine the welfare of their children during and after apprenticeship. Nevertheless, the primacy of children's well-being and the profound parent-child bond were not unique to the West African cultural context, and blacks' efforts to assert their parental prerogative should be assessed with this in mind.

The Fate of Free Children during Apprenticeship: Parental Visions of the "Freedom Road"

During the period of apprenticeship, which was itself an aspect of state-supported control, children under six years old, by virtue of being free, remained outside the ambit of the estate's jurisdiction. As established in chapter 2, the effort by estate management to effect command of free children's labour was met with the virtually universal refusal of parents to relinquish their control over this aspect of their children's lives. Parental rejection of these schemes not only indicated the premium which they attached to their children's liberty, but also denoted an awareness of the potential of the colonial state to deprive their children of freedom. Thus, as articulated by apprenticed parents, most of them fathers and former headmen on the Plantain Garden River Valley properties, surrendering control over their children even for a short while would be tantamount to an admission of their inability to care for them, and the governor would use his power to "have their children bound to the busha".[9] This declaration served as an important indicator that as persons soon to be fully freed, they had every intention of safeguarding the liberty and welfare of their children and would not relinquish control over them. Significantly, too, such initiatives provide evidence which challenges the view (discussed in earlier chapters) that black men were rendered ineffectual and inconsequential, especially as fathers, by systems of domination.[10] Indeed, this negative perception was perhaps best articulated by James Anthony Froude forty-four years after apprenticeship, when he cast black men as "disclaiming all responsibilities . . . after the babies have been once brought into the world".[11]

In an effort to retain jurisdiction over them, many parents removed their free children from the estates, sometimes to live with relatives in the towns and sometimes to attend schools as many as eleven to thirty miles from home. Although blacks regarded this decision as their parental right, this practice provided the occasion for the earliest calls by pro-planter stipendiary magistrates for legislative interference by the state to compel parents to keep their free children resident on the estates to which they were attached. The rector for the parish of St Thomas-in-the-East, Reverend Stephen H. Cooke, reporting to Governor Sligo from Morant Bay in 1836, argued that apprenticed parents' removal of their free children from estates without the approval of the proprietor or his attorney was an issue "which appears to call loudly for legislative interference". Cooke further recommended that the state make compulsory the residence of free children on the estate to which their parents were attached, their attendance at estate schools and, most importantly for "the future prosperity of the island", their daily labour on the estates.[12] The implications of these suggestions for parental prerogative were that as apprentices, parents would not have the authority to make decisions regarding the removal of their children and would be accountable to estate management in this respect, and that failure to comply would be met with punitive measures imposed by the colonial state. However, any effort at using legislation to limit the liberty of free children would have raised the ire of the abolitionist interest in Britain, and thus parents continued to exert ultimate control over their children, a prerogative and a vision which they would not surrender at any cost.

In the face of almost universal refusal on the part of parents to apprentice their free children, many stipendiary magistrates accused the parents of dereliction of duty. Interpreting the eighteenth clause of the Imperial Act of Abolition as a mandate to all apprentices to consent to the binding of their free children, magistrates such as Special Justice Gregg of Trelawny bemoaned the fact that parents had not "complied with the spirit and meaning of that clause". Gregg expressed a frequently voiced view that "until such laws are enacted as may compel them to do so",[13] black parents would never agree to apprentice their children. Such a proposal for legislative measures to coerce parents to apprentice children who had just been freed by imperial statute would have negated the spirit of abolition and would not have found favour with British humanitarian interests. Moreover, such a show of legislative force would have abrogated both the rights of parents and their vision for their children's future. In any respect, Stipendiary Magistrate Palmer's assessment that the eighteenth clause was "intended to be limited to those cases where the parent, from poverty or infirmity, is unable to provide for the support of the child"[14] indicated that apprentices, far from being delinquent in refusing to submit to the clause, were in fact justified in exercising their parental right not to do so.

Proposals for state measures to compel parents to apprentice their children may have been too draconian; hence, a more subtle, but still invasive, suggestion which gained much support among stipendiary magistrates during the apprenticeship was that of governmental provision of "schools of industry" and enforcement of attendance by free children. Stipendiary Magistrate

Cocking, like many other magistrates and custodes, warned of "the very worst results" which could be "expected from this numerous and rising generation" if "Government does not very soon establish schools of industry".[15] Thomas McCornock, attorney for several properties in St Thomas-in-the-East, expressed a commonly held perception of black children when he indicated that they would not attend the schools without compulsion. Similarly, the custos of St Catherine argued for compulsory industrial education to avert the possibility that the free children would grow up as "useless, if not dangerous members of society".[16] The proposed dual role of the state – its provision of industrial schools and its enforcement of attendance – would serve to inculcate in free children the appropriate work ethic and "habits of industry" necessary to "their station in life", and would promote economic stability through the provision of labour. All discussions on the need for state provision of compulsory industrial training were regarded as highly suspect by parents, who viewed the twin objectives of industrial training and enforced attendance as a ploy to gain dominance over their free children and, eventually, to re-enslave them. They regarded the maintenance of their children's freedom as a parental responsibility of the highest order and asserted their right to have their children educated under their terms, not those of the government. Thus, if necessary, they were prepared to send their children over great distances to attend school rather than support dubious estate-based training.[17]

The imperial government was clearly concerned about the many stipendiary reports they had received regarding the "idle and ignorant" condition of the free children. The request of secretary of state Lord Glenelg to governor Sir Lionel Smith in early 1838 for an update on "enactments to secure the attendance of the children of apprentices at school" conveyed the imperial state's tacit recognition of the importance of legislative intervention on the issue of black children's education. However, Governor Smith's response to Glenelg revealed a difference of opinion, as he indicated that a "compulsory law" (his emphasis) would not be "practicable" during apprenticeship and would create parental suspicion. Importantly, Smith's rationale for not agreeing to compulsory industrial education at that time was centred on a concern for parental prerogative, as evidenced in his claim that "a compulsory law would now alarm [apprenticed parents] and create suspicion and distrust if it interfered with their children".[18] For the time being, the supporters of compulsory education would have to be satisfied with the efforts, particularly by missionary bodies, to make elementary – though not industrial – training available to some free children.

As indicated earlier, perspectives which suggested that black parents were generally debased, corrupt and incapable of uplifting the moral tone of their children were quite pervasive, and these were reflected by the frequency of stipendiary complaints to this effect. Special justice John Daughtrey, reporting from St Elizabeth in 1835, bemoaned the prevalence of "indolence and dishonesty" among the free children of his parish. He further stated, "Little good will be done by any plan for the improvement of this class, which does not embrace their separation from their parents, and regular employment as well as instruction."[19] Given the considerable evidence of the strong ties that bound apprenticed parents to their children, Daughtrey's call for physical separation of free children from their parents would have necessitated legislative intervention by the state to make this a reality.

However, an examination of stipendiary reports issued during apprenticeship indicates that calls for the state to enforce physical separation were not widespread. This may be explained by the comparatively greater reliance on religious bodies to effect moral change in blacks during this period, and by the fact that the concept of legislative enforcement of separation of children from the home environment through reformatory education did not gain currency until the middle of the nineteenth century. Although intended as a criticism, Daughtrey's observations on another occasion convey the essence of parental opposition to any plan to wrest from them control over their children: "They are jealous of everything that seems to place their free children within the power of others."[20] Certainly, this was unwitting testimony to the black perspective on family ties and parental rights which challenged stereotypes of parental nonchalance. Daughtrey's earlier suggestion of physical separation was an idea whose time had not yet come.

The Evolution of State Control of Black Children

REFORMATORY AND INDUSTRIAL SCHOOLS, 1838–1882

Reformatory and industrial schools represented the ultimate attempt by the colonial state to assume official control over children who were adjudged to be lacking in "proper parental upbringing". Although black children were not the sole targets of these efforts, the pervasiveness of complaints about the children of the formerly enslaved indicates that they were the primary group of interest. This section examines the evolution of these elements of domination by the colonial state and the implications for parental prerogative.

From 1843 onwards, a recurring theme of stipendiary complaints was the decreased school attendance by the children of formerly enslaved people. While prolonged droughts and family labour requirements no doubt contributed to this decline, many stipendiary magistrates attributed it to parental indifference and "carelessness about their children".[21] The decline, coupled with the belief that the colony's welfare was inextricably tied to the inculcation of habits of industry among the "rising generation", prompted renewed and widespread calls for governmental action. The state's response to this was the passage by the Jamaican Assembly in 1843 of an act to encourage the formation of industrial schools and to promote attendance through the offer of monetary incentives to teachers with large enrolments.[22] Though clearly not a coercive measure, this piece of legislation held no attraction for parents, who continued to regard all talk of industrial schooling as indications of plans to re-enslave their children.

However, the increased stipendiary reports of children being brought up in "idleness and vice" and the concurrent reports of declines in school attendance fostered a climate of opinion which prompted appeals to the colonial state for enforced separation of such children from their homes. Thus, in 1846, on the eve of his departure as governor of Jamaica, Elgin underscored the support of the colonial state for the forcible removal of some children from the home environment. For those children "brought up as outcasts in idleness", he recommended that they "be conveyed by authority" (his emphasis) to industrial seminaries. However, Elgin suggested two important limitations to the state's power in such cases: first, such drastic action should only be taken where it could be proven that the children were not being educated and, second, the state could only intervene after "appeal to the better feelings" of the parents had been exhausted.[23] Elgin's emphasis on the cautious use of state authority implied his recognition of the rights of freed parents as well as his awareness of the potential of parental opposition to such measures. Nevertheless, perspectives such as Elgin's widened the pool of arguments in favour of governmental intervention to enforce "habits of industry", and these views would be mirrored in subsequent developments in reformatory and industrial education.

In 1851, the passage by the Jamaican Assembly of the Orphan Asylum Act heralded the first post-slavery attempt by the colonial state to effect, through legislative and judicial means, the forced removal of some children from their homes. Originally conceived as a measure to aid children orphaned by the cholera epidemic, the act enabled the state to legislatively sanction the transfer of parental authority – not only in the case of orphans, but also in the case of "certain other destitute children" – to the board of management of the orphan asylum. Thus, the law empowered the chairman of quarter sessions to recommend the commitment to the orphan asylum of any child under twelve years who was considered to be "deserted and destitute, and without any visible employment or means of subsistence . . . whether . . . orphan or not".[24]

Two important cornerstones of reformatory legislation were present in this act: that of state sanction of the forcible removal of children from their home environment, and that of state implementation of alternative mechanisms of control over children found "wandering and destitute" and hence lacking in "proper parental upbringing". The Orphan Asylum Act was in many respects a significant state-sponsored negation of black parental rights and it resulted in petitions for its disallowance, mainly from Baptist representatives on behalf of black congregations in several parts of the island. These petitions, though written by Baptist missionaries, conveyed the spirit and message of the freed parents for whom they spoke, who pointed to the infringement upon parental rights and the disintegration of the family unit by state-approved legislation. Thus, they claimed, the committal to the asylum of children who were not orphans, without the prior approval of their parents or relatives, was "subversive to the natural rights of parents". If the act was enforced, parents would be powerless to prevent the forcible removal of their children and their detention away from home until they reached the age of twenty-one. Even the detention of orphaned children, the petitioners felt, was in contravention of relatives' wishes, as many of those orphaned by cholera had been adopted by relatives from the wider kinship network who feared that committal to an institution was a move towards reapprenticing and possibly re-enslaving the children. These adoptions were an important affirmation of the support system provided by the extended familial network, even if they were not recognized as such by the colonial state. Also, as Baptist ministers pointed out, the majority of poor black children likely to be affected by the act were from dissenting congregations, and as such, the state's insistence on their being brought up in the Anglican faith until the age of twenty-one would have been an essential affront to the religious principles of their parents, dead or alive. Moreover, the legislative enforcement of apprenticeship until the child attained the age of twenty-one ensured that parents, if they were alive, would also be deprived of the right to direct their children away from forced agricultural labour, a right which they had fought so hard to secure during the apprenticeship.[25]

Hull Terrell, secretary of the Protestant Dissenting Ministers, emphasized the predicament of parents when he pointed out that the state, by way of the Orphan Asylum Act, had invested too much power in the hands of magistrates, and that temporary economic distress on the part of parents could result in prolonged separation from their children. Herman Merivale at the Colonial Office, like most of his colleagues, missed Terrell's point about the fate of children pivoting on the delicate economic balance facing most black parents in the drought-plagued, economically depressed period of the 1840s and 1850s, and thus concluded that "no rights of parents who are themselves discharging their duty to their child could be interfered with".[26] Additionally, Governor Charles Grey's views coincided with those of the Colonial Office when he argued that the act did not infringe on parental rights because parents or relatives, after a child's committal, could apply for a writ of habeas corpus to have the child released by submitting proof of their ability to maintain the child.[27] Blind to the fact that a denial of parental rights would have already occurred by that point, and that sheer economic reality would militate against most black parents being able to afford writs of habeas corpus, the Colonial Office declared that it failed to see sufficient grounds on which to disallow the Orphan Asylum Act. Consequently, within a few short years, the establishment of reformatory and industrial schools would be a natural progression from the concept of the orphan asylum.

In the wake of the Orphan Asylum Act, increased stipendiary reports of large numbers of children seen to be living in a "state of destitution" and growing up in "ignorance and vice" enhanced local receptivity to precedents of reformatory education that existed in England. In 1856, Richard Hill, stipendiary magistrate for St Catherine, suggested to Lieutenant Governor Bell that reformatory education was "one of the most urgent demands of the colony" and pointed to the need for the establishment in Jamaica of a reformatory union for two groups of children who were implicitly lacking in beneficial parental influence. These were "the destitute and uninstructed children and youths and the juvenile culprits from the surrounding townships".[28] Among the many voices clamouring for state legislation on reformatory education was that of stipendiary magistrate Charles Lake of St Andrew, who argued that legislative intervention was necessary to educate the "large number of children of the peasantry . . . seen wandering about in idleness".[29]

The passage in 1857 of the Industrial Schools' Act, "to make better provision for the care and education of vagrant, destitute and disorderly children", placed the stamp of state approval on reformatory education, with all its ramifications for parental prerogative. Although the act launched a period of privately organized rather than state-administered reformatories and industrial schools, it nevertheless established the parameters within which the state, through its judicial arm, could commit children to these institutions. Thus, any child under the age of sixteen found in "want and distress", begging or "wandering in the streets and highways", asleep in an unoccupied building or "not having any home . . . or lawful or visible means of subsistence", would be sent by parochial authorities to certified industrial schools, regardless of whether the child's parents, relatives or guardians were alive. Such a mandate, based on European standards of proper attire and appropriate public conduct for children, as well as on the prevailing philosophy that black children of "responsible parentage", when not in school, should be gainfully employed (preferably on the estates), was clearly conducive to the abuse of parental rights. Subjective assessments of whether a child was "in want and distress" or presumptions of homelessness could easily result in the separation of a child from a parent who had no other limitation but that of economics. Most importantly, consigning a non-criminal child to such an institution because he or she had no "lawful or visible means of subsistence" was a blatant interference with the rights of black children, who had no less of a claim on the right to enjoy their childhoods than did their white counterparts, and with the rights of parents to determine whether their children spent their time in work or leisure. As Sidney Turner, inspector of reformatories in England, noted, allowing the state to define child vagrancy in this way gave "powers of interference which might easily be abused, to the injury or annoyance of a very different class of persons".[30]

Similar in many respects to its antecedent, the Orphan Asylum Act, the Industrial Schools' Act also provided some legal leeway for parents wishing to reclaim their children. The act entitled parents to the return of their children provided that they could afford the payment of a bond or security, the value of which was left to the discretion of the presiding magistrate; later, it would require the approval of the governor himself. Children who had broken the laws of the state were also to be sent to reformatory or industrial schools, and the Industrial Schools' Act provided for their separate accommodation. Such children, by virtue of having been adjudged guilty of a criminal offence by a court of law, were legally deprived of parental control, as the organization in charge of reformatory and industrial schools (which remained private until 1869) assumed the role of the parent; that is, it acted *in loco parentis*. Although this organization was private, the Industrial Schools' Act, by providing for governmental subsidies to all reformatories and industrial schools, allowed for some measure of state influence over those institutions, however restricted. Thus, for example, punitive measures for criminal children sentenced to the reformatory were decided on and incorporated into the criminal code by the government.[31]

The first girls' reformatory, the Kingston and St Andrew's Reformatory, was opened on East Queen Street, Kingston, in October 1857, two months before the passing of the Industrial Schools' Act, and the St George's Industrial Home and Reformatory for Boys was opened on Upper Knight Street, Kingston, in July 1858. Although these institutions were privately organized, the reports issuing from these two state-certified and state-assisted bodies indicate the extent to which the whole concept of the reformatory and industrial school attempted to denigrate black parental influence and promote an alternative agency of control. The administrators saw it as their mission to first eradicate "adverse" parental values formerly "ingrained" in them, and to then educate the children in acceptable (Victorian) standards of behaviour. Most of the children were, according to these reports, "offspring of careless, deranged parents . . . reared in utter idleness . . . inmates of ill-regulated houses, and subjected to all the contaminating influences of vice and ungodliness".[32] One year after the formation of the St George's Industrial Home and Reformatory, its administrators were able to report that "the humanizing influences of home and family life have had a marked effect".[33]

In providing for the committal of children to government-certified industrial schools and reformatories, the Industrial Schools' Act of 1857 had set out no provision for the "future care of children" after their discharge from these institutions. Given that reformatory philosophy attributed committal to parental "deficiencies", it was crucial, from the colonial government's point of view, to institute pre-emptive measures against the possible resumption of adverse parental influence or neglect upon the child's release. Thus, in 1861, the state took steps to shape the future reality of these children through the passage of the Act in Aid of the Industrial Schools' Act. This empowered the managers of certified industrial schools, with the governor's consent, to apprentice to householders children who had reached the age of thirteen or whose terms were about to expire and whose parents were either unable or unwilling to provide for them. A minimum of three years and a maximum of five years were established for the apprenticeship.[34] In light of reports of children being left to find their way home upon discharge from reformatories, it seems doubtful that the managers of these institutions would have made any exhaustive efforts to determine parental ability or willingness before apprenticing the children.[35] Consequently, the rights of parents to be reunited with their children would be thwarted by state enforcement of this legislation. In 1868, reflecting the reactions of blacks to the practice of apprenticing these children, the managers of the boys' reformatory explained the eventual failure of the 1861 act in aid and the practice of apprenticeship which it enforced on the grounds that "it created an unjust suspicion that we desired to bring back a system of slavery". Moreover, the householders to whom the children had been apprenticed proved themselves to be no models of substitute parental guardianship, as "the children under their care were neglected, ill-treated, overworked and generally ran away".[36]

By the late 1860s, the privately organized girls' and boys' reformatories were clearly unequal to the task of coping with what was reported to be a growing problem of child and juvenile vagrancy and idleness. Within a few years of their inception, private funding for these institutions had all but disappeared and the numbers of children being ordered into these facilities greatly exceeded available space. Within this context, more appeals were made for the colonial government to undertake greater responsibility for the task of reforming children of "neglectful parents". The recommendation of the Royal Society of Arts in Jamaica was an accurate reflection of public (Eurocentric) views on the issue: "It may well become a question whether those who utterly neglect their children, do not forfeit their natural right to the charge of them, whether the state should not assume the duty and become their parent."[37] Moreover, as Governor Grant argued in 1869, the reformatory – and, by extension, its role of social reformation – had "become so large and so important" that full governmental control was justified. Indeed, to the colonial state, the need for mechanisms of social control, judiciously implemented, seemed even more critical in the aftermath of 1865. The passage of Law 11 of 1869, also known as the Reformatories Law, gave the governor complete jurisdiction over the existing industrial and reformatory school system as well as the power to constitute other government reformatories. The colonial state thus signalled its readiness to stand *in loco parentis* for those children whose parents had purportedly neglected them.[38]

As noted earlier, black parents' opposition to the idea of their children being apprenticed in general, and to the probability of their being detained in reformatory-related apprenticeship in particular, had contributed to the eventual failure of the 1861 effort to enforce this type of apprenticeship. Governmental cognizance of continued parental criticism of the notion of apprenticeship for their children led to the termination of this practice by Law 11 of 1869.[39] The British government was also concerned that the apprenticeship of minors under these conditions could be open to abuse and stated that it was not advisable that this provision of the law "in the present very critical state of the island be allowed to remain any longer in force".[40] In an apparent concession to parental rights to reassert control over their children at the expiration of their terms, Law 11 of 1869 further ordered that no child could be detained in a reformatory beyond the age of fifteen years. Additionally, the rights of parents, under special circumstances such as illness, to regain jurisdiction over their children while they were confined at the institution was recognized by this law, which allowed parents to petition the governor for their children's release. That parents were well aware of this provision of the law is illustrated by the case of a boy, Alfred Godson, who became ill while in the reformatory in 1874. His mother, having petitioned the governor, was informed by the superintendent that her son could not be released as he was ill in hospital. Godson's mother returned, armed with a cart in which to transport her sick son, and, showing the letter which she had received from the governor's secretary, demanded and obtained the release of her son.[41]

However, in most respects, Law 11 of 1869 enforced state dominion over parental rights. Not only did the law empower the government to deprive some parents of their children for a specified period, but it also imposed a doubly punitive measure on them by making it mandatory for parents to contribute towards the financial support of their children during their detention. Intended as a measure of state deterrence of parental neglect, this law remedied what critics saw as a weakness of the reformatory legislation of 1857. Under Law 11, the government was also authorized to bring legal action against parents who defaulted on payments. Like its predecessor of 1857, the law of 1869 targeted children who had "no visible means of subsistence" and who appeared to be destitute and therefore, by implication, lacking in parental care. Evidence given before the Commission on the Juvenile Population in 1877 makes it clear that many black parents were anything but docile in response to the state's efforts to deprive them of jurisdiction over their children. The rector of Spanish Town, Reverend C. Douet, pointed out that because of black parental perception of the reformatory as a place for punishment of criminal children, "there would be a great row" if the authorities tried to remove their children there on the basis of financial need alone. Parents, Douet stated, would be quick to ask, "Who dares to say that we cannot support our children?" He continued that they would "defy you to prove it".[42]

However, by 1872, renewed concerns about the future of children released from the reformatory contributed to the colonial state's decision in that year to reintroduce legislation to facilitate the apprenticeship of inmates. In an effort to forestall the relapse into "idle and degenerate" ways that was anticipated by so many, the superintendent of the boys' reformatory, Melville, had emphasized the importance of skills training, especially for boys. However, the 1869 law prohibiting the detention of children in the reformatory beyond age fifteen would militate, Melville argued, against completion of training before the expiration of the term. Since the "dispositions of their parents and their own" against industrial training would make voluntary completion of such training unlikely after departure, Melville suggested that the government act to reintroduce apprenticeship for boys committed after age thirteen. In this way, they would be "compelled to continue in the reformatory and learn such a trade as should be suited to their abilities".[43] Law 30 of 1872 resolved this dilemma by investing the superintendent of the government reformatory with the authority to subject the inmates to apprenticeship, and by extending the maximum age of detention from fifteen to sixteen years of age.[44] In its paternalistic bid to mould members of the rising generation within the context of utilitarian training for blacks, the colonial state had negated some parents' rights to influence the economic endeavours of their children and had renewed the spectre of prolonged separation of parent from child. Melville, however, rationalized the issue from the state's perspective when he argued that since the government stood *in loco parentis* in the case of the reformatory, parents did not have the right to object.[45]

In its 1877 mandate to the commissioners appointed to inquire into the condition of Jamaica's juvenile population, the colonial state reaffirmed its philosophy of exercising dominion over children who were deemed to be neglected or otherwise in need of state intervention. Among the instructions given to the commissioners in 1877 was the request to "consider and report upon the subject of state interference for the protection of orphans and neglected children".[46] Witnesses before the commission detailed a picture of widespread neglect of children as a result of what was perceived as both parental indifference and parental incapacity. In an effort to address this concern, the commissioners recommended that the state strengthen and extend its legislative guidelines for reformatories and industrial schools. Law 34 of 1881, the Reformatories' and Industrial Schools' Law, incorporated most of the commissioners' proposals while effecting further inroads into parental prerogative. This law also solidified reformatory philosophy for years to come, providing for the official designation of the reformatory as a habitat for criminal children only and the industrial school as a training ground for "vagrant and destitute children".[47]

While retaining all previously established criteria for the committal of children, Law 34 of 1881 provided additional grounds on which the state could remove children from the care of their parents. Thus, under the new law, any child under sixteen years of age who was "habitually ill-treated or neglected" by the parent would be sent to the industrial schools. In 1879, the Commission on the Juvenile Population had recommended that the definition of "neglect" in the law be expanded to include "the omission without valid excuse to send the child regularly to school". This suggestion reflected the prevailing view of witnesses before the commission that parents had a duty to send their children to school, and that if they "habitually" failed to do so, then punitive measures should be applied and the state should remove the child to the appropriate institution and assume responsibility for his or her education. However, this interpretation of what constituted neglect could not be explicitly stated in Law 34 of 1881 without the existence of supportive legislation to implement compulsory education. Nevertheless, clause 7 of the new law, by subjecting to committal any child "habitually left by its parents or guardians without proper supervision", indicated a tacit acceptance of this interpretation of neglect, since being "habitually left without proper supervision" implied that the child was not being educated.[48]

Cases of excessive flogging and "undue punishment" by parents had always been the subject of legislative and judicial action by the state. Significantly, clause 7 of Law 34 pioneered (in Jamaica) the principle of state intervention to rescue children from situations perceived as abusive. Hence, the law stated that any child under sixteen years of age who was habitually treated "with cruelty" by parents could be sent to the industrial school. This new criterion for state removal of children from their homes was prompted by the testimony of several witnesses before the Commission on the Juvenile Population and by increased reports of excessive punishment of children.

Additionally, Law 34 of 1881 established that as of that year, the state should stand *in loco parentis* in the case of any child whose surviving parent was imprisoned. While the government justified this move by pointing to the absence of any parental control in such a child's life, this was a clear rejection by the state of any possibility of relatives assuming responsibility for the child, implying as it did that among black families, at least, the extended familial environment was not conducive to "proper upbringing".[49]

Testimony of witnesses before the Commission on the Juvenile Population that some parents, especially mothers, requested the authorities to send their children to the reformatory because they could not control them, strengthened the perception that black parents were unfit to raise their children.[50] Thus, clause 10 of Law 34 provided for the voluntary transfer of the parental domain to the state by enabling the committal to the industrial school of any child whose "parent, step-parent or guardian claims inability to control" him or her. However, in order to guard against "negligent parents" trying, through this channel, to offload their charges on the government, the law provided that such parents should be requested to maintain their children during their tenure at the school, at a cost not to exceed five shillings per week.

The controversial issue of apprenticing children in the reformatory or industrial school was fine-tuned by Law 34 of 1881, in order to protect the state against charges of intent to renew slavery and to secure the stamp of approval on the apprenticing of inmates. Clause 21 of Law 34 thus allowed the superintendent of an institution to apprentice any child who had been there for twelve months, with the important proviso that the "child's consent" was necessary and that the apprenticeship must cease when the child was eighteen. This was clearly a clause which risked facilitating abuse of both the rights of the child and parental prerogative, and it raised the issue of a child's competence to make such decisions in the absence of parental guidance. By placing the burden of consent on minors, the state also indicated its lack of regard for parental opinion on the matter of apprenticeship. Cumulative experiences from 1834 to 1880 had proven that if parental consent to apprenticeship was sought, there would be only one reaction, and thus the state moved to pre-empt this reaction through legislation. However, because clause 21 had the potential to contravene the guideline of mandatory release at age sixteen, and also in an effort to protect itself against charges of renewed slavery, the state introduced clause 34, which allowed for the retention of children in the institution beyond age sixteen provided that the child's written consent was given. As with clause 21, no provision was made for consultation between parent and child. This indicates how thoroughly the parental prerogative had been subjected to state control, and demonstrates that in a paternalistic context where children, and in particular black children, were viewed as incapable of making wise decisions, the state was prepared to utilize those children for the realization of its goals of social and economic assimilation.

One of the enduring themes in the evolution of reformatory philosophy during this period was the need to inculcate "habits of industry" in children, especially black children. However, this was twinned with another concern of equal importance to the elitist perspective: that on departure from the "civilizing influence" of the reformatory or industrial school, black youth would most likely revert to lives of idleness and crime. This philosophy had informed every attempt at apprenticing inmates during this period. It is instructive, therefore, that clause 22 of Law 34 implemented a novel mechanism to promote the continuation of "industrious habits" after the expiration of the child's term at the school. In response to the recommendation of the Commission on the Juvenile Population, this clause introduced an embryonic version of the modern probationary system. This facilitated continued state management and surveillance after departure from the institution, requiring that every juvenile who had not been apprenticed should continue for two years to periodically report to the superintendent with proof that he or she was "gainfully employed". Failure to honour the terms of this probationary period would result in a charge of vagrancy being brought against the juvenile. This feature of the latest reformatory act was the object of enthusiastic approval by Lord Kimberley, Edward Wingfield and others at the Colonial Office.[51]

This probationary clause of Law 34 demonstrates how far the lengthy arm of the state could be extended into what was still regarded by some parents as their domain, even though their children were juveniles of sixteen years of age. In fact, witnesses before the Commission on the Juvenile Population had testified to the tendency of some black children to free themselves from their parents' control as soon as they could earn some money. Importantly, clause 22 reflected the state's expectation that "after the money expended on the education of the boy in school, the state has a right to exact some guarantee against his relapsing into vagrancy and crime as has often hitherto been the case".[52]

TOWARDS COMPULSORY EDUCATION AND THE APPRENTICESHIP OF MINORS, 1834–1882

Reformatory and industrial schools, by their definitions and terms of operation, could only affect a relatively small portion of the population of black children, with numbers in the government reformatory ranging, for example, from 272 in 1877 to 258 in 1878.[53] However, white society perceived that a far greater number of children were growing up in "idleness and vice", and that these children could only be adequately reached through compulsory education. Embryonic during the apprenticeship period, the issue of compelling black parents to educate their children resurfaced during the 1840s with increased stipendiary reports of considerable declines in school attendance.[54] The question of state enforcement of education and particularly industrial education, a recurrent theme throughout this period, sparked controversy over the boundaries of governmental intervention in what was perceived as the parental domain.

In response to reports in 1846 of government plans to implement compulsory industrial education, black parents in Lacovia, St Elizabeth, demonstrated their antipathy to such schemes by withdrawing their children from the curate's school. By so doing, they asserted their parental right to control the direction of their children's education and emphasized that "they would not consent to the children again being enslaved".[55] Influenced by the perception that the freed blacks had neither an understanding nor an appreciation of education, some stipendiary magistrates recommended governmental imposition of punitive fines for parents who failed to educate their children. By the mid-1850s, the imperial state, convinced of the importance of school attendance to the maintenance of social stability in the colony, supported the view that "education should be made imperative and obligatory".[56]

However, partly out of anticipation of parental opposition and partly in recognition of the financial constraints imposed upon governmental expenditure in the aftermath of free trade, Governor Henry Barkly urged a cautious approach to any schemes for compulsion. He alternatively suggested the imposition of a special tax for educational purposes, and reliance on inculcating "in the peasantry the duty of securing the benefits for which they pay".[57] Referring in 1854 to an education bill which promoted the idea of compulsory educa- tion and penalties for negligent parents, stipendiary magistrate Richard Hill pointed out that objections to the bill had some basis in concerns for parental prerogative. In the "public discussion" on the bill, which ultimately was not passed, it was noted that "duties of parents have a right of privacy which cannot be transgressed without wrong and mischief . . . this bill overstepped that right".[58] Opponents of the bill argued that once education was made accessible, black parents would regard the education of their children as their duty. This view, Hill argued, was reinforced by the fact that "thousands of the working people's children were attending the schools" even though they were not compelled to do so. Hill's observation proved a testament to the priority which black parents, of their own accord and without state com- pulsion, attached to their children's education. Further, it underscored the importance of education, on their terms, to the vision of freedom which the people had for their children.

While much of the rationale for objecting to the bill seems to have been cen- tred on the primacy of parental rights, the expense of implementing machinery to make education compulsory also militated against such a move, not only in 1854, but for quite a while thereafter.[59] The economic and constitutional crises facing the colonial government in the aftermath of the Sugar Duties Act affected its ability to fund many projects considered vital to colonial development. Scarce resources were allocated to perceived areas of priority such as immigration. Educational schemes for blacks continued to suffer from inadequate funding, precisely because the Jamaican Assembly had never regarded education for the black masses as a priority. In the context of these constraints, calls for state implementation of compulsory education abated until the establishment of the Crown Colony regime and the paternalistic administrations of governors like Grant and Musgrave. Thus, an economically necessitated laissez-faire approach remained the order of the day. Such economic constraints explain why the colonial state continued to rely on denominational groups to effect educational schemes in the colony, and why, in spite of its commitment to reformatory education, it was prepared to leave this enterprise to private charitable groups up to 1869.

During this period of relative state inactivity on the issue of compulsory education, it was nevertheless the hope of both the metropolitan and the colonial governments that black parents would gradually overcome their antipathy to industrial education, which, according to the rationale, would facilitate economic and social assimilation and promote the welfare of the colony. However, parents continued to resist the direction in which both state and denominational interests attempted to take their children. Thus, reacting to efforts to introduce manual labour into the elementary schools, parents insisted that "they [did] not send their children to school to learn to work . . . they [could] teach them that themselves".[60] It was therefore not surprising that the state's efforts to convince rather than coerce parents to enlist their children at the government model schools in Falmouth and Montego Bay met with little success.[61]

By 1877, several factors contributed to the resurgence of discussions on compulsion in education. The continued parental opposition to industrial training necessitated alternative strategies to implement utilitarian education. Also, the presence of a paternalistic administrative climate, both in Britain and in the colony, favoured the imposition of schemes deemed conducive to black welfare. Moreover, the adoption of compulsory education in Britain in the 1870s facilitated a renewal of British governmental interest in applying this coercion to the colonies. Also influential was what was perceived as a worsening problem of child and juvenile vagrancy and the rationalization of this as the consequence of parental indifference to education.

In 1879, the Commission on the Juvenile Population, in delivering its report, accused parents of contributing to societal ills by not sending their children to school, and called upon the government to devise machinery to compel parents to do so. In spite of testimony from persons like Reverend Enos Nuttall, incumbent of St George's Anglican Church in Kingston, who attributed non-attendance at school to poverty rather than nonchalance, the commissioners recommended draconian judicial action against parents who failed to comply.[62] Ensuing discussions brought to the forefront the issue of the limits of state interference in parental rights and highlighted the divergence of views between the imperial and colonial states. In expressing his reservations about compulsion, John Savage, the inspector of schools, emphasized the duty of parents to educate their children but pointed out that any state effort to enforce education would entail insuperable difficulties. His observations convey the depth of parental ties and the significance which blacks attached to their rights as parents: "The extreme sensitiveness of the people, to any interference between them and their children and their readiness to resent the slightest attempt to control them [in trying] to enforce the attendance of their children at school . . . would produce immense irritability among the people, which might lead to disastrous consequences."[63]

Governor Musgrave, concurring with Savage's views, informed Lord Kimberley of the Colonial Office in June 1880 that any attempt at compulsory education was not advisable, as it would be "abortive" and would result in "much dissatisfaction among the population".[64] The Colonial Office, desirous of implementing compulsory education, was unimpressed with Musgrave's stance. Insisting that compulsion was urgently needed "both for the sake of the children and for the general good of the community", Kimberley advised Musgrave to report promptly on the procedure by which compulsory education could be implemented in Kingston.[65]

Musgrave was unable to promptly inform the Colonial Office of such plans, as the arrangements had to be deferred until the newly appointed inspector of schools had arrived and assessed the situation. However, in a clear endorsement of parental prerogative, Musgrave informed Kimberley in October 1880 that the state should encourage parental cooperation rather than legislatively enforcing compliance. Convinced that education was a "matter of faith and conscience" and that parents "should be led, not driven", Musgrave concluded that state coercion and punishment of parents could only lead to disaffection on the part of blacks. He reminded Kimberley that the enormous expense involved would necessitate more burdensome taxation on the very people whose cooperation on the education of their children was being sought.[66]

In a subsequent communication a few months later, Kimberley tacitly acknowledged Musgrave's concerns about the potential of black parental opposition and argued that "great circumspection should be used in introducing compulsory education". However, it was clear that the views of the imperial government would eventually prevail, as Kimberley agreed only to postpone giving the governor any final instructions while he awaited the arrival and report of the new inspector of schools.[67] By 1882, no final decision on compulsion had been made because the anticipated report had not been submitted by that year.

However, in 1881, in a token experiment with compulsion, the colonial state, under the new poor-relief regulations, made school attendance mandatory for any child between ages five and thirteen whose parents had applied for outdoor relief (not inmates of the poorhouse). By making the continuation of relief conditional on the provision of proof of school attendance to the relieving officer, the government was able to enforce education on this comparatively small population of poor-relief applicants.[68] The expense and potential opposition entailed in implementation of compulsory education for the mass of the black population meant that by 1882, neither legislation nor infrastructure to this end had been undertaken by the state.

The ability of the colonial state to impose apprenticeship on minors after 1838 was restricted by law to the confines of the reformatory and industrial schools. Outside of these spheres, the apprenticeship of a minor – that is, the indenturing of a person under sixteen years of age to a "master craftsman" for the purpose of acquiring a skill or a trade – was a voluntary affair and one which resided within the parental domain. According to the terms of the early laws governing such voluntary apprenticeships of minors, (4 Vict., 30, and 5 Vict., 35), a parent could enter into an agreement or contract to have his or her child, usually a boy, apprenticed. These arrangements were usually non-residential and subject (in practice) to alterations by either party. Elite society viewed these contracts of apprenticeship as opportunities for the exercise of a "morally beneficial" influence on children and for training them in industrious habits, opportunities perceived as being absent from the homes of black children.

Such voluntary arrangements received mixed reactions from black parents and children. As a rule, most black parents regarded apprenticeship, like industrial education, as a preparation for a servile future which was alien to their vision of their children's "freedom road". Not surprisingly, therefore, most were adamant that they would "not be a party to the arrangement". However, parents without a means of support, such as some mothers of "illegitimate children", sometimes had to resort to apprenticing their children to tradesmen.[69] Some boys, especially, resisted their parents' attempts to have them apprenticed because it interfered with their freedom.[70]

In the period 1838–82, there were two significant departures from the status quo in which the apprenticeship of non-institutionalized children was accepted as a voluntary affair and seen as the province of the parent. The first occurred during the first half of the 1850s, in response to the cholera and small-pox epidemics. Calls were made, usually by stipendiary magistrates, for state enactment of legislation to sanction the apprenticeship of children orphaned by these epidemics, but who were not in institutions. Charles Lake, stipendiary magistrate for Portland at the time, supported this call for state approval of substitute parental authority figures that would "arrest the further progress of idleness and vagrancy among a large number of children whose parents are separated from them by death". Supporters of state-enforced apprenticeship sought to legitimize their request by pointing to the duty of the state to stand *in loco parentis* in the case of orphans. In so doing, they disregarded the support provided by other family members, who in many cases had moved to adopt these orphans. The proposal did not move beyond the discussion stage, however, as by 1857 the issue of the "orphaned and destitute" had been incorporated into reformatory legislation.[71]

The second departure from the status quo occurred in 1865 when, in response to growing requests for state action in the face of escalating praedial larceny, the colonial government sanctioned the apprenticeship of children who had been convicted of stealing. By the Indenture Act (28 Vict., c. 19) the colonial state empowered any two justices of the peace to apprentice for five years any child under the age of sixteen who was convicted of petty larceny. Although the act targeted all offending juveniles regardless of race, from a governmental perspective, the likely pool of offenders would have been the children of the poor black masses. This draconian measure by Governor Eyre's administration further eroded black parental prerogative. In providing for the physical removal of the child from his or her home for five years, the Indenture Act thereby denied the parent a role in the child's development for this period. This was clearly Eyre's objective, as the act was based on the presumption of derelict or non-existent parental influence. Influenced by a philosophy similar to that employed in the apprenticing of children in the post-bellum United States, Eyre argued that apprenticing a child "to a planter or householder" would provide "better care and training" for that child.[72] The Colonial Office's recommendation that such an apprenticeship should extend beyond one year only if parental consent was given may have been a limited acknowledgement of parental rights, but it also indicated the support of the imperial state for enforced apprenticeship of minors.[73] However, when British member of Parliament Edward Cardwell announced the disallowance of the act in 1866, after several months of operation, this was more in response to concerns about the vulnerable state of post–Morant Bay society than it was an expression of respect for parental rights.[74]

In passing the Apprenticeship Law of 1881, also known as Law 3, the colonial government sought to give effect to the recommendations made by the Commission on the Juvenile Population for stricter regulation of apprenticeship contracts, while at the same time implementing mechanisms to secure the rights of parties involved in these voluntary arrangements. Thus, the law stated that an apprenticeship contract could only be binding on a minor if it had been agreed to by both parent and child in the presence of a justice of the peace or clerk of petty sessions, who had to ensure fulfilment of all requirements before countersigning. This was an effort to halt unregulated apprenticeships, protect the state (as author of the law) against charges of abuse and ensure the rights of parents and children. However, this clause was not applicable to the apprenticing of minors in reformatories.

The government tried to ensure that the law did not ignore parental prerogative by enabling any parent or guardian who had not consented to an indenture to apply to the district court judge for an annulment within three months of the start of the contract. However, even if an unsuspecting parent discovered an indenture within the specified time, the time and expense of district court proceedings would make it difficult or impossible to obtain an annulment. Meanwhile, by making all private apprenticeship contracts terminable at age twenty-one, the law forestalled "adverse parental influences" until that age, by which time, in keeping with the colonial state's agenda, "habits of industry" would have already been instilled.

Two final effects of Law 3 of 1881 – again, with the goal of stricter regulation of apprenticeships – were that apprentices were empowered to complain of their masters' mistreatment (if they could find the time and money to do so) at courts of petty sessions, and that justices of the peace were given the right to terminate contracts of apprenticeship if, for example, the contract had not been undertaken in the presence of a justice of the peace or clerk of petty sessions. They could also terminate a contract if the legal guardian had not consented to the apprenticeship.[75]

Conclusion

Among the many adversities imposed upon blacks by the system of slavery had been the abrogation of their control over their children. The activism of parents on behalf of their free children during the apprenticeship period shows the primacy of the parent-child bond and indicates that a very important meaning of freedom for black parents was their unfettered right to determine the welfare of their children. This analysis has demonstrated that as the nineteenth century progressed, the colonial state, informed by elitist perceptions of black parents as inept and a utilitarian approach to the raising of black children, sought once more to negate parental dominion under circumstances which it deemed appropriate. Thus, the state, backed by elitist opinion, attempted to control and reform the children of blacks – and, ultimately, black society – by means of subjecting "neglected, abandoned and criminal" children to confinement in reformatory and industrial institutions, promoting compulsory and industrial education and legislating for the apprenticeship of minors after 1838.

However, the state's justification for its attempts to assert control over black children was permeated by contradictions. Black parents were indicted for failing to educate their children, when in fact the colonial authorities did very little to fund educational facilities after the expiration of the Negro Education Grant in 1845. The government's criticism of black parents also failed to recognize the persistent efforts of many fathers and mothers not only to educate their children, but also to provide the infrastructural facilities which would allow them to do so. As discussed in chapter 2, there is significant evidence of parents, especially fathers, volunteering their labour to construct schools for their children and working hard to ensure their children's educational and material welfare.[76] Certainly, this evidence of black parental initiative is reflective of an enduring commitment to the welfare of kin and especially of the strong parent-child bond which characterized a black Jamaican familial culture influenced by West African traditions. Importantly, such initiatives also indicate that some black fathers were activists on behalf of their children; their actions negate the assertions of writers such as Froude that black men were disinterested and insignificant in issues relating to the welfare of their children.[77] As further evidence of its selective stance regarding the best interests of black children, the state characterized black parents as "wanton" and "careless" and charged them with allowing their children to grow up in "destitution", while choosing to ignore the role of harsh taxes and low and uncertain wages which confined many black families to a cycle of poverty. Most importantly, efforts by the colonial state to exercise dominion over these children constituted a denial of the existence of constructive black parenthood and of black parents' right to raise their children according to their own standards, in the context of their own vision of the meaning of freedom.

This assessment has shown that when confronted with attempts to control their children, whether by estates or by the state, parents adopted all means necessary to resist them.[78] During the period of modified slavery referred to as the apprenticeship, black parents were virtually universally successful in countering efforts by others to determine their children's future. In the post-slavery period, although the state initiated efforts to assume parental authority through reformatory institutions (affecting, however, only a comparatively small number of children), black parents were by no means powerless in this context; as seen in this discussion, they were able to resist attempts to detain their children in these institutions beyond the specified term of confinement. Certainly, the spectre of black parental opposition to state-supported efforts to retain children in these institutions under a system of apprenticeship contributed to the withdrawal, albeit temporarily, of such measures by the late 1860s.

Utilitarian efforts by the colonial state to equip black children for their "station in life" through industrial education were stoutly resisted by parents during the entire period under consideration, as both an infringement of parental vision and a restriction of their children's freedom. Similarly, few parents permitted their children to participate in the system of voluntary apprenticeship which was established after 1838. For those who did, they regarded this system as a means to an end – that is, a means by which their children could acquire marketable skills. In this respect, these parents were exercising their prerogative rather than conceding the right of others to do so. For much more than a generation after emancipation, black fathers and mothers demonstrated their belief that freedom was an ongoing process which was to be assiduously guarded, and in this context, their resistance to state encroachment on their natural rights to determine the best interests of their children constituted an enactment of this vision of freedom.

Chapter 5

Tragedy at Morant Bay
A WINDOW INTO THE WORLD OF BLACK FAMILIES

> The soldier told the child to go out of the house, and the little boy said his father
> had not done anything that they had killed. A constable came up and said that my
> husband was a good man. I have five children.
> — *Testimony of Grace Cherrington, victim of the suppression following the Morant*
> *Bay Rebellion*[1]

A GREAT DEAL HAS BEEN written about the events which occurred at Morant
Bay in 1865, and the historiography of the rebellion is replete with analyses of
a causal nature. Some of these emphasize the critical unfolding of socio-economic events leading up to 1865. Others focus on the pivotal roles of leaders
like "Bogle and his men", while Swithin Wilmot has sought to highlight the
contributions of women to this most important protest of nineteenth-century
Jamaica. Accounts of the event's aftermath have tended to focus on the political
path which ensued, and analyses of the suppression that occurred as part of
this have been, for the most part, of a general nature, punctuated by statistical
references to its toll in lives and property.[2]

Both Clinton Hutton and Gad Heuman brought greater visibility to the
human suffering occasioned by Governor Eyre's "prompt and . . . terrible"
retribution.[3] However, neither work examined the impact of the suppression
within a detailed thematic context of the family. Further, there is the salient

Figure 8. *Court House, Bath (St Thomas in the East).* Adolphe Duperly, *Daguerian Excursions in Jamaica* (1840), reprinted courtesy of the University of the West Indies Library, Mona.

issue of historical emphasis; as Roy Augier observed, in commenting on the indiscriminate and violent nature of the suppression, "Since so many were innocent the act of October 1865 was not retribution, it was murder. Ought we not to remember Morant Bay in greater measure for the many who suffered, rather than exaggerate the achievement of the few who rioted?"[4]

This chapter extends the discussion on the impact of the events at Morant Bay by examining the effects of the consequent suppression on black families in St Thomas-in-the-East. Their own testimony before the Royal Commission, despite certain limitations (to be addressed shortly), indicates that for an inordinate number of blacks, the aftermath of the rebellion at Morant Bay was indeed a family tragedy. Many families from Morant Bay, the Plantain Garden River district, the Blue Mountain Valley, Port Antonio and Manchioneal suffered sudden and violent loss, and sometimes multiple losses. In many cases, the severity was heightened by the centrality of the victims to the economic base of the family. Indicators of family stability such as the acquisition of homes and the duration of unions were adversely affected. Nevertheless, under the most traumatic of circumstances, many affected family members devised survival strategies and demonstrated the resilience which enabled their families to continue after Morant Bay.

Importantly, the evidence presented here also allows us a window into the world of black families of St Thomas-in-the-East, indicating, through black testimony, important signifiers of commitment to family and kinship ties, longevity of unions, profound attachment to family property and consistent reliance on family networks, both consanguineous and conjugal. Certainly, the evidence presented here overturns negative stereotypical representations, discussed earlier, of the black family as dysfunctional and chaotic and of black men and women as disinterested and negligent within familial contexts. In particular, the evidence challenges assertions of male marginality by demonstrating the centrality of sons, fathers, husbands, partners and brothers within their families. What becomes abundantly clear in this assessment of black survival strategies is an enduring commitment to kindred, a world view which had characterized familial culture in traditional West Africa and which proved to be foundational in shaping the black experience in Jamaica during this period.

Reliance upon the minutes of evidence of the Jamaica Royal Commission of 1866 as the evidential base for this analysis has its own inherent limitations. The immensity of the undertaking – a three-man commission heard and recorded 730 witnesses in fifty-one days – in itself created room for reasonable error. Additionally, the cultural divide between white commissioners and black witnesses, even with the aid of interpreters, would have led to some cultural or linguistic misinterpretation on both sides. Furthermore, a time lapse of well over three months between the revolt and the commencement of the inquiry would have been conducive to lapses of memory and confused recall. (On the other hand, given the shock and violence of their experiences, many of these witnesses may have been undergoing stress-related "recurrent and vivid recollections of the event".)[5] It is also possible that some witnesses may have been prompted or may have lied or exaggerated in anticipation of some beneficial outcome.

In spite of these limitations, the minutes of evidence remain a valuable tool with which to construct, as far as possible, a picture of the effects of the suppression imposed after Morant Bay on black families. It was possible, in several instances, to confirm the veracity of witnesses' accounts by comparing them with statements made by others at the scene. Ultimately, the shortcomings of individual witnesses and the limitations discussed above, especially the possibility of cultural or linguistic misinterpretation, would not have altered the validity of the general testimony nor the vivid images of the event generated by so many. Because this chapter makes use of these testimonies to a significant extent, this analysis of the impact on black families of the suppression following the Morant Bay Rebellion makes an important contribution to the project of giving voice to the black experience, especially in the anglophone post-slavery Caribbean. Coming almost a generation after "full free", this is one of the comparatively few bodies of evidence in which blacks directly convey to us their experiences, emotions and efforts to cope with crisis.

Selecting black family members for this analysis required that several determinations be made based on their testimonies. Determining the race of the witnesses was facilitated by the commission's categorization of each person as "black" or "coloured". Witnesses' references to relatives in their testimonies gave a picture of their family situations. Some may well have had family members affected by the events, but as they made no reference to family in their statements, these persons were not considered in the analysis. A total of 212 witnesses were called under sections C (witnesses as to deaths) and D (witnesses as to destruction of property by burning), and of this total, 97 were classified as black family members using the criteria noted.[6] This examination of the impact of the suppression on black families is therefore based on the accounts of these 97 black family members, and it is their experiences, not those of the black population of St Thomas-in-the-East in general, which are analysed here. It is hoped that this discussion will give greater visibility to all these families. At the same time, it is clear that the experiences of these 97 family members during and after October 1865 are a mere microcosm of what was occurring in the wider black population of St Thomas-in-the-East, and any conclusions drawn as to the quantitative and qualitative impact of the suppression on black families must be conservative.[7] Nevertheless, the fact that almost half of those who gave statements under sections C and D were blacks who had encountered disastrous family consequences supports the conclusion that Morant Bay was indeed a family tragedy.

The Impact of the Suppression on Black Families

The suppression of the Morant Bay Rebellion exposed a considerable number of black families to extreme trauma, which Victor Reus defines as events "associated with either actual or threatened death or injury to oneself or another".[8]

Seventy-one out of ninety-seven, or 73 per cent, of the black family members studied testified that they had lost one or more of their own and/or that they or other family members had been threatened with death or injury or had been injured during the course of the suppression. This experience was exacerbated by the sudden and violent nature of the events.

Certainly, the worst cases of extreme trauma were occasioned by multiple deaths in one family, especially when the victims were immediate family members whose deaths were witnessed by the surviving relatives. Henrietta Bailey of Notts River lost her son, William, and her husband, Robert, when both were shot within seconds of each other, in full view of Henrietta, who recounted her experience to the commissioners: "The boy was lying down on the bed got fever . . . I stood up at the door mouth and see him shot." This event was devastating to a family unit which had been together long enough to produce "a grown son".[9] Losses such as these were especially hard for elderly family members, such as Maria Robinson of Mount Lebanus, who was deprived of her three sons as well as her grandson. Although she gave no evidence to this effect, it is likely that because of her advanced age, her sons and perhaps her grandson, who was grown, had contributed to her welfare. At any rate, it appears that her sons either lived with her or were visiting her on "the last day she ever saw them" as they ran into the woods.[10] Confronted with the shooting deaths of both her husband, Simon Wilson, and her brother, James Stewart, Francis Wilson of York Village was especially worried about her uncertain economic future. She remarked, "Wilson, is that the way you . . . going to dead wrongfully and leave two little children for me to maintain?"[11]

Multiple deaths within a family also linked extended families in tragedy. Thus, when the Berry brothers, Joseph and Robert, were shot, they left behind Eliza, Joseph's wife, and their seven children, as well as Mary, Robert's wife. Similarly, when the Bryan brothers of Long Bay, Ned and James, were shot, they left behind Ned's wife and baby as well as a third brother, George, who lived next door and survived only because he hid in the bushes. Both sets of extended families had lived at Long Bay in contiguous dwellings suggestive of yard formation, similar to the pattern which existed in traditional West African compounds (see chapter 1).[12] Mary, Ned's wife, having witnessed the killings of her husband and brother-in-law, had herself been threatened by one of the black volunteers, who informed her that she would have met a similar fate had it not been for the baby in her arms.[13] Although only nine out of ninety-seven black family members, or 9 per cent, testified to multiple losses, the repercussions were nevertheless devastating.

Loss of one member of the family unit was, however, just as crushing. Many children were left without one of their parents – usually, but not always, the father – under the most tragic of circumstances. Any attempt to represent the number of young children deprived of a parent during the suppression would be conservative, as black family members who testified to the loss of a spouse or partner did not always indicate the number of children left behind, if any. Nevertheless, based on the testimony of the ninety-seven black family witnesses studied, a total of forty-one children were left with only one parent as a result of the deaths of thirteen parents from different households.

Grace Cherrington, whose husband was shot in their home while she was next door, returned home to see her young son being harassed for money by the soldiers who had shot him. She testified that her son, who had witnessed his father being killed, "took frightened" and not only showed the soldier a chest of valuables, but demanded of him why they had shot his father, as he had done nothing. The irony of this situation was that the couple had provided hospitality for other soldiers from Newcastle on the preceding Friday night into Saturday morning. On Sunday morning, a different group of soldiers visited their house and left Mrs Cherrington's five children fatherless.[14]

Several adults were also deprived of their parents or parents-in-law. Nine out of the ninety-seven witnesses, or 9 per cent, fell into this category. Sarah Tyne was afraid to stay with her father after he had been shot by soldiers because she felt that a similar fate might befall her. Obviously affected by feelings of guilt that she could not comfort her father, she told the commissioners that she "left him there to die" even though "he was grunting and not yet dead". Later that night, when she had determined that it was safe to return to the cow pasture where he had been shot, Sarah found that she was too late.[15] Clearly, such cases of extreme trauma also left family members with a sense of helplessness and guilt. Susannah McGregor expected to find her father, the sexton of the church at Barracks, at her home where she had left him when she went to work her grounds. Instead, on her return, she learned that he had been killed and found that soldiers were in the process of threatening her sick husband with a similar fate.[16]

Adult children also testified to what they viewed as the unjustifiable circumstances under which they lost their parents or parents-in-law. In several cases, the data indicate that elderly relatives resided either in the same house as the younger members of the family, as seen with Susannah McGregor, or on the same premises in a nearby house. This suggests a desire to maintain close physical links with elderly parents or parents-in-law. Additionally, some adult children testified to their continued support of elderly family members, a fact which indicates the endurance of the commitment to kin which had characterized black familial values over generations. Stephen and Rebecca Telford of Mount Lebanus lost a father and father-in-law respectively when John Telford was killed. During a heated exchange between Rebecca and some soldiers who were insisting that she "come into the house", John Telford, who lived in the same yard, came to the door to inquire "what was all the noise". Rebecca testified that "just as they saw the old man they shot him down and he dropped . . . I took up the two children and ran to the bush".[17] Similarly, Thomas Duncan of Port Morant could not understand why his father-in-law, John Noble, had been killed because "he was a sick man and had been lying in his house for many years". Although Noble explained to the maroons that he could not manage to go outside, he was taken out, tied to a tree and shot. This incident made Duncan decide that he no longer wished to remain a constable.[18]

Events at Morant Bay altered the expectations of many parents that their children would survive them. Of the ninety-seven black family witnesses, 14 per cent testified to losing their children during the suppression. Hannah Aspitt, whose first husband had predeceased her and whose second husband had been arrested, lost her sixteen-year-old daughter, Amelia Stewart, approximately one week after she was shot while they were both hiding in the bushes.[19] As they were under martial law, she was unable to get help for her daughter. In this case, the explanation given by the maroon who shot Amelia that he had detected a movement in the bush and fired at what he anticipated was a man about to attack him seems indefensible.[20]

Though hiding in the bushes was a common survival strategy during this period of unrest, it also proved to be a health hazard, particularly for children, during the rains of October 1865. After her house was burned and her life threatened because she would not inform on her husband's whereabouts, Sarah McKindo narrowly escaped rape by two soldiers who wanted "one or two rounds with her". Thus, she took the decision to hide herself and her small child in the bushes for eight days. Sarah testified that she was afraid to light a fire to keep them warm; subsequently, "the child took cold, and the inside of the child went bump, bump like a watch beating . . . and the poor child died".[21]

Other parents lost their children under more violent and inhumane conditions. William Shann, son of Charlotte Ross of Barracks, was confined to bed with "a lame leg". In spite of his mother's plea that "it is a sick person . . . it is my son who is sick", he was shot dead by soldiers who later said that they were "truly sorry to have shot an innocent person, they thought he was a rebel".[22] For many parents similarly affected, the trauma of being suddenly and permanently separated from their children was doubtless intensified by the absence of a trial or any opportunity for their children to defend themselves. This must have been the experience of Sophia Bates when she was informed that her sixteen-year-old son, Henry Bonnyman, had been shot by soldiers while trying to escape into the sea.[23]

After Robert Beecher of Harbour Head was given a pass and sent home from Morant Bay, his mother, Rosa Johnson, must have anticipated a long life for her son, with whom by her own testimony she was close. This hope was terminated as he was rearrested and hanged shortly after his return home. Rosa told the commission that he "sent a handkerchief to make me have remembrance". Deaths of adult offspring like Robert sometimes left the bereaved parent in an economically endangered position as well. Rosa Johnson's husband had been dead for eleven years and she had no other means of support besides her son.[24] Although Robert Davis of Manchioneal lived with his daughter, he, like Rosa Johnson, was very close to his son, John. Thus, when John was taken to Manchioneal Bay and shot, the loss was acutely felt, and Davis testified that he was "very dependent on his son who supported him".[25] John McLaren, a native Baptist, was told that he was being arrested because "his son was James McLaren and he knew Bogle and Gordon and he must know something about it". The elder McLaren, in reminiscing about his son, conveyed that sense of achievement and worth which for many parents was cut short by 1865: "Me can't read or write but James McLaren him could read and write . . . I put him to school when he was a little bit of a boy."[26]

By occasioning the death of spouses and partners, the suppression after the Morant Bay Rebellion not only resulted in extreme trauma for many but also abruptly terminated several unions which had been the nucleus of stable family units for varying lengths of time. Thirty-four of the ninety-seven black witnesses, or 35 per cent, testified to the loss of a spouse or partner as a result of the suppression. Wilmot has indicated that women were by no means "marginal to the events at Morant Bay", and as such, some men must have lost their partners, whether or not they were participants in the rebellion. For example, David McBean's wife left home on 14 October to visit the market at Winchester, but during the course of the day, he heard that she had been shot. David testified that, having organized a rescue party, he, along with other men, transported her home, but she died on her arrival there.[27] However, the vast majority of deaths among spouses or partners were male heads of families, and this would have reduced the income of the surviving members even if the wife or partner usually worked. This also shows that men were seen as the primary instigators of the rebellion and were therefore the main targets of the suppression. Survivor George Mac Murray testified that he hid for two weeks because he had heard that soldiers were coming to burn every house and "kill every man in Bath".[28] Similarly, Jacob Davis hid because he had heard that if the soldiers "saw any man in the house they would shoot him".[29]

From testimony given by surviving spouses and partners, it is clear that many of the affected couples had been together for a significant period of time, thus challenging the stereotypical characterization of black unions as unstable and short-lived.[30] Other indicators of extended unions, such as the number of biological children affiliated with a couple and their length of residence on land of their own, support this conclusion. Testimony from some black witnesses also underscored the fact that many of the victims of the suppression were from smallholding and peasant families. For example, Charles and Lianta Logan had lived at Duckenfield for a long time, on "buy land of their own". Therefore, when "black soldiers" shot her husband and burned the family's home, this terminated a relationship of some duration. However, Lianta had clearly made an effort to continue the process of survival on the family property, as she was still living there (although she did not say under what conditions) when she appeared before the commission.[31]

The family unit of Charles and Ann Mitchell displayed signs of stability and durability before the events of October 1865. Charles was a bowlmaker by trade and a native Baptist, and he sometimes "kept a school at Spring". The couple had been together long enough to have a grown son and the family had been able, in difficult times, to save enough to buy land at Harbour Head, on which Charles had built their home. There is also evidence to indicate that Charles took care of his mother, who resided with them. When volunteers shot him in their yard, this traumatized his mother, who was forced by the soldiers to go and look at his body. Having lost her husband of many years, Ann Mitchell was further confronted with the burning of their home. Aware of her own tragedy and uncertain future, she summarized her predicament: "They burnt my house and left me in distress." As was the case with other bereaved relatives, she was denied the traditional forms of burial for her husband's body because workers were "afraid to come and dig the hole" during martial law. Eventually she was forced to wrap his body in calico, and with someone's help, she disposed of his body in the sea.[32]

John and Lucretia Mullens had been married for a long time by 1865. Although Lucretia was not sure of either of their ages, both were clearly of advanced years. Moreover, their daughter, Mary Mitchell, was grown and had her own family. John had worked very hard to support his family, having worked as a labourer at Pera Pen and earned additional income from fishing and working his provision grounds. During the suppression, he was severely flogged for failing to follow orders to come to Golden Grove, and he died from the infected wound within a week after he returned home. In her testimony, Lucretia emphasized her husband's strength, saying that he was "a grey man but a strong man", and blamed the authorities who had administered the flogging for his death; as a strong fisherman, she said, he could "go out anywhere on sea and catch fish and work in the provision ground", but after the flogging, "his back was really smashed". She was never told what her husband had done to deserve his arrest and eventual death. Unlike many other families, however, the Mullens' home was not burned and Lucretia was able to get assistance from her daughter, who came to live with her at Pera.[33]

Some unions did not have the benefit of longevity before being cut short by the suppression. Catherine and James Johnson of Garbrand Hall had not yet been married a full year when James was shot by soldiers, leaving Catherine with a newborn baby.[34] A similar fate befell Isabella Francis, who lived with Andrew Clarke and their month-old child.[35] In both of these cases, the houses were burned, leaving the young women without immediate shelter.

We may speculate, based on the testimony, as to the fate of these families after the male head of the family had been removed. In many cases, the surviving spouse or partner showed evidence of distress or of desperate attempts to start again. Prior to October 1865, many, though not all, of these women had adhered to the Victorian model of female domesticity. In some cases, the suppression engineered a shift in socio-economic roles, with bereaved spouses or partners assuming the dual responsibility of head of the household and income producer. Ann Cargill's husband, William, had been on his way to Oxford to work when he was shot, allegedly by maroons. After this tragedy and the subsequent burning of their home, she was left with two small children to support. She emphasized to the commission how difficult life had become for her and her children; her main concern was that on most days, they could not get enough to eat. Thus, it is an indication of their great resilience that bereaved family members like Ann Cargill were able to effect strategies of recovery. Ann informed the commission that she was able to get a job at the Bay (a reference to Morant Bay), and that subsequently she was able to regain access to grounds from which she could maintain her children.[36]

A similar level of self-reliance was demonstrated by Rosey Young, whose husband, Thomas, was hanged. Left with four children to maintain, she attempted to do so by working land which she had rented at Pembroke Hall.[37] For other survivors, such as Henrietta Bailey, who had suffered the double tragedy of witnessing the shooting deaths of her son and her husband, the contrast between their previous standard of living and that imposed by the suppression was stark. Whereas she had lived with her husband and adult son in their house on "buy land of their own" and had had recourse to a stable family income, Henrietta was now alone, her life relegated to "a little hut because they burned the house".[38]

In some cases, women who had contributed to their household income before 1865 now found themselves not only deprived of their partners, but also faced with economic uncertainty because of the suppression. Thus, in the immediate aftermath of martial law, some women who had worked on estates found that they were unable to collect wages owed to them. For others, obtaining employment on estates in the troubled environs of St Thomas-in-the-East was too much of an obstacle. A few women, bereaved and hungry, resorted to their wider family networks for assistance. Ann Wedderman had resided and worked at Holland estate with her partner, Samuel Walker, and their two children. After Samuel was killed, Ann was unable to collect the two weeks' wages owed to her by Mr Stewart, overseer of Holland estate. Under the circumstances, she could no longer continue to live at Holland. Thus, alone, unemployed and unable to care for her children, she turned to her father for help. She testified, "If it had not been for my father I should not have been able to live, me and my picaninnies would have died of hunger."[39]

The ability of some bereaved women to become or remain self-reliant in the aftermath of the suppression was certainly diminished, and in some cases made impossible, by the destruction of shelter. Mary Ann Williams, without a way to support herself after her husband, James, was shot, lost everything of value in her house and ultimately found herself entirely without shelter. She testified before the commission that she stayed some of the time with her mother at Prospect and at other times with neighbours.[40]

It is highly probable that many of these witnesses, having experienced extreme trauma, suffered from what medical science later defined in the twentieth century as post-traumatic stress disorder. Certainly, most of them would have met at least one of the criteria, in that they were confronted with the death, threatened death or injury of loved ones, or threats or injury to themselves. Symptoms of this disorder include nervousness, distressing and recurrent recollections, nightmares and feelings of detachment or estrangement from others. These symptoms must persist for over one month to be classified as post-traumatic stress disorder.[41] Several of the witnesses testifying before the commission referred to either themselves or family members being made sick by the impact of the suppression on their family circle. Jane Brown, married to William Brown and living at Harbour Head Road, was arrested along with her daughter and released for lack of evidence against them. Subsequently, however, the family experienced the loss of one son by execution, the destruction of all the food on their grounds and the burning of their family home. After the suppression, Jane, her husband, and her younger son had to seek shelter in "a little house" where her adult daughter already lived under cramped conditions with her own family. Jane testified before the commission that William was "sick now from all this thing".[42]

No doubt, for William Brown and other surviving male heads of families, the trauma of losing their homes and family members must have been intensified by anxiety over their ability to continue in their traditional roles as providers for their families. Sarah McKindo, whose child had died from exposure after they were forced to hide in the bushes for eight days, testified that before October 1865, her husband, Abraham, had worked at Coley estate as well as on the public road to provide for his family. However, Abraham, who had survived only because he had successfully hidden in the bushes, had been sickened by the loss of his child and the burning of his house. Sarah testified that he was "at home, but not very well". Although she concluded that "so much rain made him knock up", her husband may very well have been experiencing post-traumatic stress. Anxiety over shelter likely played a large part in his concerns, as although the couple had been able to make a small hut, they had not yet built a large house; as Sarah said, "we don't know that we shall be able to get that now".[43]

The burning of more than one thousand houses during the suppression was not only "wanton and cruel",[44] but also part of a calculated strategy to undercut the opposition of blacks by striking at their economic base. In the process, it unravelled a tragedy of significant dimensions for the black families. The burning of homes struck at the core of much that was crucial to the existence and development of the family. Further, it signified material loss for many families who had bought land and built their homes. This assault rendered futile the many years of difficult labour in harsh times, the frugal savings and the investment of family labour which had gone into the construction of these dwellings, however simple. Material loss also resulted from the destruction of the contents of homes or from robberies prior to burning, as mentioned by some witnesses. Further, the property around peasant and smallholding homes was crucial to the economic bases of these families, yet many experienced the loss of livestock and provisions during these incidents of burning. Of the ninety-seven testimonies assessed, fifty-two witnesses, or 54 per cent, testified to their houses being burned.

Importantly, these houses had allowed families to fulfil what Abraham Maslow referred to as "security needs" by creating in family members, especially children, a sense of safety.[45] Yet when so many were forced to watch helplessly, sometimes with children beside them, as their homes were consumed by flames, the very thing that had made them feel secure became a source of anguish. Moreover, the loss of shelter under such conditions further endangered the financial security of surviving family members who had already been economically marginalized by harsh conditions prior to October 1865.

For these families, the home also represented a focal point for the creation and dissemination of memories. The devastation of their houses, especially when this was preceded by violence against family members, replaced ordinary and pleasant memories with tragic ones. Further, the destruction disrupted their ties to the past and to their ancestors. The dwelling symbolized the connection between past and present generations in two ways: first, some testified to having inherited their homes and properties from parents or relatives, and second, for many black families who owned land, the property around the house contained the burial sites of dead relatives. This chain of connection, reminiscent of West African vertical links of kinship with the dead (discussed in chapter 1), was interrupted by the force of the suppression.

Adverse consequences occasioned by the burning of houses were intensified for those who had undertaken the task of house building without any assistance from relatives. Such was the situation of Ann Mackenzie of Long Bay, whose husband had deserted her about nine years prior to 1865. Having never received any money from her husband, who had "gone away to St Mary's parish", she had by dint of her own efforts constructed a new house on her property. Thus, when "black soldiers" visited in search of her husband and subsequently set fire to her house, the effect was too much for Ann: "Poor me! I'm destitute. I have nobody to do anything for me. I make new building, new house and you come and this done to my poor building."[46]

The devastation of the burnings was also magnified for family members rendered vulnerable by pre-existing problems such as bereavement or physical handicap. Having lost her husband in July of 1865, Jane Wilson of Long Bay had again experienced loss with the death of one of her two children the night before her house was burned. Her pleas to Codrington, a local magistrate and a planter, to spare her house because she was innocent and had "no husband now" and, by implication, no way of rebuilding, had no effect.[47] Physically handicapped, Ann Ogilvie not only lost her son and sole means of support, but also faced a harsh future without shelter after the burning of her house and the removal of "every bit" of her worldly goods from it.[48] Similarly, Henrietta Piercy's husband was blind and housebound, making the couple's need for secure shelter all the more crucial. Having been spared the burning of their house on two occasions because "a poor old blind man lived in it", their future was endangered by local magistrate and estate manager Arthur Warmington's orders to "haul out the blind man and put fire to the d——d house" (*sic*).[49]

Ironically, some people's homes, particularly those of females living alone or with young children, were preserved from burning because their occupants were seen as solitary and defenceless. Rosa Johnson, whose husband had been dead for eleven years and whose son had been hanged in the conflict, was spared the loss of her house by a maroon named Woodrow, who informed the others that "this is the house of a poor woman, her husband is dead and she has no man".[50]

Family exigencies, however, did little to halt the indiscriminate nature of the burning, as Esther Williams, who lived at Weybridge with her baby's father, discovered. Finding herself in the throes of labour as Codrington and others approached her house, she explained her plight and pleaded with Codrington not to burn her house, as she did not know where she would live with her child when it was born. However, Esther's pleas fell on deaf ears: "He set my house on fire and I was in childbirth." She tried to make it to her sister's house, and just as she got there "the child dropped".[51] The widespread nature of the burnings and the general fear inspired by the activities of white soldiers, black soldiers and maroons alike also discouraged other women in labour from remaining in their homes for the births. Thus, when Agnes Stewart Davis of Roselle heard that the soldiers were approaching her district, she hid in the bushes for three days. During this period she gave birth, assisted by her "little child", and returned to find her home burned.[52]

In the face of extensive burning, some people sought to save their homes by making a variety of appeals to those conducting the destruction. Some women petitioned on the basis of the welfare of their large families. Sophia Davis of Font Hill, whose husband had retreated to the bushes, unsuccessfully pleaded with a soldier not to burn her house because she had so many children: "I rose with the child in my arms and said, 'Massa, I beg you not to burn my house with my nine children.' "[53] Others appealed to the perpetrators on the basis of character or who their family members were, but this was usually to no avail. Thus, when white soldiers attempted to burn Betsy Buckley's house in Fair Prospect, she appealed to Codrington on the dual basis of her husband's occupation and her own innocence: "I said my husband was a constable and I was an innocent creature, and I said, 'Do massa, save my poor soul.' "[54] Codrington, unmoved by her plea, said, "D——n the constable and d——n you too" (*sic*), and set fire to the house. John William Hamilton, who was at home with his wife and mother when the soldiers came, narrowly escaped being shot when a passing constable vouched for his character. Hamilton, the constable said, was not a rebel and he always tried to "work honestly for his bread". In spite of this testimonial, his house was still burned.[55] Similarly, even though Abraham Francis's life was spared because his father, Joshua Francis, was known to be the sexton of the church at Barracks and "a good old man", this did not prevent his house being burned. Ironically, his sister, Susannah McGregor, subsequently had her house preserved when she told one of the officers that her father, the sexton, had just been killed.[56]

As previously discussed, material losses occasioned by burning were exacerbated by the fact that for some, their lost homes had represented connections to previous generations and in some cases had been the only material legacy bequeathed by deceased family members. When their home, along with their outhouse, was burned, Thomas and Mary Worgs and their five children were deprived of shelter and a focal point for family memories, especially for Thomas. Their house had been home for two generations of the Worgs family, as he recounted: "It was my father's before me."[57] For widows like Jane Wilson, the burning of their homes eliminated the only form of security left to them by their deceased husbands.[58]

For others who had acquired their homes through their own efforts rather than through inheritance, the emotional component of the loss could be just as significant, especially for those who had lived in their homes for a lengthy period of time. Thus, Lianta Logan, whose husband had been shot, had lived with him in their home on "the buy land at Duckenfield for a long time". Similarly, Gilbert Francis, his "poor sick wife" and their nine children had resided in their home on twelve acres of "buy lands" at Mount Lebanus for over ten years.[59] Certainly, an integral aspect of losses like these was the extent of these families' efforts in acquiring and maintaining their homes over many years. Phoebe Ennis of Airy Castle emphasized the value which she and her husband had attached to their home and their willingness to fulfil their responsibilities as homeowners when she pointed out that they had paid their taxes every year.[60]

The economic devastation and misfortune accompanying the destruction of houses were augmented by the attendant losses of possessions in and around the houses as a result of the unmitigated and wanton plunder unleashed by the enforcers of the suppression. From 11 October, the day of the rebellion, until retribution took its effect, considerable looting occurred amid the chaos of the conflict. It is equally clear, however, that the categories of goods which black witnesses identified as having been taken from their homes were consistent with their status as small farmers, peasants and labourers. As such, the confiscation of smallholders' lawful property prior to the burning of buildings significantly aggravated the loss and suffering resulting from the suppression. Most witnesses complained of the removal of men's, women's and children's clothing and of thus being left not only without shelter, but with only the clothes on their backs. Especially for large families, this caused great hardship, particularly during the rainy season. For George Mac Murray and his wife, whose house was not burned on the enforcers' first visit, the confiscation of everything of value was too much to bear: "I found my wife was crying because the things were taken away, and I was forced to cry myself, we staid [*sic*] in the house all day . . . when my mind was cooled a little, I went out into my garden field."[61]

Family members also suffered the theft of poultry and livestock important to both their domestic economy and livelihood. James Stewart, small settler of Thornton and father of seven children, testified that prior to burning his house, the maroons smashed his furniture, took out all his clothes and those of his children as well as two horses and saddles. Stewart was fortunate enough to have his horses returned to him. Sophia Davis of Font Hill, who admitted that the distress of having her house burned had prompted her to appear before the commission, testified that in addition to losing her home, she had also been deprived of all her clothes, her barrow, her fowls and her hog.[62]

Whereas some of these losses were the result of outright robbery on the part of the enforcers of the suppression, some degree of confiscation was also influenced by the perspective that blacks could not afford anything other than pedestrian items. Thus, any item external to that category was deemed to be stolen and hence was confiscated. Ann Mackenzie, discussed earlier, had proven that she could support herself after her husband had deserted her nine years prior, and had even built herself a new house. Therefore, when, prior to burning her house, one of the soldiers insisted that her pillow was "a white man's pillow", Ann not only retrieved it but also justified her possession of it: "Freedom come a long time and it is time to buy a tick and a pillow. . . . I took it from him."[63]

Items of monetary as well as acutely sentimental value were taken, usually from female family members – many of whom, like Sophia Davis, had their "married ring" removed under threats of "having their brains blown out". For too many women, the wedding ring was one of the few, if not the only, material reminders of a union abruptly terminated. Invariably, small but crucial family savings were also taken by soldiers, volunteers and maroons, thus multiplying the deprivation for the families involved. For many such families, this meant that they literally had no resources to command, as they saw their small savings wiped out once the burning and pillaging were complete. Catherine Wilson of Golden Grove, having lost her husband to the suppression, sought to set the record straight as to how she had come by the five pounds which had been confiscated from her: "It was my labour that I labour for on the estate. . . . I continually saved it when I worked."[64]

Serious though its consequences were for all the black families involved, the destruction of property was especially detrimental to those who had more than one property affected. In the particularly challenging economic environment of the 1850s and early 1860s, acquisition of property, maintenance of peasant-based enterprises and small-scale shopkeeping were all indicators of persistence, endeavour and a level of stability on the part of some black families. For many, the events of 1865 placed serious limitations on this progress. Indicative of this level of enterprise were Rebecca and Stephen Telford, who together owned fifty acres of land at Mount Lebanus, on which they had constructed a large dwelling, a smaller house and a shop. Between them, this small-farming couple had ten children and utilized family labour to assist with the shopkeeping and farming endeavours. As noted earlier, tragedy visited the Telfords with the shooting death of Stephen's father, John, who also lived on the property. In addition, the family enterprise was completely wiped out with the pillaging of barrels of flour and mackerel from the shop and the burning of both the shop and their large dwelling.[65]

A similar fate befell John Hamilton of Manchioneal, who lived with his wife and his "old mother" and tried to make a living from shopkeeping. In spite of a constable's efforts, as previously discussed, to vouch for his character as one who worked "honestly for his bread", Hamilton's house and shop were burned. He testified that his savings of eighty-two pounds were also destroyed in the fire. George Mac Murray, like many others, supplemented his income as a labourer by renting additional grounds, in this case with a house on the property. He also owned a home in the mountains at Friendship. Both homes were destroyed in the suppression, and all clothing and material goods belonging to him and his wife were either pillaged or burned. As seen in Mac Murray's testimony, previously detailed, the devastating losses engendered by the indiscriminate burnings had reduced the couple to tears.[66]

In the face of such utter devastation, the resilience and perseverance which had characterized black activity since 1834 enabled some family members to undertake initial steps towards recovery from loss of shelter. The first efforts at rebuilding were small-scale, as indicated by the testimony of Sarah McKindo, who along with her husband had already started the rebuilding process: "We made up a little hut . . . a little bit of a one. We don't make up any large one yet, we don't know that we shall be able to get that now." Similarly, Lewis Orr, who had worked as a shopkeeper but was at that time unemployed, was nevertheless rebuilding "a little place" for himself and his wife. Some received assistance from the most unlikely quarters. For example, Sophia Davis, her husband and their nine children were able to remain in Font Hill because "a good massa" gave them "half a house" fairly close to where the family's home had been burned.[67]

The force and speed with which "retribution" was implemented relegated many to virtual incapacity as their relatives were put to death or their homes burned. Nevertheless, amid the fear and helplessness, some were able to devise strategies to ensure their own survival and, in some cases, that of their entire family. When residents of Prospect Village heard that soldiers were coming in the night "to consume the village with fire" and that "the children was to be runned [*sic*] through with bayonets", several of them went to Leith Hall estate for protection. Among these was Elizabeth Millet, who lived with John Peters, the father of her children. Upon hearing the news, she tied her child on her back, held another in her arms and went to Mr Espeut, the proprietor of Leith Hall, where she worked. She and her family took refuge in the bookkeeper's barracks and stayed there for three weeks. Elizabeth and several others who worked at Leith Hall preferred to take their chances with Espeut rather than risk death at the hands of the soldiers. Elizabeth informed the commission that there had been many other women and their children at the bookkeeper's barracks and that "their husbands kept guard". It seems that this strategy of preservation worked, as no harm befell these men, women or children, most likely because they had voluntarily gone to Leith Hall and were known to Espeut. However, several of the men, including Elizabeth's partner, were forced to dig graves for others who were brought to Leith Hall for execution.[68]

Although fraught with difficulty, the strategy of hiding in the bushes was widely utilized by men, women and children alike, with varying degrees of success. Concealment in the woods, especially during the rainy season of October, could lead to illness and even death, as seen in the case of Sarah McKindo's baby. Other outcomes of attempted seclusion could be equally fatal, especially for those being hunted by men familiar with the area. Nevertheless, this was the strategy of choice for most men, who saw themselves as the primary targets of the suppression. Indeed, most black men who survived visits to their homes by enforcers of the suppression were able to manage this either because they were arrested and released or because they successfully eluded capture in the woods.

The latter was the case for George Mac Murray, who along with his wife had been so distressed by the confiscation of all their material goods from their home. After this event, he managed to successfully hide himself for two weeks, only to find upon his emergence that both of his houses had been burned.[69] Some men left their women and children in the house when they went into hiding, either because they surmised that escape and successful concealment might be easier if they went alone or because they believed that their families would not be harmed by the soldiers. Other men sent their family members to stay with relatives while they hid in the bushes. Charles Walker sent his wife and children to his wife's sister's house at Rocky Point while he took to the bushes at Airy Castle. When he returned safely to Rocky Point, he found that their home had been burned and "everything gone, only my life saved".[70]

William Christy Sr and William Christy Jr, father and son, both utilized this avenue of survival, but with a slight variation. William Jr successfully hid himself until it was safe, but William Sr took to the woods "to assist a young constable" who had persuaded him to help in commandeering other would-be escapees. Others adopted more creative strategies before retreating to the woods, such as the Graham brothers, who pretended to be fatally shot and then made their escape through the canes.[71]

Contrary to the expectations of many men, their womenfolk, when left behind to confront the enforcers, were not necessarily safe. As seen earlier, Sarah McKindo, whose husband survived only because he too "went to the bushes", was threatened and subjected to attempted rape. No doubt, some enforcers of the suppression utilized rape as a punitive measure; thus, incidents of rape were anything but random and, indeed, likely occurred more frequently than was reported to the commission. Chloe Munroe of Font Hill devised her own strategy to survive a rape at gunpoint. After her husband had "gone to bush", she was raped by one of the soldiers who remained behind. Although the line of questioning used by the commissioners was accusatory and deliberately worded to elicit an acknowledgement of compliance on her part, the message conveyed by Chloe's testimony was clear: the attack upon her person was brutal, but her strategy was intended to guarantee her survival. She testified that "him fix me on to the wall . . . he tore up all my front. I can't pea pea [*sic*] for two days". Chloe told the commissioners, "I took my knee and shove him off", but she had evidently taken the decision that she could do little else because, as she informed them, "the gun lean up against the wall".[72]

Black women, on many occasions, adopted the strategy of acting as inter-cessors in the interest of protecting their families and preserving their property.

Figure 9. *Holland Estate (St Thomas in the East).* Adolphe Duperly, *Daguerian Excursions in Jamaica* (1840), reprinted courtesy of the University of the West Indies Library, Mona.

Men also interceded, but this happened on comparatively few documented occasions, and it was usually on behalf of strangers, as in the instances in which constables saved John Hamilton's life and Grace Cherrington's house.[73] Female family members more frequently assumed this role because the males were usually either not in the house or were the ones requiring intercession. Cecelia Victoria Stewart of Font Hill pleaded, ultimately unsuccessfully, with local magistrate and planter Francis Bowen to save her husband Thomas's life, since Bowen intended to burn their home. Rebecca Telford, whose husband Stephen had been arrested, was threatened with death because she would not give the soldiers her wedding ring. She got down on the ground and begged them to spare her life for her children's sake: "Good massa, don't shoot me . . . if you shoot me, who is to take care of my little children?"

Mothers such as Charlotte Ross and Henrietta Bailey appealed to the soldiers to spare their sons' lives because they had been sick and had done nothing to deserve death. Neither was successful.[74] As shown previously, women such as Sophia Davis and Betsy Buckley also tried, though unsuccessfully, to preserve their families' houses from being burned. Ultimately, the outcomes of most such efforts were shaped by the circumstances of the suppression. Appeals to preserve life and property were secondary to the authorities' concerns to quell the rebellion and to institute "swift and terrible" retribution. Within this context, efforts at intercession by black family members were, for the most part, destined to fall on deaf ears.

Ironically, under the circumstances of the suppression, but perhaps in an instructive example of their commitment to collective welfare, blacks attempted to assist not only their own during the difficult days of October 1865, but they also extended help, in some instances, to white families who were trying to reach safety. Eleanor Shortridge, wife of Samuel Shortridge, and her six children, governesses and nurse were among several other white families who were attempting to escape the dangerous conditions they faced at home. They were guided by a young black man named Wood to the family home of Diana Blackwood, a black woman, and allowed a brief respite. However, Mrs Blackwood's warning of the "advancing mob" enabled Mrs Shortridge and her group to escape. At the Amity Hall "negro houses", they were allowed to stay at the home of "an old man and his daughter", who shared their meal of breadfruit with Mrs Shortridge and her children. From there, they were guided to yet another black family home, where they spent the night before making it to relative safety at Rhine estate.[75]

The Search for a Just Resolution

For many blacks, it was painfully evident that the cause of justice had been derailed by the forces of the suppression. Indeed, emerging out of the "voluminous evidence" taken by the Royal Commission was a clear picture of serious offences perpetrated in the name of suppression. However, the ability of the victims of these offences to obtain a just resolution, through civil action, to cases of wrongful death or injury was limited by two considerations. First, the majority of allegations of wrongful death or injury were against military officers, and as Governor Grant theorized, such cases would be "for the consideration exclusively of the military authorities".[76] Second, the Act of Indemnity legally exempted from penalty all persons who "in good faith . . . had acted for the crushing of this outbreak".[77]

In spite of these constraints, however, some of the affected family members undertook the pursuit of justice in the aftermath of the suppression. They were aided in this respect by the anxiety of the paternalistic Crown Colony government to "select for . . . the condemnation of the government such abuses of power as have tended to bring discredit upon the administration of the colony".[78] In February 1866, for example, the family of George Marshall requested attorneys Nathan and Burke to undertake proceedings against George Ramsay for the murder of Marshall during the suppression. His family, through the lawyers, argued that without authority or the benefit of court martial, Ramsay had ordered Marshall hanged because after receipt of the forty-eighth lash, he had faced Ramsay and groaned.[79] The case was dismissed by a vote of five to three of the sitting magistrates in Spanish Town. Attorney General Heslop, almost immediately thereafter, issued a warrant for the arrest of Ramsay to answer a bill of indictment for the murder of Marshall.[80]

At the proceedings before the grand jury at the Morant Bay circuit court in October 1866, Judge Kerr emphasized that martial law – and, by extension, the Act of Indemnity – had sanctioned only those actions deemed "necessary in the judgment, not of a violent or excited, but of a moderate and reasonable man". Ramsay's response to Marshall's clearly anguished grinding of his teeth and agonized groans was decidedly contrary to Kerr's criteria of moderation and exercise of reason, and he therefore instructed the jury to return a true bill. However, the grand jury's composition – being seven whites, seven of mixed descent and one black man – and its finding of "no bill" proved detrimental to the Marshall family's chances of gaining an equitable outcome on this occasion.[81] Secretary of state Lord Carnarvon, sharing in the colonial governor's desire to use cases such as Marshall's to condemn abuses of power during the suppression, contemplated the institution of criminal proceedings against Ramsay in England. However, this did not come to fruition due to the Colonial Office's concern that the renewal of the case after the delay necessary for British prosecution "might stir up emotions again in Jamaica".[82] Indeed, the only "just" outcome for the Marshall family was a decision that Governor Storks had made previously to suspend Ramsay from his position as superintendent of police.[83]

Other family members sought judicial recourse in response to cases of cruel and unwarranted flogging administered by civilians during the suppression. They initiated this process by testifying before the Royal Commission, and in so doing exposed the abuse of power that was prevalent during October 1865. In this effort, they were assisted by Governor Grant, who had instructed two agents, Ewart and Lindo, to interview affected persons from St Thomas-in-the-East and, if they wished to prosecute, to obtain sworn depositions. Family members were also informed that their cases would be investigated free of expense to them.[84]

Both Elizabeth Collins, a widow from Long Bay, and her daughter, Charlotte Scott, gave sworn depositions that they had been brutally flogged on the orders of Christopher Codrington, without authority and for reasons which had nothing to do with the rebellion. In Elizabeth's case, the whipping resulted from a dispute between herself and Codrington over a hog. Charlotte was whipped because she allegedly told Codrington that she "wished the flies would blow the arses of all the whites and coloureds as they did in Morant Bay". Betsy Lucas of Duckenfield, who had lost both her husband and her home, deposed that she was whipped on the orders of William Pitt Kirkland, a magistrate and merchant from Bath. She stated that Kirkland had indicated that since the constables had not bothered to shoot her, she should be given "fum-fum" (a whipping) instead. Also giving a sworn deposition was Ann Galloway, who was pregnant when James Codrington ordered her to receive thirty-five lashes because she was found on Charles Hunter's property.

Lucretia Mullens, discussed earlier in this chapter, whose husband had died from infected wounds within a week after a severe flogging, also initiated steps to obtain judicial resolution. However, when she and her daughter, Mary Mitchell, informed Lindo that the flogging had been administered by soldiers and not by Ford as originally presumed (Captain Ford had a business in Bath and was in charge of volunteers in the St Thomas-in-the-East irregular troops), Lindo was forced to terminate her case, which was a military matter and thus covered by the Act of Indemnity.

Lindo, who undertook to be the solicitor for all the aggrieved family members, submitted all of these cases except that of the Mullens family to the attorney general for prosecution before the grand jury at the sitting of the St Thomas-in-the-East circuit court, scheduled for 18 October 1866. However, the same jury which had returned a "no bill" finding in Marshall's case returned a similar result in *The Queen v. Woodrow*, in which the defendant, John Woodrow, an engineer from Bath, was charged with unlawfully flogging women. Meanwhile, cases brought by Elizabeth Collins and Charlotte Scott against Christopher Codrington, Ann Galloway against James Codrington and Betsy Lucas against William Kirkland were all adjourned because of the inability of Crown witnesses to attend during the heavy rains of October.

Given the composition and predisposition of the jury, even if the cases had not been adjourned, it is highly unlikely that justice would have been served to the family members.[85] However, persons like Betsy Lucas may have received some semblance of satisfaction from the removal of Kirkland from his positions as magistrate for St Thomas-in-the-East and collector of dues.[86]

A final dimension open to blacks in their search for equitable outcomes was in the area of compensation. Guidelines which had been established by the Compensation Commission and the colonial government allowed for the payment of £2,426 for damage done in the suppression to persons who were "not implicated in the disturbances". At the same time, the claims of "implicated" persons, amounting to approximately £542, were rejected.[87] Although Governor Grant made reference to the existence of "many similar cases", the effort of William Kelly Smith was the only documented case of a black person requesting compensation for unlawful arrest during the events of 1865. However, it seems as if Smith's efforts to gain justice were doomed to failure from the outset, as although Grant admitted "the unlawfulness of the seizure and deportation to Morant Bay of the petitioner", he concluded that the Act of Indemnity seemed "to have closed this and all similar cases".[88]

Associated with the *Jamaica Watchman and Free Press* before his arrest "for conspiracy with George William Gordon, Paul Bogle and others", Smith subsequently made three separate petitions for compensation in which he emphasized the adverse impact of his arrest on himself and his family. He argued that his "wife, three daughters, a son and a widowed blind mother" faced considerable pain and deprivation as well as the forced sale of their property and furniture in order to afford a writ of habeas corpus, bail and legal fees. In view of his subsequent acquittal, Smith had requested compensation of £182 17s. for all expenses and for the damage done to his health by his protracted false imprisonment. Smith's persistence in the face of constant disappointment, first in petitioning the governor and then the queen and finally in visiting England (financed by "humane friends" in Jamaica) to present an equally unsuccessful petition to the Earl of Kimberley, were all indicative of his commitment to what he summarized as "Negro self-help".[89]

Conclusion

In answer to his own query, "Who would have remembered the Morant Bay rioters?", Augier posited that they are remembered because, in the words of Eyre, "The retribution has been so prompt and so terrible that it is never likely to be forgotten."[90] It is also for this reason that we should never forget those families of St Thomas-in-the-East who became victims of the suppression. For them, the events of October 1865 embodied the visitation of tragedy in its ulti-mate form. Irrespective of the rationalizing perspective of martial law, for too many black families, the suppression epitomized justice gone awry. Contrary to the elitist stereotyping of the black family in freedom as dysfunctional, disinterested and neglectful of kin, the testimony of the blacks who witnessed the events of Morant Bay pointed to the existence of stable, enduring and functioning family units, the material foundations of which had been based on years of hard work and frugality in harsh economic circumstances in the period preceding the events. Within the sample of black families discussed in this chapter, there is a preponderance of evidence of men and women for whom the continued care of family, especially of elderly relatives, and the maintenance of close, sometimes co-residential, extended kinship networks were prioritized, as had been the case in their societies of cultural origin in West Africa. Isolated references to desertion by family members in the years prior to 1865 may have been explained by factors such as economic distress or relational crises. The evidence presented here shows that in the construction and reconstruction of their family lives, both men and women played central rather than peripheral roles. Further, the testimonies of many witnesses challenged assertions of the marginality and indifference of the black male in familial contexts and indicated that many black men in St Thomas-in-the-East viewed themselves as integral to the well-being of their families, and were valued in this light by their family members, as demonstrated in their fulfilment of their responsibilities as sons, grandsons, husbands, partners, fathers and grandfathers. Ironically, however, for too many families of the parish, the force of the suppression, by targeting black males in particular, resulted either in the decimation of these men, thus permanently removing them from their families, or in the significant curtailing of their material and emotional ability to continue in supportive roles within their family groups.

For the black families of St Thomas-in-the-East, October 1865 was a watershed. The suppression engineered a tragedy of significant proportions for these families, devastating hard-won material foundations, decimating kinship networks and, in the process, inflicting personal and emotional trauma on so many. Out of disruption and disintegration, however, arose opportunities for regrouping and reconstruction, and in this respect, both men and women, but women in particular, utilized their surviving family networks as support mechanisms, thus demonstrating the enduring legacy of the link with West African traditions, as had been the case for preceding generations of black families. It is clear from their efforts to survive the crisis and to reactivate their lives that the resilience and commitment to kin and community which had allowed many black families to weather the difficult decades prior to 1865 would again enable them to move forward. It is for this show of resilience and centrality of kinship ties, as well as for their suffering, that we need to remember the families of 1865.

Chapter 6

Family Legislation, 1838–1882
IN PURSUIT OF CULTURAL CONFORMITY

> There is great distress among women whose husbands or paramours have deserted
> them and their children on account of there being no law in this island to compel
> men to support their own children.
>
> – *Reverend H. Clark, 1865*[1]

IN THE POST-SLAVERY PERIOD TO 1882, laws relating to the family in Jamaica
were a reflection of imperialist ideology and metropolitan precedents, as well
as a response to the perceived need to strengthen mechanisms of social control and cultural compliance in the aftermath of slavery. From a Eurocentric
perspective, emancipation, with its potential release of blacks from the "civilizing" milieu of the plantation environs, raised the much-feared prospect of a
descent into an amoral and barbaric existence, with its attendant social chaos.
Thus, for white society, the maintenance of hegemony and social stability was
inextricably linked to its attempts to mould the freed people to its normative
patterns. The principal mechanisms for implementing these twin tasks of cultural conformity and social control were the school, the religious bodies and
legislative intervention.

This analysis will demonstrate that legislation on the family in Jamaica
evolved in response to the perception that blacks were morally depraved, irresponsible and lacking in "habits of civilization", and as such, although the laws

were not intended solely for blacks, they were the primary targets. Therefore, in its conception and purpose, family legislation was greatly influenced by considerations of class and cultural control. By legislating penalties for certain behaviours and enforcing others pertaining to family life, elitist society sought to impose its normative framework on blacks while promoting the ideal of the Victorian family as the centrepiece of total societal stability.

Within the context of Victorian thought, a crucial prerequisite for societal order was the promotion of the family based upon Christian, legal marriage. By the same token, non-married unions (informal unions) were viewed as the very antithesis of social progress. Consistent with this typology was the assumption that certain behaviours were characteristic of each category of family. Thus, non-married parents were stereotypically "careless", profligate and neglectful of their responsibilities to their children and other members of the family. Legally married unions were, for the most part, supposed to symbolize the very opposite in behaviours and values. British Victorian philosophy and legislative precedence, imposed upon the colony, placed the stamp of legitimacy upon the progeny of legal marriages and fostered the "curse of illegitimacy" on the children of non-married unions. Within such a conceptual framework, it is hardly surprising that pivotal to emerging legislation on the family during this period was a body of laws which had as their central objective the promotion of Christian marriage, especially among the newly freed black population, who by elitist perception were woefully in need of this institution. This body of legislation included the Dissenters' Marriage Act of 1840, a series of marriage laws passed between 1879 and 1880 and, ironically, the Divorce Law of 1879.

The earliest post-slavery legislation pertaining to the family in Jamaica sought to sanction the body of marriages which had been performed by dissenting clergy during slavery and immediately afterwards, which previously had been unrecognized. With full freedom imminent, the view that the interests of "civilized society" would best be assured with the encouragement of the "married state" gained greater currency both in metropolitan and colonial circles. Thus, the 1836 report of a select committee of Parliament appointed to investigate the apprenticeship system emphasized that "strong objections have been urged against the present state of the law with regard to marriages, which confines to clergymen of the Church of England the power of solemnizing the marriage ceremony". The report further urged that "all grounds for these complaints should be speedily and completely removed".[2] Indeed, this report echoed the sentiments earlier expressed by Lord Glenelg in his instructions to colonial governors to work towards a law which would validate marriages previously celebrated by Nonconformist missionaries.[3]

This mandate to facilitate the spread of "civilized behaviour" among the newly freed people was implemented in early 1840 with the passage of the Dissenters' Marriage Act (4 Vict., c. 44). By recognizing all marriages performed by dissenting missionaries prior to and following the act, this law was unequivocally intended to further the adoption of the "married state" among blacks, who had been the main constituents of the missionaries both during and after slavery. As such, this was an astute political move by colonial authorities, who understood the centrality of these missionaries, particularly the Baptists, to the lives of the black majority and, by extension, to elitist goals of cultural and social control. Thus, the framers of this law were especially anxious that the body of marriages performed by dissenting missionaries during slavery not be allowed to remain outside the realm of official recognition.

By the terms of this law, two important criteria for the legalization of dissenters' marriages were the production of registers for those ceremonies performed prior to 1840 and the posting of banns for those celebrated thereafter. However, Baptist missionaries in particular viewed the first criterion as an obstacle to the progress of their "civilizing mission" and to the legalization of those marriages for which no registers had been kept or for which the registers had been destroyed during the burning of Baptist chapels in 1832. The attorney general argued that the act would not illegalize marriages for which registers could not be provided; rather, the determination of legality would be left to the common law and the court.[4] From the perspective of missionaries like Phillippo, the Dissenters' Marriage Act succeeded in its mandate to encourage "habits of civilization" in blacks, resulting, Phillippo claimed, in "not fewer than 14,840 marriages" occurring annually.[5]

In spite of optimistic missionary pronouncements about the increase of marriages in the immediate post-slavery years, by the mid-1840s it was evident that for a variety of reasons, the majority of blacks were intent on organizing their families in unions external to the married state. These reasons included the expense entailed in the ceremony, a desire not to be tied to one person and an expressed preference for "faithful concubinage"[6] (this issue is discussed further in chapter 1). Stipendiary magistrate Hall Pringle, for example, reported from Vere that although "a prodigious number of the black people got married in 1838, 1839 and 1840 . . . since that period marriages in this country district among the lower classes become more and more uncommon".[7]

Mounting concern over this decline in marriages among blacks, as well as the view that "concubinage" and "illegitimacy" were the root of societal ills, led to legislative efforts to increase the available options for the celebration of marriages. Thus, Law 15 of 1879, the Marriage Law, had as its main objective the establishment of machinery for the celebration of marriage as a purely civil rite, while retaining provisions for the traditional religious observation. Whereas only ministers of the various denominations could perform the marriage ceremony prior to 1879, by the Marriage Law, civil officers were now invested with this power as duly authorized marriage officers. Ministers of religion wishing to marry persons as of 1879 had to be appointed marriage officers. This provision of a secular alternative may also have been a response to the growing disenchantment of many blacks with both established and non-established churches by the 1870s.

Missionaries and other Eurocentric observers seeking to provide explanations for the decline in marriages among freed people theorized that couples who had lived in "sinful concubinage" for several years usually avoided church marriages in a bid to escape the "moral embarrassment" attendant upon publication of banns within the church. Therefore, the Marriage Law of 1879, in providing for a civil ceremony, was directed primarily at the "lower orders" of black Jamaicans who were seen by the colonial authorities as the main contributors to the "scourge of concubinage". According to this perspective, blacks were now expected to take advantage of the removal of this potential obstacle to legal marriage because the law allowed a more private posting of banns within the office of the superintending registrar. The law also provided a third option for persons wishing to get married by providing for the application to the governor for a marriage licence. At a cost of ten pounds per licence, however, this was hardly an option feasible for poor persons.[8]

In mandating that persons under the age of twenty-one had to provide proof of consent by the father or, if he was deceased, by the legal guardian, and in allowing the mother's consent only if these other sources were non-existent, the Marriage Law of 1879 remained true to the principles of patriarchy. However, this provision of the new law immediately became the object of concern of the secretary of state and the attorney general, who both argued that this requirement of parental consent might discourage rather than encourage marriages, as was the intention of the Marriage Act. Concerned with the growth of the "scourge of concubinage" among "the country people", where the custom was to "set up house and cohabit together" at the age of seventeen or eighteen, Attorney General O'Malley pointed out that "anything that offers an impediment to marriage means . . . a premium upon concubinage".[9] Therefore, Law 11 of 1880, an amendment to the Marriage Law of 1879, sought to remove this obstacle to curbing "concubinage" among young blacks. The amendment provided that the "unreasonable withholding of consent" by a parent or guardian could be adjudicated by the Supreme Court, and if the judge's decision was favourable, his certificate would be a valid alternative to parental consent. Also, by reducing the fee for the governor's marriage licence from ten pounds to five, the amendment of 1880 was intended to make this option more viable than had been the case under the Marriage Law of 1879.[10]

Just over two decades before the 1879 Marriage Law, the passage in 1857 of the Divorce Law in England had generated discussion on the possibility of introducing similar legislation in Jamaica. Governor Darling, in responding to Colonial Office queries in 1858 on the feasibility of introducing a divorce bill there, had opposed the idea on the grounds that such a move would only aggravate a situation in which "the marriage tie is already so lightly held amongst the body of the population of Jamaica".[11] On the other hand, the impossibility of acquiring a legal divorce in Jamaica was increasingly perceived, particularly among the "moral elites", as a disincentive to marriage, especially among blacks. Governor Sir John Peter Grant, representing this view in 1871, commented, "This state of the law, as it affects the Negro population, has been a source of frequent complaints in petitions to me." Grant further stated that especially among "those who are guided by strong religious feeling", this inability to get a divorce acted as "a discouragement to marriage".[12]

This sentiment was echoed by others – among them, the Reverend Josias Cork, rector of Westmoreland and acting rector of St Ann's Bay Parish Church in 1877. Bemoaning the relative scarcity of marriages among the people of St Ann's, Cork attributed the people's reluctance to enter into legal marriage to the absence of a divorce law.[13] His explanation was in keeping with the views of many blacks. As seen in chapter 1, men and women had had equal access to divorce in traditional, pre-colonial West Africa; therefore, given the foundational influence of West African culture on the familial norms of blacks, as well as the Euro-Christian endorsement of the permanency of marriage without recourse to divorce before 1879, it would have been logical for some blacks to be opposed to Christian marriage under these circumstances. Furthermore, for some who were already married, but unhappily so, the impossibility of getting a divorce increased the potential of living in "sin and vice" with other partners. This was the predicament of James Grant, who had been married for eighteen years, but deserted by his wife eleven years prior. Unable to remarry and "join the church", he was hopeful in early 1879 that the governor would soon pass a law "to let me and others like me marry again and save us from sin".[14]

Paradoxically, therefore, the Divorce Law of 1879 had its genesis partly in elite society's continuing quest to promote legal marriages, especially among blacks, and also, by extension, in the desire to reduce the twin "evils of concubinage and illegitimacy". Closely patterned off the English law of 1857, the Divorce Law (Law 14) of 1879 enabled the Supreme Court to grant decrees of nullity of marriage based on grounds such as absence of mutual consent, presence of fraud, mental or physical incapacity, or the existence of a living spouse at the time of marriage. Grounds for judicial separation, as with grounds for nullification, were equally applicable to men and women, with adultery, cruelty or desertion without cause for two or more years being sufficient to warrant a separation.

Influenced both by Victorian concerns of protecting the "weaker sex" and by principles of patriarchy, the Divorce Law allowed orders of alimony to be payable to the wife in cases where judicial separation was granted on the wife's petition, as well as in cases of dissolution of marriage. Evidently shaped, too, by a desire to maintain the married state wherever possible, the law allowed for the reversal of decrees of judicial separation. The welfare of children, as with that of women, was to be safeguarded within the context of Victorian philosophy, and thus the court could grant orders for the custody, maintenance and education of children in cases where the marriage was dissolved.

Patriarchal considerations as well as Victorian ethics, with their emphasis on the woman as the crucial transmitter of moral values within the family, dictated that, in establishing grounds for the dissolution of marriage, the Divorce Law would highlight the woman's greater culpability and "fall from grace". Thus, whereas adultery under any circumstances on the part of the woman proved sufficient grounds for dissolution of the marriage, the law overlooked and implicitly condoned "ordinary adultery" on the part of the husband. By clause 14 of the act, the wife had to prove her husband's "bigamy with adultery", acts of sodomy or bestiality, "incestuous adultery"[15] or rape before she could obtain dissolution of her marriage. By excluding as grounds for dissolution ordinary adultery on the part of the husband and by requiring proof of these comparatively infrequent or not easily corroborated offences, the law promoted gender inequality as well as the prevailing philosophy that women should tolerate their husbands' "indiscretions". However, in making the burden of proof greater for the wife contemplating dissolution of her marriage, this provision (clause 14) served as encouragement for her to remain married, for better or for worse. This would seem to be supported by the fact that in suits of judicial separation, which were not characterized by that "air of finality" associated with divorce, ordinary adultery by either party was acceptable grounds.[16]

Contrary to the expectations of those who had supported the need for a divorce law, blacks did not embrace this opportunity to end one marriage and begin another. Neither did the Divorce Law result in the anticipated significant increase in marriages among the general population. Thus, whereas the rate of marriage per thousand for the entire island for 1879–80 was 3.7, the rate remained the same for the period 1880–81 and increased slightly to 4.0 for the period 1881–82. Patrick Bryan's explanations for the very low rate of divorce among all populations certainly may have held true for blacks in particular. No doubt, as Bryan suggested, some couples remained married, in spite of problems, because of the economic dependence of some wives, or because divorce would have meant social embarrassment for those who had internalized the association of marriage with respectability.[17] However, the low rate of divorce among blacks may also have been a reflection of the attendant expenses of court hearings and alimony. Ultimately, however, both legal marriages and legal divorces remained low among blacks because the majority displayed a preference for organizing their families outside of legal marriage, and therefore for persons living in these informal unions, the Divorce Law had no relevance. As William James Gardner observed in 1870, when blacks living in informal unions wished to separate, they often utilized their cultural tradition of the division of the cotta. The cotta, according to Barbara Bush's description, was a circular pad, traditionally made from dried and plaited plantain leaves, that enslaved workers often wore on their heads when carrying loads. Bush traced the "ceremony of the cotta" to a West African–inspired tradition practised under slavery. According to Edward Long, the circular shape represented eternity and "perpetual love" to the enslaved, and therefore when they wished to separate, the cotta was divided into two halves, with each partner retaining one half to symbolize separation. Gardner's reference to the ceremony of the cotta as late as 1870 indicates the durability and appeal that this tradition held in the lives of blacks who wished to terminate their informal unions.[18]

The ideological context within which European elites sought to influence black familial norms was expanded in the later nineteenth century, as Bryan observes, by the concepts of social Darwinism and positivist thought. Social Darwinism, in theorizing the racial and cultural inferiority of blacks, provided the rationale for exercising both political and cultural hegemony. Positivist thought, with its emphasis on "the moral order of society", helped to shape British family laws, some of which set the precedent for local family legislation. Bryan notes that "as a British colony Jamaica absorbed not only ideas but laws and institutions, which had emerged out of British positivist thought. The passion for the creation of a new moral order was evident in policies that encouraged stable family life and legitimacy."[19]

Therefore, within the dual contexts of Victorian Christian philosophy and the later nineteenth-century positivist emphasis on improving the moral order of society, it is logical that there were widespread calls for colonial legislation to enforce social obligations to family members irrespective of the type of family unit in question.

However, the prevalence – especially, though not solely, among blacks – of unions organized outside of legal marriage remained a serious obstacle to elitist efforts to improve the "moral tone" of society. These unions not only offended the moral sensitivity of elite society, but from this perspective, the progeny of these "careless parents" were the root cause of the growing problems of poverty and juvenile vagrancy, as well as a potential burden on the public purse. Most colonial policymakers viewed these perceived problems of "concubinage" and "illegitimacy" as the province of blacks and, hypocritically ignoring their existence among the elite, resorted to legislative solutions. Thus, the rationale went, if Christian, legal marriage could not be universal among blacks, then legislative means could be used to enforce the behaviours which Victorian thought associated with such marriages, such as maintenance of family members and responsible parenting. Between 1869 and 1882, a series of maintenance, bastardy and registration laws were passed, the common objective of which was to promote conformity, especially among blacks, to those family values regarded by European society as the norm.

From the 1840s onwards, increased reports of neglect and destitution of family members, especially the elderly and deserted women and children, prompted early discussion on the need to address these issues through legislation. In 1846, Governor Elgin, in commenting on reports of the old and infirm being abandoned by their relatives, ascribed this to "moral and social rather than economical causes" and to the absence of a sense of family obligations among the peasantry, who "since they became free have not always shown a disposition to assume them".[20] Given these racist, elitist claims as well as the stereotypical categorization by elite society of unmarried or informal black unions as "irresponsible and immoral" and of the children of these unions as "neglected", it is hardly surprising that reports of destitution among some children and old people should have been interpreted as evidence of familial neglect and as an extensive problem applicable to black families in general. A great deal of the evidence presented so far in this work certainly contravenes any assertion of generalized neglect within black families. Given the harsh economic circumstances of low and uncertain wages that followed the contraction of the sugar economy after the Sugar Duties Act of 1846,[21] cases of destitution or neglect were more likely to have been occasioned by economic constraint rather than, as alleged by Elgin, by "moral and social causes". Operating within a similar conceptual context, in 1845, the custos for St Catherine, William Ramsay, attributed the "immorality and depravity of the present day" to the neglected children of deserted women and emphasized the absence of an affiliation act in Jamaica to force fathers to support their "illegitimate" children.[22]

While conceding that persons should ideally support their family members out of care and duty, Richard Hill, stipendiary magistrate for St Catherine, argued in 1858 that legislative compulsion of these family responsibilities would "go far to check a great deal of prevalent heartlessness and indifference". Citing the English precedent of 43rd Elizabeth (the Poor Relief Act of 1601), Hill accordingly suggested that in cases where neglect of any family member resulted in a burden on "parochial bounty", overseers of the poor should be empowered, as in England, to effect a prosecution of the offending family member for compulsory allowance.[23] Although Hill's suggestion did not bear legislative fruit in 1858, this was a conceptual antecedent of the later laws of maintenance.

Although agreeing in principle with Hill's call for compulsory support of family members, Governor Darling concluded that efforts to legislate on this issue would be "utterly impracticable". Identifying what was to prove a serious obstacle to any such legislation prior to the termination of representative government, Darling anticipated the legislature's opposition to the idea, as any discussion on maintenance, he argued, would also raise the thorny issue of "bastardy". Indeed, Hill's suggestion, if carried forward, may have opened up a veritable can of worms for some members of the legislature and other elites who were themselves, in spite of their sanctimonious pronouncements about blacks' moral deficiencies, potential targets of bastardy and maintenance laws. For the time being, however, Darling preferred to offer to a Victorian patriarchal and racist society an immensely more acceptable explanation for the "impracticability" of the measure in 1858. He argued that "the laxity of morals which exists amongst the female population . . . would render affiliation extremely difficult".[24]

The presumption that reports of increased praedial larceny and general social malaise by early 1865 were directly linked to the neglect of children in particular led Eyre's administration to respond legislatively to some aspects of the latter problem. Thus, the act, 28 Victoria, cap. 5, "for the punishment of idle and disorderly persons, rogues and vagabonds" passed in February 1865, amended the earlier 4 Victoria, cap. 42, which went by the same title. Extending the original meaning of "rogues and vagabonds" to include a "husband or father" whose desertion or abandonment of his "wife or children" resulted in their becoming dependent on charity, the amending act also increased the duration of punishment from twenty-eight days to three months.[25] However, given the elitist perception that neglect of family members was more predominant among persons "living in concubinage" than among married persons, this legislative response, because it applied only to legally married men, was limited in scope. As on previous occasions, the legislature had stopped short of dealing with problematic questions of "bastardy and illegitimacy".[26]

In April 1865, in the wake of the distress accentuated by Underhill's letter, Governor Eyre reiterated the view that the high incidence of pauperism was largely the result of "fathers almost invariably deserting their illegitimate children" and of relatives neglecting and "throwing upon the parish" family members unable to care for themselves. Conveniently blind to the impact of government-endorsed high levels of taxation on the poor, Eyre, like many other colonial state officials, sought to rationalize the societal ills of poverty and destitution as products of black indifference to family. Although neither poverty nor "illegitimacy" were exclusive to blacks, Eyre, in articulating a view which was representative of racist, elitist perspectives, attributed the problem of poverty among the underprivileged classes (which were predominantly black) specifically to irresponsible fathers who – in this view, almost without exception – deserted their "illegitimate children". Recurrent throughout this period, this view of black men as disinterested and generally irresponsible in familial contexts was explicable through the lens of a cultural framework which equated the Christian, legal married state with responsibility and support of children and other family members. Conversely, therefore, black men and women who chose to organize their families outside of these established boundaries were characterized as irresponsible and neglectful of their families. In reality, although harsh economic circumstances no doubt made it difficult, and at times impossible, for some black men and women to adequately maintain their families in a material sense, this did not preclude their continuance of emotional and moral support. The pervasive claims of black familial irresponsibility and the constant efforts by the colonial authorities to enforce cultural conformity through legislative pressure must be assessed within this context. It is hardly surprising, therefore, that Eyre bemoaned the absence of "the discipline and obedience exacted by the masters in slavery" and argued for legislation to enforce support of "illegitimate" children and the maintenance of elderly and infirm family members. Eyre's words conveyed the unmistakable conclusion which had been made by white society that "illegitimacy" and neglect were black problems, and that in the absence of compulsion by the whip, a legislative solution had to be enforced against these black "perpetrators" of the problem.[27]

However, as previously noted, any discussion on maintenance predictably raised the issue of "bastardy". Exhibiting a fine distinction between the two issues, maintenance laws were usually aimed at enforcing support for children, "illegitimate" and legitimate, as well as for other destitute and helpless family members. Bastardy legislation provided the means by which a woman could seek to establish a man's affiliation to her "illegitimate" child as a prelude to pursuing maintenance. The two categories of legislation were, however, interconnected. Because elite society in general, and some members of the assembly in particular, opposed the idea of a bastardy law as an invitation for a "greedy and debased" woman to swear an oath of affiliation against any man of her choice, the spectre of such a law almost invariably aborted discussions on maintenance while representative government was in force.

Thus, while agreeing that a bastardy law in addition to a maintenance law would be "extremely useful", Governor Eyre, like Darling before him, explained the non-enactment of these measures by citing the prevailing concern about "abandoned" females who "would swear children to any person for the purpose of extorting money". Reverend Henry Clark, island curate of Trinity, Westmoreland, gave a more telling explanation when he argued that the assembly's failure to contemplate this legislation in 1865 was in order "to cover their own tracks".[28]

By 1869, therefore, with the "impediment" of the assembly having been removed, and given the determination of the paternalistic Crown Colony government to effect societal reform, the way became clear for the enactment of a law of maintenance, Law 31 of 1869. One of the objectives of this law was to discourage "concubinage" by placing the legal responsibilities of unmarried parents on par with those of married parents. Since black Jamaicans were identified by elite society as generalized practitioners of "concubinage", blacks became the principal targets of the laws relating to maintenance. Whereas prior to 1869, legally married parents had been mandated by laws such as 28 Victoria, cap. 5 , "for the punishment of idle and disorderly persons, rogues and vagabonds" to support their legitimate children, the parents of "illegitimate" children had been bound by no such dictates. According to the Eurocentric rationale, black parents in particular had remained unmarried so as to escape the responsibilities of maintenance, and from that perspective, this discrepancy in the law had for too long placed "a premium on concubinage".[29] Such a rationale at best underestimated other variables, largely socio-cultural factors (discussed earlier in this chapter), which helped to explain why so many black families lived outside the confines of legal marriage.

The Maintenance Law of 1869 established the obligation of both unmarried parents to support their "illegitimate" children. While it was especially aimed at fathers whose failure to extend material support forced mothers to appeal to parochial authorities for help, the law did not release mothers from their responsibility to maintain their children. By empowering the parochial authorities, through legal action, to recover parochial funds spent on the child – from both parents if both had the means, or from one if only one was able – the law was also clearly intended to alleviate the burden which "illegitimacy", in particular, had placed on public funds. Perhaps in reaction to reports that black mothers often left their children in the care of a grandmother, rather than as a tacit recognition of the importance of the extended family among blacks, the Maintenance Law also provided for the parochial recovery of funds, where possible, from grandparents. While not specifying punitive measures for default of payment, this maintenance law, by equating the responsibilities of unmarried and married parents, implicitly subjected unmarried fathers to the same three months' imprisonment as married fathers under 28 Victoria, cap. 5 (a law to punish "rogues and vagabonds").

In an effort to address the issue of abandonment of elderly family members, another trend which elite perspectives attributed to blacks, the Maintenance Law of 1869 also obliged "illegitimate" children to support their elderly parents as well as their grandparents. Provision was also made for recovery, through the courts, of parochial funds spent on neglected parents and grandparents. On the thorny issue of men who refused to either acknowledge or maintain their "illegitimate children", the 1869 law established a legal precedent in the colony by enabling the mother to identify and take action against the reputed father for maintenance.[30] However, the immense difficulties associated with the enforcement of this clause rendered this groundbreaking aspect of the Maintenance Law a virtual dead letter. The attorney general, perhaps naively, predicted that "questions of paternity are not likely to be frequent".[31] By placing sole reliance on the oath of the mother, the law raised serious doubts among those convinced of "female duplicity" as to whether paternity could be fairly established in this manner.

Moreover, even if paternity was acknowledged, the circuitous route which an unmarried mother had to take to establish a claim for maintenance seriously diminished her capacity to benefit from this provision. Not empowered by the law to herself initiate legal action for maintenance, the unmarried mother was dependent upon the municipal board to do so, but only after the child had been declared indigent and granted relief. This requisite declaration of indigence was itself an obstacle to the operation of the Maintenance Law, as "indigent" was not a categorization which most black parents wished for their children. Black opposition to being labelled "poor", "indigent" or "pauperized" could be seen in the resistance of parents to their children being sent to "ragged schools" (a term denoting schools for the very poor) and their refusal to send their children to school in tattered clothing. They were adamantly opposed to becoming "indoor poor" (residents of poorhouses) and preferred instead to collect alms as "outdoor poor" to avoid the stigma which they attached to poor relief.[32] Subsequent to a declaration of indigence, the chairman of the municipal board had to apply to two justices of the peace for an order to enforce payment from the negligent father. If this failed, the churchwardens of the parish had to undertake similar steps. It is therefore hardly surprising that most municipal boards "treated the law as unworkable".[33]

This deficiency in the Maintenance Law of 1869 meant that although the intended focus of maintenance legislation had been the population "living in concubinage", ironically, the earlier law to punish "rogues and vagabonds" (28 Vict., c. 5) directed at legally married fathers proved more workable in practice than the 1869 law. This was largely because, under the earlier law, married women could directly initiate legal action. The relative frequency with which suits for maintenance were brought by married women before the police magistrate's court in Kingston in the 1870s, for example, may indeed have indicated, as Eric Foner suggested of black women in the United States, that some women in Jamaica did not "placidly accept the increasingly patriarchal quality of black family life", and that they were "more than willing to bring family disputes before public authorities".[34] The frequency of suits brought under the earlier law by married women invalidated the elitist perception that "neglect and desertion" were the province of unmarried men – stereotypically, black men. Although the race of the men involved in these examples could not be ascertained in the sources, examples of court cases involving charges of neglect by married men include that of Ellis Howell, who in 1873 was sentenced to twenty-eight days' hard labour for refusing to support his wife, whom he had deserted seven years prior,[35] and Frederick Wood, sentenced in 1877 to four weeks' hard labour for refusing to support his wife and five children.[36] In stark contrast, every witness who testified on the issue of maintenance before the 1877 Commission on the Juvenile Population pointed to either the non-implementation or the extremely rare prosecution of cases by the municipal board under the Maintenance Law of 1869.[37]

Thus, the impracticability of this aspect of the Maintenance Law of 1869 – its failure to curb episodes of abandonment of women and their children – as well as persistent elitist concerns that the "scourge of illegitimacy" threatened both the public purse and the fabric of society contributed to the passage of the bastardy laws of 1881 and 1882 and their complementary enactment, the Maintenance Law of 1881. Influenced particularly by reports made in 1877 to the Commission on the Juvenile Population of the widespread neglect of vulnerable family members, this body of legislation reflected the persisting preoccupation of the administration, in the last years of pure Crown Colony rule, with effecting moral reform through the inculcation of Eurocentric family values.

Patterned off metropolitan precedents, the Bastardy Law of 1881 invested the mother of a "bastard" child with the power to directly initiate steps to affirm the paternity of her child by her oath before a district court judge. Additionally, the judge's reliance on evidence from the putative father as well as the mother, and the assurance of the man's right to appeal to the Supreme Court if he was adjudged to be the father and ordered to pay maintenance, helped to allay fears of extortion by "dissolute" women. Women's efforts to affirm paternity of their "bastard" children were rendered less expensive and time-consuming by the Bastardy Law Amendment Act, Law 26 of 1882, which provided for the oath and the evidence to be heard additionally by a justice of the peace or a clerk of petty sessions. Once paternity was established by any of these officials, the father was ordered to pay a maximum of five shillings weekly for maintenance, a portion of which was to be spent on the child's education and, by extension, the "task of civilizing" him or her.[38]

However, the bastardy laws were not merely the acknowledgement of the right of single mothers to assert claims for support of their children, if indeed this could be argued. Certainly, these laws empowered single mothers insofar as the maintenance of their children was concerned, but the laws were predicated on a false Euro-cultural presumption that unmarried men who did not reside with the mothers of their children extended neither material nor emotional support. The bastardy laws also betrayed a subtle layer of racist stereotyping which suggested that black men were the predominant offenders on this issue. Therefore, the bastardy laws were aimed not only at achieving social and moral reformation along Victorian lines, but also at radically altering forms of black family organization. Importantly, colonial policymakers clearly intended this "empowerment" to serve the ulterior purpose of making "promiscuous unions" just as expensive as legal marriage and, according to the rationale, thereby reduce the incidence of these unions and improve both the rate of marriages and the "moral habits" of the black majority. Moreover, by implementing effective machinery by which the mothers of "bastard" children could directly establish claims to maintenance, the bastardy laws were intended to alleviate the burden on poor-relief funds. Elite society, in spite of the "indiscretions" of many of its own, had never looked favourably upon the children of unmarried unions. Indeed, the concept of "illegitimacy" had developed into a construct attended by disapproval at every level, from legal to societal. The Bastardy and Maintenance Laws of 1881, by reserving the term "bastard" for children of unmarried parents who were not living together and "illegitimate" for those of unmarried parents living together,[39] fostered greater levels of disapprobation for those children termed "bastards". This strengthening of a pre-existing disapproval of "bastard" children and, by extension, their mothers, was evident among the "moral elite" and others who had internalized Eurocentric values which equated non-married (in the Christian, legal context) unions with social disgrace.

The bastardy legislation of 1881 also held other serious implications for black families headed by single mothers. In the eyes of the law, the mother of a "bastard" child was the primary caregiver, because she was a single mother and her child resided with her. Therefore, in instances of alleged neglect – that is, failure to adequately take care of the child – the Bastardy Law assigned greater responsibility and hence more culpability to the mother. Though contrary to the Victorian ideal in which the male bore the main responsibility, this aspect of the Bastardy Law represented an uneasy elitist accommodation to the social reality in Jamaica. Thus, the Bastardy Law of 1881 made the mother liable to imprisonment for a maximum of twenty-eight days if her child became a burden to parochial charity as a result of her negligence. Since he was not, in the eyes of the law, the primary caregiver, the father of the "bastard" child was merely forced to compensate the parochial authorities for funds disbursed on behalf of the child.[40] Because no clear guidelines for determining what constituted neglect were written into the law, and because subjective assessments by police magistrates or local justices were used to decide such cases, the Bastardy Law of 1881 at times served to reinforce the very chain of neglect which it was framed to halt by imprisoning mothers whose only "offence" may have been their inability to cope under difficult economic circumstances. Importantly, by providing for the imprisonment of the mother only, the law also raised the discomforting prospect of depriving the child of the only parent which he or she had in residence. Moreover, some single mothers who worked had neither extended family nor friends living nearby, and were thus open to charges of child neglect while working to support their children.

Law 16 of 1881, the Maintenance Law, while similarly focused on the issues of "illegitimacy", child neglect and the consequent strain on poor-relief funds, was a far more comprehensive and draconian measure than its predecessor of

1869. Unmistakably influenced by persistent elitist stereotyping of the black masses as shiftless, irresponsible and neglectful of family, this law was designed to force cultural compliance not only on black men, but on black women as well by making "living in sin" an extremely expensive proposition. The objective of making "illegitimacy" a costly affair, a purpose of the old Law 31 of 1869, was applied even more extensively in the Maintenance Law of 1881. Thus, a man (by virtue of the stereotype, black) "living in concubinage" was bound to support not only the children he had with his partner, but also all the children his partner may have had previously. This provision of section 2 of the 1881 Maintenance Law can be understood within the context of Victorian patriarchy, which viewed the man living in "concubinage", unlike the father of a "bastard", as the primary parent. Clearly a strategy to enforce Christian, legal marriage, as well as to reduce the numbers of abandoned children and thus the burden on poor relief, the emphasis on the man's responsibility to his partner's children as well as his own also reflected an accommodation to the reality of family life in Jamaica. Wingfield of the Colonial Office, although he viewed this clause of section 2 as "rather a strong measure", conceded that "it is perhaps necessary in Jamaica where cohabitation out of wedlock seems to be the rule".[41]

Reflecting the concern expressed before the Commission on the Juvenile Population that "illegitimate" children were often neglected by their mothers, the 1881 Maintenance Law also held mothers living in "concubinage" responsible for the maintenance of their own children. The principle of making unmarried cohabitation expensive so as to "induce more marriages" also shaped the provision relating to married men, who were now obliged to maintain not only their own children by their wives, but also their wives' previous children, whether they were legitimate or not. By Victorian precepts, then, married women were not legally responsible for the support of their children. However, widows left behind with legitimate children were obliged to maintain them, as they were the sole caregivers. In the continuing quest to end the "premium on concubinage", Law 16 was also intended to discourage widows from having children without remarrying, as this would mean that they would have to maintain them.

The all-inclusive nature of the 1881 law was reflected in the clauses mandating support of parents and grandparents (although this had been included in the 1869 law, it had lacked clarity in that version). By legislating that all persons born in wedlock were obliged to unreservedly support their parents and grandparents, the Maintenance Law of 1881 was intended as an endorsement of the benefits of legal marriage. However, in the context of reports of widespread desertion of women and children, "illegitimate" children, although bound to maintain their mothers, were only required to afford the same to their fathers in cases where the father had recognized and treated the child as his own during "its tender years".[42]

In requiring grandparents to maintain their grandchildren, the law provided an important safety net for children whose parents were unable to care for them. However, in restricting this benefit to legitimate grandchildren only, the 1881 measure reflected the pervasive negative stereotyping that was associated with "illegitimacy". Since white society perceived this as a black problem, it was felt that the law should discourage "the children of illegitimacy" from experiencing "material comforts" through legally enforced support from grandparents. Witnesses before the 1877 Commission on the Juvenile Population attributed the increase in "illegitimacy" to the tendency of "wanton" women to leave their children in the hands of "some old grandmother".[43] The proponents of this Eurocentric perspective were clearly not cognizant of the central role played by the culturally derived extended family among blacks.[44]

Unlike its predecessor of 1869, the Maintenance Law of 1881 met all the criteria for effective enforcement. Thus, any family member entitled to maintenance who was not in receipt of such could either personally or with help make a report to a justice of the peace, who was empowered to issue a summons to the negligent relative. In respect of punitive measures, the 1881 law was unambiguous and virtually universal in its application. With the exception of fathers of "bastards",[45] any family member who left home in order to avoid payment to a relative who was entitled to compensation was liable to either a maximum fine of twenty pounds or imprisonment for a maximum of three months. It is indeed possible that this aspect of the law excluded fathers of "bastards" out of concern that members of elite society who fell into this category would have been subjected to the same penalties as the presumed black offenders. It was more likely, however, that in keeping with the definition of "bastardy", the father would not have been living with the mother; hence, the issue of his leaving home to escape his financial obligations would not apply.

In the second half of the nineteenth century, the high infant mortality rate held serious implications for the growth and well-being of the family, especially the black family. In the absence of an official system of registration of birth and deaths, the subjective reports of custodes, clergymen and others attributed infant deaths to a mixture of black parental neglect and incompetent midwives, and indeed presented these deaths as a "black problem", even though infant mortality was by no means exclusive to blacks. The governor, Sir John Peter Grant, announcing in 1868 his administration's imminent introduction of legislation to enforce registration of births and deaths, claimed that this would be the panacea for the high infant mortality rate, which he too attributed to the "culpable neglect on the part of the parents".[46] Both Grant and the Colonial Office vastly underestimated the contribution of factors such as socio-economic hardship, the cycle of malnutrition and contagious diseases, rationalizing instead that registration would induce greater parental accountability and care of children.

Insufficient funds to finance the machinery of registration delayed the bill until Governor Musgrave's administration. Law 19 of 1877, the Births and Deaths Registration Law, emphasized the duty of both married parents to report a birth within forty-two days and to sign the register. In order not to discourage from this practice the very persons whose alleged neglect had been perceived as the cause of the high mortality rate, the law exempted the father of an "illegitimate" child from giving pertinent information to the registrar and from having his name recorded. Only a joint request from both the mother and father of an "illegitimate" child could overrule this exemption. Influenced in the latter respect by the Imperial Act, the purpose of this joint request was to prevent the mother from naming a man who was not the father of her child. Clearly, concerns that "wanton" women would exploit "innocent" men were still influential.[47]

However, in the first six months of registration after the law took effect, the problem posed by this requirement of both partners' consent to the man being named as the father became evident. According to the registrar general, although it was the "almost universal practice" for the father of the "illegitimate" child to come forward to register his offspring, he was usually sent away to return with the mother and as a result, the completion of the registration process was delayed. Importantly, this observation by the registrar general conveyed, perhaps unwittingly, instructive evidence that within six months of the passage of the act, fathers of "illegitimate children", who by elitist perception were predominantly black, were virtually universally initiating the process of registration, thereby not just acknowledging their children but also indicating their willingness to undertake the responsibility for their care. Coming from the registrar general, who had nothing to gain by misrepresenting this trend, here was a crucial contradiction of the stereotype of the uncaring and irresponsible black father who rejected responsibility for his children once they were born – part of the larger stereotype of black familial irresponsibility upon which most of the legislative efforts at moulding the cultural and normative patterns of the people had been predicated.

Law 13 of 1881, the Registration Law, re-enacted most of the clauses of the 1877 law, providing deadlines for registration of both births and deaths, while addressing the issue of delays occasioned by fathers being sent away to return with the mothers. Clause 18 of the 1881 law removed the prerequisite of joint approval before the father's name could be used, thus enabling fathers of "illegitimate" children to register their births. However, Lord Kimberley's insistence that clause 18 created a potential opportunity for abuse by either party led to the amending act, Law 8 of 1882, which reinstituted the joint approval by both parents as a prerequisite for registering the father's name.[48] While colonial administrators remained convinced that the high infant mortality rate was inextricably bound to the "scourge of illegitimacy", paradoxically, they were – up to 1882, at any rate – forced to tread lightly on this issue in order to facilitate compliance on the matter of registration.

Conclusion

Nigel Bolland has observed that "the shaping of social codes, identities, relationships and the creation of social values"[49] are some of the means by which hegemonic power is wielded. This analysis has demonstrated that legislation on the family in the post-slavery period to 1882 was clearly utilitarian in purpose and designed to implement these pathways to cultural and political hegemony.

For the most part, it has been seen that laws on the family evinced both a prescriptive and ameliorative intent on the part of the colonial state to address what it perceived as the "scourge of illegitimacy, vice and immorality"[50] among "the lower orders". By promoting Christian marriage with its attendant values, and by withholding legitimization from family forms outside of this elitist ambit, the laws were intended to marginalize and even denigrate these informal unions which had been adopted by the majority of the masses of Jamaican people. To the extent that blacks comprised the majority of the population, they were the main targets of these legislative efforts to achieve cultural conformity in familial organization, regardless of the fact that the informal unions prevalent among blacks were not unique to them. The rationale behind these legislative efforts pivoted on the misconstrued premise that all blacks had internalized the Eurocentric value system and thus could be shamed into adopting Victorian family patterns and values.

Some blacks had indeed, over the years, evidently imbibed these European-based familial norms. As seen previously, the idea that Christian, legal marriage invested one with a certain degree of "respectability" was accepted by some blacks from as early as the apprenticeship period.[51] Additionally, the upsurge in Christian marriages in the initial post-slavery years when missionary activity was at its greatest suggests that some blacks, at least those within the scope of missionary control, had adopted this ideology.[52] There is also evidence that some couples exhibited an accommodation to the Eurocentric model by getting married, but only after many years of living together out of legal wedlock. By the late 1870s, evidence of this acceptance of imposed family values was largely to be found among older blacks who had experienced enslavement and who themselves had adopted Christian marriage. For some of these blacks, the passage of time and the process of creolization had clearly diminished the influence of West African–derived familial values. Thus, for example, Nathaniel Beckford, himself a former slave, and by 1877 a married father of seven and grandfather of five, expressed the view that he was "very much troubled" by the news that his son had fathered a child outside of marriage.[53] At the same time, the decision by some blacks to refrain from Christian marriage did not always indicate their rejection of Eurocentric values, nor did it always demonstrate their continued acceptance of African cultural traditions. For some, economic concerns such as the "inability of the man to provide a house and furniture", the expenditure involved in the provision of a "grand entertainment on the day of the marriage", or uncertainty by either party about the ability to provide or obtain economic security for the future may have been the real deterrents to the adoption of Christian, legal marriage.[54]

Despite official attempts in this direction, the majority of blacks in Jamaica had not been swayed by Eurocentric forms of family organization. This is evident from the consistent reports of a decline in legal marriages among blacks, previously discussed in this chapter. The rate of marriages for the island, inclusive of all racial groups, was extremely low throughout the 1880s; as cited previously, for example, the marriage rate per thousand for 1881–82 was only 3.7.[55] Based on the reports of declining marriages among blacks in particular, we can extrapolate that this rate would have been even lower for the black population. In fact, so perturbed had white society become by the general failure of blacks to embrace marriage that radical suggestions were offered, such as that of a clergyman named Reverend Hine, who proposed in 1865 that a grant of land should be given by the government to every young woman who got married.[56] For many blacks, however, there were important socio-cultural reasons to refrain from entering into the legal married state. Among these were the continued belief that their African-derived forms of familial organization invested them with more independence, equality in status and flexibility with regards to divorce or separation, especially before the advent of legal divorce in 1879. Other contributory factors were the fear of loss of independence, a desire not to be tied to one woman (or man) and a concern on the part of many women that legal marriage would give their husband the "license to ill-treat" them.[57]

By continually withholding legitimization from the informal family forms practised by many blacks, colonial policymakers and legislators had hoped to "shame" blacks into accepting the norm. This had not been very successful. Statements from the "moral elites" bore unwitting testimony to this fact. Reverend E. Reinke, Moravian missionary from Fairfield, Manchester, declared, for example, that "mothers of illegitimate offspring feel no disgrace whatsoever".[58] In this respect, blacks' acceptance of having children in family settings organized within their own cultural parameters, without the supposed legitimacy conferred by legal marriage, was comparable to the views of black families in post-slavery America who "did not consider it wrong for a girl to have a child before she married".[59] Barbara Bush's observation, discussed earlier in this analysis, that this acceptance of child-bearing outside of Christian, legal marriage may well have been explained by African cultural retentions which did not attach a social stigma to having children out of wedlock, no doubt continued to hold true for some blacks during this period.[60]

Although having children outside of legal marriage was not unique to blacks, the greater ratio of "illegitimate" to "legitimate" births in Jamaica in the period under review indicates that blacks were quite content with their own forms of familial organization. Thus, for example, the percentage of "illegitimate" births for the entire island for the quarter ending 30 September 1878 was 60 per cent, while for the period 1881–82, the figure was 58.2 per cent.[61] Judging by these statistics along with the foregoing discussion, it is evident that blacks on the whole remained unaffected by legislative attempts to alter their family forms and, from the colonial state's perspective, their morality.

According to elitist stereotypes, failure by some black Jamaicans to support children and other family members was usually explicable by a generalized indifference to family ties. Legislative efforts such as the maintenance laws reflected this stereotype and were largely directed against the "lower orders" of blacks, especially those who lived "in states of concubinage", even though failure to materially support family members was not limited to the black experience. Further, the failure by some blacks to support their families may have resulted from an inability to do so, bearing as they did the burden of harsh economic times. This was especially apparent after natural disasters, such as the cyclone of August 1880 which devastated farming communities in St Mary and other parts of the island. Reports indicated widespread suffering among persons, largely black peasantry, who "under ordinary circumstances . . . can by industry maintain their children, but at present they have no food".[62] Kinship bonds, so central to West African cultural traditions, in some cases may have been severely tested or even severed by interpersonal disagreements, economic deprivation or out-migration. Nevertheless, evidence discussed elsewhere in this analysis demonstrates that most blacks cared about the well-being of their family members, especially that of their children and the elderly, and that many who had migrated to places such as Limon, Port-au-Prince and Navy Bay continued to support their families, especially "their old people", in Jamaica.[63] From this standpoint, black Jamaicans did not need legislative reminders of their familial responsibilities, as they demonstrated the continued centrality of kindred that had existed in the societies of their cultural origins. Indeed, this assessment has shown that elitist attempts to influence the familial norms and values of blacks through legislative measures were founded upon pervasive but largely invalid assumptions of irresponsibility by both black men and women who chose to organize their families outside the realm of the Euro-Christian norm, and that these stereotypical claims were negated by the abundant evidence presented throughout this work of black activism on behalf of family.

Ultimately, the principal objective of the body of family legislation which emerged during the period under review had been to effect a transformation in the familial organization and normative patterns mainly of the black majority.

The very fact that by 1882 most blacks continued to organize their families in a cultural context outside of the Eurocentric paradigm lends credence to the failure of this elitist objective and to the persistence over time of black familial culture.

Figure 10. *Market Women.* Cousins Hereward Postcard Collection, reprinted courtesy of the University of the West Indies Library, Mona.

Concluding Thoughts

THIS ANALYSIS HAS DEMONSTRATED THAT activism on behalf of family was a persistent hallmark of black family life during the period 1834–82, and that some of these initiatives were undertaken even under the severe constraints of the paradoxical system of the apprenticeship. Indeed, we have seen that the commencement of the transitional period termed the apprenticeship, but more realistically assessed as a period of modified slavery, marked the start of a dichotomous course for the black family. Virtually every aspect of family life was endangered by the labour-maximization priorities of estate management. Yet as shown by this discussion, the legal termination of slavery on 1 August 1834 provided opportunities through which apprentices could initiate the process of consolidating the pre-existing black family. Decidedly, during this transitional period, blacks were neither helpless nor apathetic regarding their familial concerns, despite the continuance of serious limitations upon their freedom and family lives.

It has been shown that when confronted with exploitative measures inimical to their families' welfare, apprentices acted both individually and collectively to articulate and advance familial interests. Paramount among these were their concerns for the safety and dignity of their family members, their assertion of their rights of motherhood, their entitlement to conjugal visits and the rights of their children to freedom in perpetuity. These measures of advocacy, as seen in this assessment, were important to apprentices' familial rights and had implications for the very existence of the apprenticeship.

In examining these implications, it may be useful to do so within the context of Michel de Certeau's model of resistance and opposition to domination. He theorized that oppressed peoples, termed "the politically weak", employ a variety of actions and strategies which, as they persist over time, may contribute to the undermining of some aspects of oppressive control.[1] As illustrated in this work, black family advocacy influenced British humanitarian opinion, helped to shape legislation intended to curb the abuse of apprentices and eventually contributed to the termination of apprenticeship itself. Many instances of family activism during apprenticeship – particularly the apprentices' extensive complaints and testimony about the flogging of pregnant women on the treadmill, but also the complaints by female family members against sexual harassment and the quest of the Recess plantation families for safety, among other initiatives – were shown to have exerted the erosive influence which de Certeau described. By contributing to the dismissal of corrupt officials, or by achieving legal restraint on abusive estate management, these family members played a vital, albeit unacknowledged, role in wearing down some aspects of domination which had proven inimical to family welfare.

Nigel Bolland, in his assessment of de Certeau's model, notes that actions of this sort by oppressed peoples are "generally invisible" in the records, because documentation has been "written for and left by the strong".[2] It is hoped that this discussion has given greater visibility to the contributions of these black family advocates who "are no less important . . . simply because they are obscured, unsigned and unacknowledged by posterity".[3] Ultimately, it has been demonstrated that although designated powerless by the colonial state, apprentices, by virtue of their constant striving against injustices directed at their families, were engaged in political activity of their own, intended to effect change to an oppressive way of life. To the extent that their family-based activism contributed to the premature ending of this system of modified slavery, black apprentices played a vital role in shaping their own evolving reality of freedom.

Such activism was not only reactive to abuses against the family but was also initiatory on behalf of family objectives. Apprentices therefore accorded preference to a variety of measures which, as illustrated in this work, allowed them to reunite with separated family members, whether on a temporary or permanent basis. Indeed, it is now clear that a significant foundation for the post-slavery reconstruction of the family was laid during apprenticeship and that the process continued unabated within the context of full freedom. It may be concluded that their efforts at reconstituting and strengthening their families, their collective initiatives to construct schools for their children and to gain access to health care on their behalf, and their insistence on preserving the liberty of their children enabled blacks during the period of the apprenticeship to establish for their families "meaningful spheres of freedom in the face of extraordinary opposition and repression".[4]

As illustrated by this evaluation, a preponderance of black family activism on issues central to the family such as fair tenancy policies was conducted through legal agencies ranging from the stipendiary courts to the Supreme Court. The implications of this focus on legal resolutions to family issues extend beyond the superficial rationalization of "a love of litigation". Despite the tendency towards adverse outcomes for these cases, the unremitting use of the stipendiary courts, by apprentices in particular, as a medium for family action established a clear recognition on their part of their unfolding right to justice as persons soon to be fully freed.

The continuance, throughout the entire period under study, of this focus on the legal process allows us to make important conclusions about black family activism. It indicates that the concept of "legal personhood" among formerly apprenticed families – that is, their belief in the need to develop relationships with legal persons and the legal process,[5] which had been embryonic during apprenticeship – had become fully established as a black family strategy by the end of this period. It also demonstrates that these families were fully committed to their belief that "access to justice was an attribute of citizenship" and hence a crucial tool with which to forge "the unfinished business" of emancipation.[6] In view of the impediments associated with blacks' pursuance of justice through the courts, their continued use of this medium "forcefully belied the commonly held theories about a race of moral cripples who placed little value on marital and familial ties".[7]

As this analysis has demonstrated, groups of freed families undertook collaborative action on many occasions between 1834 and 1882, in pursuit of maternal rights under apprenticeship, in protest against unfair evictions, in support of health and education concerns, and in defence of the security and continued liberty of their families. This investigation has also shown that collaborative action sometimes had its genesis in one community (as in efforts to build schools or promote health care) and was sometimes generated across communities (as in joint efforts by parents from several parts of a parish to resist attempts to subject their children to industrial education). Such prominence given by blacks to collective family advocacy allows us to make important inferences about their perceptions of family and community, and about the strategies which they prioritized.

It is clear that whether they were seeking autonomy or protection, freed people valued community-based family action as a strategy which empowered individuals, their families and their communities and enhanced their chances of success. Given the foundational influence of West African cultures upon the familial norms and values of blacks, this post-slavery demonstration of collective responsibility in action must have been, in part, a reflection of the enduring influence of the "notion of commitment to the collectivity",[8] which, as seen in chapter 1, had been the genesis of community-based systems of support in West Africa. Collaborative, family-based activism was also an adaptive response, honed by experiences of enslavement and the post-slavery challenges highlighted in this analysis. Black people's consciousness of community was strengthened by the removal of physical barriers at emancipation, by a cognizance of the commonality of certain familial concerns in the context of freedom and by their understanding of the need to act as a community of families in pursuit of their interests. This collaborative activism signalled awareness, at least on the part of those families involved, of the importance of the family as a foundation on which they could develop strong communities. This work has also shown that elitist notions of irresponsible black parenthood, prevailing philosophies promoting utilitarian industrial training for black children and notions of reforming society through its children contributed to an emerging effort by the colonial state to exert control over the children of ex-slaves. However, as we have seen, this effort, executed at first indirectly through private reformatories and then directly through state-controlled reformatories and extended apprenticeships, affected only a comparatively small portion of the black population because of the limited scope of these institutions. The reformatory movement institutionalized the abrogation of parental dominion by way of the state's assumption of *in loco parentis* status. Similar state efforts to influence the development and futures of black children through plans for compulsory education bore no fruit during this period, partly because of lack of infrastructural and financial support for the schemes and also, significantly, because the colonial government anticipated strong opposition from black parents.

This evaluation has shown that it was the virtually universal resistance by black parents to all efforts at influencing their children's developmental paths through industrial education and voluntary apprenticeship, both before and after 1838, which largely explained the failure of such attempts. Enslavement had made serious infringements upon black parental autonomy. Thus, the persistent advocacy by freed parents on behalf of their children's welfare, and their insistence on parental dominion throughout the entire post-slavery period in the face of a variety of elitist-sponsored efforts to exert control, were crucial components of their drive to reassert personhood within the parameters of "full free". In this respect, black parents' prioritization of their children's freedom and well-being was in keeping with the close parent-child bond which had characterized their West African societies of origin, but it was also a powerful indication that many black Jamaicans had embraced the ties that bind as the centrepiece of a familial culture forged in the experiences of post-slavery society. This commitment to familial bonds, although not unique to blacks, remained a significant characteristic of the evolving black family despite tremendous challenges.

It is now clear that developments such as the extensive emergence of peasant proprietorship and the establishment of family autonomy over the labour and education of its members contributed to the growing stabilization of the family during this period. As evidenced by this investigation, other initiatives such as the reconstitution and consolidation of families, before and after 1838, as well as black families' determined advocacy of their interests throughout this period, furthered this stabilization. The stability of many black families was also apparent in evidence of durable and productive unions, as well as in unwitting elitist commentary on the pervasiveness of "faithful concubinage". Such evidence of stability challenged the perspective, common at the time, that the black family was unstable, chaotic and dysfunctional and that the formerly enslaved were uncaring or apathetic with respect to familial well-being.

However, as this examination has revealed, developments within the post-slavery period also fostered elements of instability within the black family. Thus, worsening economic conditions, the migration of family members and the growth of personal tensions and strife within families likely contributed to instances of neglect of family members. The prevailing elitist, Euro-cultural construct, by equating family units based on Christian marriage with stability, maintenance of children and other family members, and generally "responsible" attitudes towards the family, relegated black family forms, most of which continued to be organized outside of this conceptual framework, to a behavioural code which was seen as stereotypically irresponsible, neglectful and uncaring in familial contexts. Moulded by this frame of reference, elitist perspectives represented genuine but isolated cases of neglect by some family members as the norm for blacks in general. Based upon the significant evidence of activism, commitment and support for family discussed throughout this work, it remains clear that these elements of instability were not the universal characteristics of the black family which elitist testimony represented them to be.

We have also seen that some families during this period experienced disintegration and disaster as a result of forces external to the family. Apart from the effects of natural disasters and disease, some were torn apart by the renewal of attempts after 1834 to reduce blacks to chattel slavery, this time through kidnapping and sale to external slave markets. Some family members of such victims utilized every resource available to them in an effort to be reunited with their loved ones; these endeavours demonstrated the attachment to kindred which had characterized familial culture in their societies of origin in West Africa, and which remained constant for many during the period of enslavement and into freedom. In their quest to be reunited with relatives from whom they had been separated in this way, black families received considerable assistance from both the British and local authorities and this, for several families, facilitated successful outcomes. Nevertheless, the inability to accord more visibility to the actual events of these family reunions remains a limitation of the sources. The apparent pervasiveness of these abductions makes this aspect of the investigation an area for more thorough future research.

As this evaluation has revealed, the suppression of the events of October 1865 at Morant Bay had significant repercussions for many black families in parts of St Thomas-in-the-East. The resultant adversity interrupted several aspects of the progress which they had made in the difficult years leading up to 1865 and inflicted a broad spectrum of tragic consequences on many of these families. An examination of the testimony of black witnesses indicates the continuance of extended family networks, both co-residential and non-co-residential, in the period prior to the suppression, and reveals that in several instances, these networks were tragically altered by the force of the suppression. As was the case in traditional West African societies where commitment to collective welfare was culturally significant, the surviving family networks proved invaluable as support and recovery mechanisms in the aftermath of the suppression. Indeed, the initiative and resilience which were integral to black family activity over the years were also displayed in the wake of these events, enabling survival and recovery of family members. By examining the plight of individual families, this discussion has attempted to place a more human face on the suffering occasioned by events at Morant Bay, an experience that has all too often been reduced to statistical representation.[9]

Black family forms were shown to have exhibited both elements of continuity and change during this period. Much of the family-oriented legislation which emerged after apprenticeship was influenced by the desire to alter the family forms and familial values of the black majority in an effort to enhance both hegemony and social control. As established by this analysis, for the most part, blacks continued to embrace their own forms of unions outside of the confines of legal marriage, and persisted in their attachments to their extended families, even if elite society disapproved of the role of "some old grandmother" in the rearing of their children.[10] In both these respects, it is evident that there was a continuity of traditions which had characterized familial culture in the West African societies of origin, a subsequent transmission of these values to unions among enslaved persons[11] and a persistence of some of these cultural practices over the almost half a century covered by this study. Conversely, as seen in this analysis, generational separation from West Africa, creolization and socio-economic crises also exerted some formative influence on black family life during this period. We have also seen evidence of the continuation, and in fact increase, of the single-parent family form (usually, but not always, headed by mothers) over the course of this period, generally the product of a combination of factors such as migration, death or, at times, desertion. No doubt, some women as well as men chose to live apart from their partners. Although elitists condemned this type of family arrangement as morally reprehensible and, as seen in the analysis, attempted through bastardy laws to promote ostracism and thereby create conformity, this objective was not achieved in most cases; single-parent units continued unabated, much to the discomfort of "polite" society. Moreover, as evidenced by the unwitting testimony of white witnesses before the Commission on the Juvenile Population, many of these single parents, by dint of hard work, presented a challenge to elitist stereotypes of neglect.[12]

An upsurge in Christian marriages among blacks in the immediate post-slavery years, especially prevalent in areas under missionary control, may have reflected both a desire to conform to missionary expectations and a degree of cultural accommodation or creolization by blacks. This initial upsurge in legal marriages also represented a departure, albeit short-lived, from the generalized opposition to Christian family forms during slavery, as reported in the sources.[13] As indicated in the introduction to this work, no detailed quantitative analysis of black family forms was undertaken here, as this was not the intended focus of the work. Such an analysis is recommended for future research, as this may enhance our understanding of black family forms after 1838.

When Francisco Scarano and David Sabean emphasized the need for historians of the family to shift away from the traditional focus on family forms and structure and instead to assess the relationships and interactions within the family, they accentuated the historiographical significance of such an undertaking.[14] In uncovering and assessing these interrelationships within black family networks in freedom, and in examining how activism and agency on behalf of family and community facilitated black engagement with the ongoing project of freedom, this work on the black family in Jamaica from the inception of apprenticeship to 1882 makes an important contribution to post-slavery Jamaican and, by extension, Caribbean historiography. This is especially true given the absence of any major historical evaluation of the black family in Jamaica during this period.

As discussed in the introduction, one of the most persistent concerns of present-day historians and sociologists of the family in Jamaica and the Caribbean at large continues to be the issue of the "marginalization of the black male" in the family, in both historical and present-day contexts. This apparent marginality has been represented in the literature as being characteristic of the male in the society in general.[15] Erna Brodber highlights this ongoing concern in her observation that a "similar notion of the Jamaican male as invisible [as in the past] persists today" and that social researchers are preoccupied with "trying to find him and involve him in family and community-related activities".[16] This work on the black family in Jamaica in the post-slavery period allows for a significant engagement with the current discourse on this issue of male marginality. Indeed, the ample evidence of male activism on behalf of family presented here negates stereotypical assertions of the inactive, ineffective, insignificant and peripheral black male in familial contexts in the historical setting, even as the evidence locates him, in the period 1834–82, as an effective advocate for his family and a significant and central husband, partner, father, grandfather, son and brother, both in terms of his image of self and in the activation of these familial roles. As seen in the introduction, because historians have written more about the black woman than the black man in familial contexts, the latter, as argued by Hilary Beckles, has also been made vulnerable to a historiography of neglect.[17] Therefore, in highlighting the contributions of black males to their families in freedom, this analysis has attempted to address this historiographical imbalance in a meaningful way.

At the same time, the equally substantial evidence presented here of the agency of black women on behalf of familial well-being, especially in relation to maternal advocacy, endorses the principle adopted by feminist historians and articulated by Bridget Brereton that "personal life, such as family relations and women's roles within the family" are subjects as significant and worthy of historical investigation as are "public, political relations". By demonstrating the erosive power of family-centred activism by black women (and by black men) on systems of domination during this period, this work has also affirmed one of the principal views of modern feminist historians: that is, "the personal is political".[18]

An ongoing and consequential project among social historians within the Caribbean region has been to examine, where possible, the past through the lens of the formerly oppressed. In spite of the methodological and source-related challenges involved in such an undertaking (discussed in the introduction), this enterprise remains crucial to the unfolding social history of the region, particularly because documentation was generated mainly by the politically dominant.[19] This analysis of the black family in freedom, through its extensive utilization of the testimony of black people, especially regarding their familial aspirations and concerns, enables a meaningful engagement with this project. By so doing, this work makes an important contribution to the momentous effort to give voice to the black experience in the post-slavery Caribbean.

Bolland, in differentiating between "real human emancipation" and the "change of legal status" which occurred in August 1834, reminds us that the former is a continuing process.[20] For almost half a century, black families, through their activism and resilience under the most challenging of circumstances, had endeavoured to enact their vision of freedom as an unfolding reality.

Notes

Abbreviations

BTCM *Minutes of Proceedings at Brown's Town, St Ann's*, 1837, minutes of inquiry into complaints by various missionaries

BTJW *Minutes of Proceedings at Brown's Town, St Ann's*, 1837, minutes of inquiry into the narrative of James Williams

CGR *Report of the Commissioners of Inquiry upon the Government Reformatory at Stony Hill*, 1877

CJP *Report of the Commissioners of Inquiry upon the Condition of the Juvenile Population of Jamaica*, 1879

CO 137 Governors' and Colonial Office Correspondence

JRC *Report of the Jamaica Royal Commission*, 1866

PP Parliamentary Papers (UK)

WAS *Report of the Select Committee of Parliament Appointed to Inquire into the Working of the Apprenticeship System in the Colonies*, 1836

WIC *Report of the Select Committee of the House of Commons on the West India Colonies*, 1842

Introduction

1.   James A. Thome and J. Horace Kimball, *Emancipation in the West Indies: A Six Months' Tour in Antigua, Barbados, and Jamaica, in the Year 1837* (New York: American Anti-Slavery Society, 1838), 101.

2.   Michael G. Smith, *West Indian Family Structure* (Seattle: University of Washington Press, 1962), 262; E. Franklin Frazier, *The Negro Family in the United States*, 2nd ed.

(Chicago: University of Chicago Press, 1966), 15; Fernando Henriques, *Family and Colour in Jamaica* (London: Eyre and Spottiswoode, 1953), 103.

3. Elsa Goveia, *Slave Society in the British Leeward Islands at the End of the Eighteenth Century* (New Haven: Yale University Press, 1965), 235–36.

4. Orlando Patterson, *The Sociology of Slavery: An Analysis of the Origins, Development and Structure of Negro Slave Society in Jamaica* (London: McGibbon and Kee, 1967), 167.

5. Quoted in Barry W. Higman, "The Slave Family and Household in the British West Indies, 1800–1834", *Journal of Interdisciplinary History* 6, no. 2 (Autumn 1975): 263.

6. Stanley Engerman and Robert Fogel, *Time on the Cross: The Economics of American Negro Slavery* (Boston: Little, Brown, 1974), 126–44; Herbert G. Gutman, *The Black Family in Slavery and Freedom, 1750–1925* (New York: Pantheon, 1976).

7. Higman, "Slave Family and Household", 271.

8. Patterson, *Sociology of Slavery*, 167.

9. Francisco Scarano, "Slavery and Emancipation in Caribbean History", in *General History of the Caribbean*, vol. 6, *Methodology and Historiography of the Caribbean*, ed. Barry W. Higman (London: UNESCO, 1999), 269–70.

10. David Warren Sabean, "The History of the Family in Africa and Europe: Some Comparative Perspectives", *Journal of African History* 24 (1983): 167.

11. See Patrick Bryan, *The Jamaican People, 1880–1902: Race, Class and Social Control* (Kingston: University of the West Indies Press, 1991); Brian L. Moore and Michele A. Johnson, *Neither Led nor Driven: Contesting British Cultural Imperialism in Jamaica, 1865–1920* (Kingston: University of the West Indies Press, 2004).

12. Scarano, "Slavery and Emancipation", 270.

13. See Edward Long, *The History of Jamaica, or General Survey of the Antient and Modern State of that Island: With Reflections on Its Situations, Settlements, Inhabitants, Climate, Products, Commerce, Laws and Government* (London: T. Lowndes, 1774), 2:353; Mrs A.C. Carmichael, *Domestic Manners and Social Condition of the White, Coloured, and Negro Population of the West Indies* (London: Whittaker, Treacher, 1833), 1:269–71; Bryan Edwards, *The History, Civil and Commercial, of the British Colonies in the West Indies* (London: J. Stockdale, 1793), 2:148.

14. See *Report of the Commissioners of Inquiry upon the Condition of the Juvenile Population of Jamaica, with the Evidence Taken and an Appendix*, 1879 (hereafter cited as *CJP*), West Indies Collection, University of the West Indies, Mona, Jamaica.

15. Rebecca J. Scott, "Exploring the Meaning of Freedom: Postemancipation Societies in Comparative Perspective", *Hispanic American Historical Review* 68, no. 3 (August 1988): 423; O. Nigel Bolland, "The Politics of Freedom in the British Caribbean", in *The Meaning of Freedom: Economics, Politics, and Culture after Slavery*, ed. Frank McGlynn and Seymour Drescher (Pittsburgh: University of Pittsburgh Press,

1992), 141; Bridget Brereton, "Family Strategies, Gender and the Shift to Wage Labour in the British Caribbean", in *The Colonial Caribbean in Transition: Essays on Postemancipation Social and Cultural History*, ed. Bridget Brereton and Kelvin A. Yelvington (Kingston: University of the West Indies Press, 1999), 92.

16. Barbara Bush, *Slave Women in Caribbean Society, 1650–1838* (London: James Currey, 1990), 86.

17. Sara Hawker and Chris Cowley, eds., *The Oxford Colour Dictionary and Thesaurus* (Oxford: Oxford University Press, 1996), 307.

18. Bolland, "Politics of Freedom", 142.

19. Brereton, "Family Strategies", 107.

20. "Night rambling" refers to visits by enslaved persons to relatives or "paramours" on other estates during the evenings or at night. Bush, *Slave Women*, 109; Edward (Kamau) Brathwaite, *The Development of Creole Society in Jamaica, 1770–1820* (Oxford: Clarendon, 1971), 204–5; Woodville Marshall, " 'We Be Wise to Many More Tings': Blacks' Hopes and Expectations of Emancipation", in *Caribbean Freedom: Economy and Society from Emancipation to the Present*, ed. Hilary Beckles and Verene Shepherd (Kingston: Ian Randle, 1993), 17.

21. Swithin Wilmot, " 'Females of Abandoned Character'? Women and Protest in Jamaica, 1838–65", in *Engendering History: Caribbean Women in Historical Perspective*, ed. Verene Shepherd, Bridget Brereton and Barbara Bailey (Kingston: Ian Randle, 1995), 280; Brereton, "Family Strategies", 98–102, 107.

22. Leon F. Litwack, *Been in the Storm So Long: The Aftermath of Slavery* (New York: Knopf, 1981), 230.

23. John Lean and Trevor Burnard, "Hearing Slave Voices: The Fiscal's Reports of Berbice and Demerara-Essequibo", *Archives* 27, no. 107 (October 2002): 120.

24. See Alvin O. Thompson, *Unprofitable Servants: Crown Slaves in Berbice, Guyana, 1803–1831* (Kingston: University of the West Indies Press, 2002). For examples of Swithin Wilmot's work, see Wilmot, "Black Labourers and White Missionaries: Conflict on the Estates in Hanover, Jamaica, 1838–1847", *Jamaican Historical Review* 14 (1984): 18–27; "Emancipation in Action: Workers and Wage Conflicts in Jamaica, 1838–1840", *Jamaica Journal* 19, no. 3 (1986): 55–62; "Females of Abandoned Character", 279–95. For examples of Verene Shepherd's work, see Shepherd, "Resisting Representation: The Problem of Locating the Subaltern Woman's Voice" (paper presented at the Second Conference on Caribbean Culture, University of the West Indies, Mona, 9–12 January 2002); with Ahmed Reid, "Rebel Voices: Testimonies from the 1831–32 Emancipation War in Jamaica", *Jamaica Journal* 27, nos. 2–3 (2004): 54–63.

25. "Witting testimony" is "the deliberate or intentional record or message of a document"; "unwitting testimony" is the evidence, contained in the source, which was not intended by its writer to be communicated or evidence in the source, of which

the writer was unaware. See Arthur Marwick, *The Nature of History*, 3rd ed. (London: Macmillan Education, 1989), 216.

26. Elgin to Stanley, no. 197, 20 December 1843, enclosed report of Stipendiary Magistrate Laidlaw, Governors' and Colonial Office Correspondence (hereafter cited as CO 137) 137/275.

Chapter 1

1. Niara Sudarkasa, "Interpreting the African Heritage in Afro-American Family Organization", in *Black Families,* 2nd ed., Harriette Pipes McAdoo (Newbury Park, CA: Sage, 1988), 42.

2. Frazier, *Negro Family*, 15.

3. George W. Roberts, *The Population of Jamaica*, 2nd ed. (New York: Kraus-Thomson Organization, 1979), 227.

4. See Christine Barrow, "Men, Women and Family in the Caribbean: A Review", in *Gender in Caribbean Development*, 2nd ed., ed. Patricia Mohammed and Catherine Shepherd (Kingston: Canoe, 1999), 152.

5. See, for example, Henriques, *Family and Colour*; Edith Clarke, *My Mother Who Fathered Me: A Study of the Family in Three Selected Communities in Jamaica,* 2nd ed. (London: Allen and Unwin, 1970); Raymond Smith, *The Negro Family in British Guiana: Family Structure and Social Status in the Villages*, 2nd ed. (London: Routledge and Kegan Paul, 1971); Judith Blake, *Family Structure in Jamaica: The Social Context of Reproduction* (New York: Free Press of Glencoe, 1961); Smith, *West Indian Family Structure*; Sidney Greenfield, *English Rustics in Black Skin: A Study of Modern Family Forms in a Pre-Industrial Society* (New Haven: College and University Press, 1966).

6. Barrow, "Men, Women and Family", 152.

7. Melville and Frances Herskovits, *Trinidad Village* (New York: Knopf, 1947), 287; Melville Herskovits, *The Myth of the Negro Past*, 2nd ed. (Boston: Beacon, 1958).

8. Patterson, *Sociology of Slavery*, 167, 182–259.

9. Sudarkasa, "African Heritage", 39. Other works by Sudarkasa include "African and Afro-American Family Organization", in *Anthropology for the Eighties: Introductory Readings*, ed. Johnnetta B. Cole (New York: Free Press, 1982), 132–60; and "Female Employment and Family Organization in West Africa", in *The Black Woman Cross-Culturally*, ed. Filomina Chioma Steady (Cambridge, MA: Schenkman, 1981), 49–64.

10. Bush, *Slave Women*, 87.

11. Barry W. Higman, *Slave Populations of the British Caribbean, 1807–1834* (Baltimore: Johns Hopkins University Press, 1984), 365.

12. Brathwaite, *Development of Creole Society*, ix.

13. Michael Craton, *Empire, Enslavement and Freedom in the Caribbean* (Kingston: Ian Randle, 1997), 174–81.

14. Barry W. Higman, *Slave Population and Economy in Jamaica, 1807–1834* (Kingston: University of the West Indies Press, 1995), 75; Barry W. Higman, ed., *The Jamaican Censuses of 1844 and 1861: A New Edition, Derived from the Manuscript and Printed Schedules in the Jamaica Archives* (Kingston: Social History Project, University of the West Indies, 1980), 3, 5, 16, 38.

15. Bush, *Slave Women*, 25.

16. Bryan, *Jamaican People*, 81–82.

17. Moore and Johnson, *Neither Led nor Driven*, 12.

18. Shula Marks and Richard Rathbone, "The History of the Family in Africa: Introduction", *Journal of African History* 24 (1983): 160.

19. Barry W. Higman, "African and Creole Slave Family Patterns in Trinidad", in *Africa and the Caribbean: The Legacies of a Link*, ed. Margaret E. Crahan and Franklin W. Knight (Baltimore: Johns Hopkins University Press, 1979), 45.

20. Philip D. Curtin, *The Atlantic Slave Trade: A Census* (Madison: University of Wisconsin Press, 1969), 160–61.

21. Philip D. Curtin, *Two Jamaicas: The Role of Ideas in a Tropical Colony, 1830–1865* (Westport, CT: Greenwood, 1968), 24.

22. Higman, *Slave Population and Economy*, 76.

23. Bush, *Slave Women*, 7. The term "co-residential" means residing in one house; "non-co-residential" means living in separate houses.

24. Higman, "Slave Family Patterns", 58.

25. Sudarkasa, "African Heritage", 39–46.

26. Marks and Rathbone, "History of the Family", 149; Sabean, "History of the Family", 163.

27. Sudarkasa, "African Heritage", 37–42.

28. Barry W. Higman, *Montpelier, Jamaica: A Plantation Community in Slavery and Freedom, 1739–1912* (Kingston: University of the West Indies Press, 1998), 120–23, 136.

29. Bush, *Slave Women*, 86.

30. See in chapter 2, for example, the case of Maggy Lewis, who had ten children, twenty-eight grandchildren and one great-grandchild, all resident on Orange Valley estate in Trelawny. Sligo to Glenelg, no. 103, 6 September 1835, enclosed reports of Stipendiary Magistrates Thomas Davies and Ralph Cocking, respectively, CO 137/202; *Report of the Jamaica Royal Commission*, 1866, part 2, *Minutes of Evidence and Appendix* (hereafter cited as *JRC*, part 2), evidence of Eliza and Mary Berry, 283–84, George

Bryan, 147–49, and Mary Bryan, 149–50, Parliamentary Papers (hereafter cited as PP) 1866 (5). See chapter 5 concerning the extended families formed by the Berry brothers and the Bryan brothers. Also see chapter 5 for evidence of yard formation.

31. Niara Sudarkasa, "'The Status of Women' in Indigenous African Societies", in *Women in Africa and the African Diaspora,* ed. Rosalyn Terborg-Penn, Sharon Harley and Andrea Benton Rushing (Washington, DC: Howard University Press, 1987), 39.

32. This point is developed in chapters 2 and 5.

33. Bush, *Slave Women,* 97.

34. John S. Mbiti, *African Religions and Philosophy,* 2nd ed. (Oxford: Heinemann, 1989), 139.

35. Higman, "Slave Family Patterns", 50–54; Higman, *Montpelier,* 122–23.

36. Mbiti, *African Religions,* 102.

37. Bush, *Slave Women,* 86.

38. Sudarkasa, "African Heritage", 43.

39. Simeon Chilungu, "Marriage, Family and Kinship Ties in Africa", in *African Continuities/L'Héritage Africain*, ed. Simeon Chilungu and Sada Niang (Toronto: Terebi, 1989), 63.

40. Filomina Steady, "African Feminism: A Worldwide Perspective", in *Women in Africa,* ed. Terborg-Penn, Harley and Rushing, 6.

41. Herbert S. Klein and Stanley L. Engerman, "Fertility Differentials between Slaves in the United States and the British West Indies: A Note on Lactation Practices and Their Possible Implications", *William and Mary Quarterly,* 3rd series, 35, no. 2 (April 1978): 369, 371. See also Thomas Winterbottom, *An Account of the Native Africans in the Neighbourhood of Sierra Leone* (London: C. Whittingham, 1803), 2:218.

42. Bush, *Slave Women,* 103–4, 110, 124; Higman, "Slave Family Patterns", 61.

43. Joyce Ladner, "Racism and Tradition: Black Womanhood in Historical Perspective", in Steady, *Black Woman,* 272.

44. Mbiti, *African Religions,* 141; Bush, *Slave Women,* 94.

45. Sudarkasa, "African Heritage", 45.

46. Bush, *Slave Women,* 98–101; Mbiti, *African Religions,* 141–42.

47. See chapter 6 for further discussion of this.

48. Sudarkasa, "African Heritage", 41.

49. Jean Besson, "Family Land and Caribbean Society: Toward an Ethnography of Afro-Caribbean Peasantries", in *Perspectives on Caribbean Regional Identity*, ed. Elizabeth Thomas-Hope (Liverpool: Centre for Latin American Studies, University of Liverpool, 1984), 61–66.

50. Bush, *Slave Women,* 107.

51. Barrow, "Men, Women and Family", 152.

52. Bryan, *Jamaican People,* 92–93.

53. Higman, "Slave Family and Household", 270–71.

54. Sidney Mintz, "History and Anthropology: A Brief Reprise", in *Race and Slavery in the Western Hemisphere: Quantitative Studies*, ed. Stanley Engerman and Eugene Genovese (Princeton: Princeton University Press, 1975), 493–94.

55. Bush, *Slave Women*, 86.

56. Bush, *Slave Women*, 86.

57. For example, Michael Lafitte, a former slave, resided with his "wife", his four children and his grandchild in a house at Lovely Grove. Smith to Glenelg, no. 74, 6 April 1839, enclosure, CO 137/238.

58. Higman, *Slave Populations*, 371.

59. Higman, "Slave Family and Household", 261–87.

60. Examples of this include the actions of the "black population" of Savanna-la-Mar, who in 1855 released a black man being held as a slave aboard an American vessel docked at the port. Clearly feeling an affinity to the man, they marched onto the boat and "liberated" him. The man was declared free by a magistrate in the parish. Barkly to Russell, no. 68, 20 June 1855, CO 137/326. Also see *CJP*, appendix A, evidence of Rev. William Griffiths, 55, Rev. C. Douet, 82, Rev. Enos Nuttall, 6–7, 9–10.

61. Long, *History of Jamaica*, 2:353.

62. Carmichael, *Domestic Manners*, 1:269–71.

63. Edwards, *History of the British Colonies*, 2:148.

64. Bolland, "Politics of Freedom", 116.

65. Smith to Glenelg, no. 150, 13 August 1838, CO 137/229.

66. Eric Foner, *Reconstruction: America's Unfinished Revolution, 1863–1877* (New York: Harper and Row, 1988), 87.

67. Errol Miller, *Men at Risk* (Kingston: Jamaica Publishing House, 1991), 130–36, 167.

68. Patterson, *Sociology of Slavery*, 167–68.

69. Ladner, "Racism and Tradition", 276.

70. James Anthony Froude, *The English in the West Indies, or The Bow of Ulysses* (London: Longmans, Green, 1888), 198.

71. Erna Brodber, preface to *Standing Tall: Affirmations of the Jamaican Male – 24 Self-Portraits* (Kingston: Sir Arthur Lewis Institute of Social and Economic Studies, University of the West Indies, 2003), xx.

72. Bush, *Slave Women*, 93; Higman, *Montpelier*, 119–21.

73. Hilary McD. Beckles, "Black Masculinity in Caribbean Slavery", Occasional Paper 2:96 (St Michael, Barbados: Women and Development Unit, University of the West Indies, 1996), 4.

74. Beckles, "Black Masculinity", 5.

75. Barrow, "Men, Women and Family", 159. See also Barrow, "Masculinity and Family in the Caribbean: 'Marginality' and 'Reputation' Revisited", in *Portraits of a Nearer*

Caribbean: Essays on Gender Ideologies and Identities, ed. Christine Barrow (Kingston: Ian Randle, 1998), 339–76.

76. George Beckford, introduction to Brodber, *Standing Tall*, xxxviii–xxxix. Brodber points out that the twenty-four "unmistakably black Jamaican men" whose testimonies were used in her book were born between 1883 and 1911. See Brodber, *Standing Tall*, xx.

77. Henrice Altink, " 'To Wed or Not to Wed?' The Struggle to Define Afro-Jamaican Relationships, 1834–1838", *Journal of Social History* 38, no. 1 (Fall 2004): 101.

78. Verene Shepherd, "Gender, Migration and Settlement: The Indentureship and Post-indentureship Experience of Indian Females in Jamaica, 1845–1943", in Shepherd, Brereton and Bailey, *Engendering History*, 236.

79. Catherine Hall, *Civilising Subjects: Metropole and Colony in the English Imagination, 1830–1867* (Cambridge: Polity, 2002), 137.

80. Moore and Johnson, *Neither Led nor Driven*, 136.

81. Bryan, *Jamaican People*, x.

82. Considerable evidence exists to support this conclusion. See, for example, *CJP*, appendix A, evidence of Rev. Reinke, 106, and W. Bancroft Espeut, 122–23; appendix C, evidence of Robert Pitters, 45. See also Elgin to Stanley, no. 79, 2 September 1845, enclosed report of Stipendiary Magistrate Hall Pringle, *Annual Report of the Registrar General's Department, Births*, 1881, 1882, CO 137/384.

83. This was done by simply separating, or sometimes the "ceremony" of dividing the cotta was observed (see chapter 6 for details of this custom). Also see William James Gardner, *A History of Jamaica from Its Discovery by Christopher Columbus to the Present Time* (London: E. Stock, 1873), 182; Trevor Burnard, " 'A Matron in Rank, a Prostitute in Manners': The Manning Divorce of 1741 and Class, Gender, Race and the Law in Eighteenth-Century Jamaica", in *Working Slavery, Pricing Freedom: Perspectives from the Caribbean, Africa and the African Diaspora*, ed. Verene A. Shepherd (Kingston: Ian Randle, 2002), 133–52.

84. Bush, *Slave Women*, 102; *CJP*, appendix A, evidence of E. Goldson, 29.

85. Bush, *Slave Women*, 101.

86. *CJP*, appendix A, evidence of W. Bancroft Espeut, 122–23.

87. Moore and Johnson, *Neither Led nor Driven*, 100.

88. For example, see Sligo to Spring Rice, no. 57, 1 November 1834, enclosure, *Minutes of Proceedings at Brown's Town, St Ann's, 1837* (minutes of inquiry into the narrative of James Williams, hereafter cited as *BTJW*), evidence of Amelia Lawrence and Amaryllis Gale, 163–69, CO 137/193.

89. *CJP*, appendix C, evidence of Nathaniel Beckford, 42–43, and Orgill McKenzie, 44–45.

90. Thome and Kimball, *Emancipation in the West Indies*, 101.

91. See *CJP*, appendix B, evidence of William Kerr, 1, and Michael Solomon, 28.

92. *CJP*, appendix A, evidence of Rev. George Sargeant, 116, and Rev. William Griffiths, 55.

93. See note 60.

Chapter 2

1. Smith to Normanby, no. 110, 27 May 1839, enclosed report of Stipendiary Magistrates Edmund Lyon and Daniel Kelly, CO 137/238.

2. Scott, "Exploring Freedom", 424.

3. See, for example, Bolland, "Politics of Freedom", 113–43; Brereton, "Family Strategies", 77–107; Marshall, "We Be Wise", 12–20; Scott, "Exploring Freedom", 407–28; Wilmot, "Emancipation in Action", 48–54.

4. Scott, "Exploring Freedom", 417–8.

5. Bush, *Slave Women*, 109–10.

6. W.L. Burn, *Emancipation and Apprenticeship in the British West Indies* (London: Jonathan Cape, 1937), 274.

7. Scott, "Exploring Freedom", 419, 423.

8. Elgin to Stanley, no. 9, 30 June 1842, enclosed report of Stipendiary Magistrate Thomas Dillon, CO 137/263; Barkley to Molesworth, no. 97, 2 October 1855, CO 137/327; Burn, *Emancipation and Apprenticeship*, 179; Marshall, "We Be Wise", 15.

9. See Diana Paton, *No Bond but the Law: Punishment, Race, and Gender in Jamaican State Formation, 1780–1870* (Durham, NC: Duke University Press, 2004), 178–79. For more on justice through the compound council, see Sudarkasa, "Female Employment", 49–63.

10. See Douglas Hall, *In Miserable Slavery: Thomas Thistlewood in Jamaica, 1750–1786* (London: Macmillan, 1989), 50–54, 184–85.

11. Sligo to Spring Rice, no. 57, 1 November 1834, enclosed report of Stipendiary Magistrate Charles Brown on the court case, CO 137/193.

12. Grand jurors could give one of two verdicts: *billa vera* ("true bill"), which indicated that there were enough grounds for a trial to proceed, or *ignoramus* ("we do not know"), which indicated that the bill of indictment was rejected and the accused was discharged. See Jonathan Dalby, *Crime and Punishment in Jamaica: A Quantitative Analysis of the Assize Court Records, 1756–1856* (Kingston: Social History Project, Department of History, University of the West Indies, 2000), 18; Earl Jowitt and Clifford Walsh, eds., *Jowitt's Dictionary of English Law*, 2nd ed., vol. 1, *A–K* (London: Sweet and Maxwell, 1977).

13. Sligo to Glenelg, no. 77, 7 August 1835, CO 137/201.

14. Brereton, "Family Strategies", 105.

15. Sligo to Charles Grant, no. 124, 5 June 1835, enclosed report on the case by Special Justices Marlton, Walsh and Thomas, CO 137/199.

16. Sligo to Glenelg, no. 158, 13 October 1835, CO 137/203. No other legal action was brought against Thornhill.

17. Smith to Glenelg, no. 210, 13 November 1837, enclosed *Minutes of Proceedings at Brown's Town, St Ann's, 1837* (minutes of inquiry into complaints by various missionaries, hereafter cited as *BTCM*), evidence of Edward Fearon, 208–9, CO 137/221. The term "busha" was commonly used by enslaved persons, apprentices and some freed persons to refer to those in positions of authority, especially on the plantation, such as plantation owners, attorneys and overseers.

18. Smith to Glenelg, no. 210, 13 November 1837, enclosed *BTJW*, evidence of William Dalling, 161–63, Joseph Lawrence, 167–68, and Amelia Lawrence, 168–69, CO 137/221.

19. Smith to Glenelg, no. 150, 13 August 1838, CO 137/229.

20. Sligo to Glenelg, no. 374, 10 March 1836, enclosed report of Dr Cooke, CO 137/215.

21. *BTCM*, evidence of Janette Saunders, 212–13.

22. Extracts from the *Anti-Slavery Reporter*, 10 January 1835 to 1 December 1837, from Despatches from US Consuls in Kingston, Jamaica, 1796–1906, University of the West Indies (microfilm).

23. Sligo to Glenelg, no. 523, 9 July 1836, enclosed report of Special Justice Chamberlaine, CO 137/216.

24. Thome and Kimball, *Emancipation in the West Indies*, 114.

25. Smith to Glenelg, no. 172, 8 September 1837, enclosed report of Stipendiary Magistrates Bell and Fishbourne, CO 137/220.

26. Smith to Glenelg, no. 128, 12 June 1837, enclosed report of Stipendiary Magistrate Marlton, CO 137/220; Sligo to Spring Rice, no. 121, 29 December 1834, enclosed *Report of the Committee of the House of Assembly Appointed to Enquire into the Causes of the General Discontent Among the Apprentices*, 1834, evidence of John Davy, Esq., CO 137/194; Sligo to Glenelg, no. 452, 7 May 1836, enclosed report of Stipendiary Magistrate Hawkins, CO 137/215.

27. Sligo to Glenelg, no. 182, 4 November 1835, enclosed report of Special Justice Bourne, CO 137/204; Sligo to Glenelg, no. 401, 20 April 1836, enclosed report of Special Justice Grant, CO 137/215.

28. See the discussion in chapter 1 on the views of Edward Long, Mrs A.C. Carmichael and others on the parental capabilities of blacks.

29. See chapter 1 for a full discussion on the "marginalization" of the black male.

30. Thome and Kimball, *Emancipation in the West Indies*, 103.

31. Mimi Sheller, "Quasheba, Mother, Queen: Black Women's Public Leadership and

Political Protest in Post-emancipation Jamaica, 1834–1865", *Slavery and Abolition* 19, no. 3 (December 1988): 94.

32. Sligo to Glenelg, no. 103, 6 September 1835, enclosed reports of Stipendiary Magistrates Thomas Davies and Ralph Cocking, respectively, CO 137/202.

33. Thomas Holt, *The Problem of Freedom: Race, Labor, and Politics in Jamaica and Britain, 1832–1938* (Kingston: Ian Randle, 1992), 95.

34. Sligo to Charles Grant, no. 15, 15 June 1835, enclosed report of Stipendiary Magistrate Henry Kent, CO 137/225. These cases from Old England, Trafalgar and Lower Lucky Valley are to be found in Sligo to Glenelg, no. 119, 18 September 1835, enclosed report of Dr Palmer, CO 137/225.

35. Sligo to Glenelg, no. 355, 25 February 1836, enclosed report of Stipendiary Magistrate Lyon and letter from Stipendiary Magistrate Ewart, CO 137/209.

36. See chapter 1 for a discussion of West African influences on black familial culture.

37. W. Henry Anderson to Glenelg, 20 July 1837, enclosed report of the proceedings of *Mason v. Oldrey*, CO 137/224.

38. *Report of the Select Committee of Parliament Appointed to Inquire into the Working of the Apprenticeship System in the Colonies, with the Minutes of Evidence, Appendix and Index*, 1836 (hereafter cited as *WAS*), Captain Oldrey's evidence questions, PP 1836 (560) XV, minute nos. 2874–2940.

39. Burn, *Emancipation and Apprenticeship*, 227.

40. Anderson to Glenelg, 20 July 1837, CO 137/224. Captain Oldrey believed that one of the reasons why Mason later brought an action against him was because Oldrey had brought this case to public notice.

41. See chapter 1 for a discussion of this principle of commitment to the collectivity. Also see Sudarkasa, "African Heritage", 43.

42. At a grand inquest held at the August 1836 quarter sessions in St Thomas-in-the-Vale, chaired by Nicholas Gyles, both Harris and Palmer, accused of favouritism towards the apprentices, were adjudged "incapable of administering His Majesty's Special Commission". This event may have contributed to Dr Palmer's decision to accompany the apprentices to Spanish Town. Elgin to Stanley, no. 17, 4 February 1845, enclosed memorial of solicitor Charles Harvey, CO 137/283.

43. Elgin to Stanley, no. 17, 4 February 1845, enclosed memorial along with apprentices' affidavits, CO 137/238. Although this case occurred in 1836, it was not until 1845, when Harvey requested compensation for expenses incurred on behalf of the apprentices, that the details of the case emerged in these documents.

44. Ibid.

45. Ibid.

46. Ibid.

47. Other apprenticed family members who used this medium were Peter Atkinson

and Donald Grant. Smith to Glenelg, no. 210, 13 November 1837, enclosed *BTJW*, evidence of Peter Atkinson, 166, and *BTCM*, evidence of Julian Taylor, the woman with whom Grant lived before his death, 204, CO 137/221.

48. Sligo to Spring Rice, no. 25, 28 August 1834, with enclosed deposition of Catherine Pindar, CO 137/192.

49. Ibid.

50. Smith to Glenelg, no. 210, 13 November 1837, enclosed *BTJW* and *BTCM*, CO 137/221.

51. Ibid. An examination of the minutes of proceedings reveals that at the two sittings of the commission, a total of 117 apprentices gave evidence. Of this number, 57 were verified, by their own statements or by the statements of other witnesses, as family members. One cannot conclude that the other 60 were not family members, but there was no evidentiary basis on which to categorize them as such.

52. Ibid. *BTJW*, evidence of Mary-Ann Bell, 160, Susan White, 171–72, Bella Richards, 189, Mary James, 174, Leanty Thomas, 187–88; *BTCM*, evidence of Margaret Christie, 251, and Peggy Christie, 259.

53. Sheller, "Quasheba", 93.

54. Smith to Glenelg, no. 210, 13 November 1837, CO 137/221.

55. Smith to Glenelg, no. 68, 20 April 1838, CO 137/227.

56. Smith to Glenelg, no. 210, 13 November 1837, and enclosed circular to custodes, CO 137/221.

57. Burn, *Emancipation and Apprenticeship*, 330, 343; Holt, *Problem of Freedom*, 105.

58. Smith to Glenelg, no. 74, 6 April 1839, enclosed report of Stipendiary Magistrate Walsh, CO 137/238.

59. Wilmot, "Emancipation in Action"; Douglas Hall, "The Flight from the Estates Reconsidered: The British West Indies, 1838–1842", in Beckles and Shepherd, *Caribbean Freedom*; Woodville Marshall, "Notes on Peasant Development in the West Indies since 1838", in Beckles and Shepherd, *Caribbean Freedom*; Veront Satchell, *From Plots to Plantations: Land Transactions in Jamaica, 1866–1900* (Kingston: Institute of Social and Economic Research, University of the West Indies, 1990).

60. Smith to Glenelg, no. 37, 5 February 1839, enclosed report of Stipendiary Justice McLeod, CO 137/237.

61. Smith to Glenelg, no. 74, 6 April 1839, enclosed reports of Stipendiary Magistrates Fishbourne and Hewitt, CO 137/238.

62. Ibid.

63. Smith to Normanby, no. 103, 14 May 1839, enclosed report of Stipendiary Magistrate Daly, CO 137/238.

64. Smith to Glenelg, no. 53, 25 February 1839, enclosed report of Stipendiary Magistrate Gurley, CO 137/237.

65. Smith to Normanby, no. 113, 28 May 1839, enclosed report of Stipendiary Magistrates Fishbourne and Hewitt, CO 137/238. The sixth clause of the local Act for the Abolition of Apprenticeship, 1838, exempted the very old and the infirm from payment of rental until 1 June 1839.

66. Smith to Glenelg, no. 182, 24 September 1838, enclosed report of Stipendiary Magistrate Lyon, CO 137/232.

67. Smith to Normanby, no. 117, 17 June 1839, enclosures, CO 137/239.

68. Smith to Glenelg, no. 74, 6 April 1839, enclosed report of Stipendiary Magistrate Henry Walsh, CO 137/238.

69. Smith to Normanby, no. 110, 27 May 1839, enclosed report of Stipendiary Magistrates Lyon and Kelly, CO 137/238.

70. Ibid., enclosed letter of S.G. Barrett.

71. Smith to Normanby, no. 167, 4 September 1839, enclosures, CO 137/239.

72. Ibid.

73. Ibid.; Holt, *Problem of Freedom*, 138.

74. Charles Grey to Earl Grey, no. 68, 28 July 1851, enclosures, CO 137/310.

75. Eyre to Cardwell, no. 117, 25 April 1865, enclosed "The Humble Petition of the Poor People of Jamaica and Parish of Saint Ann's", CO 137/390.

76. Eyre to Cardwell, no. 143, 7 June 1865, enclosed "Resolutions of a Public Meeting held at the Court House, Spanish Town", CO 137/391.

77. Eyre to Cardwell, no. 117, 25 April 1865, enclosed "Petition of the Poor People of Jamaica and Parish of Saint Ann's", CO 137/390.

78. Darling to Newcastle, no. 130, 17 September 1861, enclosed "The Humble Petition of the Mechanics and Labourers of Saint Joseph's District in the Parish of Saint Andrew", CO 137/356.

79. CO 137/293, Charles Grey to Earl Grey, no. 91, 20 September 1847, enclosed letter from Hon. John Salmon.

80. Barkly to Newcastle, no. 24, 21 February 1854, enclosed report of Stipendiary Magistrate Thomas Witter Jackson, CO 137/322.

81. Grant to Kimberley, no. 66, 23 April 1873, enclosed report on education, CO 137/470.

82. Barkly to Newcastle, no. 24, 21 February 1854, enclosed report of Stipendiary Magistrate Charles Lake, CO 137/322.

83. Grant to Buckingham, no. 27, 11 February 1868, CO 137/431.

84. Grant to Buckingham, no. 23, 10 February 1868, CO 137/430; Grant to Buckingham, no. 27, 11 February 1868, CO 137/431.

85. Grant to Buckingham, no. 23, 10 February 1868, CO 137/430; Grant to Buckingham, no. 24, 10 February 1868, enclosed report of the custos of St Ann's, Charles Royes, CO 137/430.

86. Grant to Kimberley, no. 102, 9 June 1873, enclosed report of Justice Bruce, CO 137/471.

87. Ibid., enclosures.

88. Musgrave to Kimberley, no. 262, 2 October 1880, with enclosed minute papers, CO 137/496.

89. Ibid., enclosures.

90. Musgrave to Kimberley, no. 324, 8 November 1880, enclosures, CO 137/497.

91. Ibid.

92. Barkly to Newcastle, no. 24, 21 February 1854, enclosed report of Stipendiary Magistrate Alexander Fyfe, CO 137/322. Also see the discussion on negative portrayals of black parenthood and male marginality in the family in chapter 1 of this work.

93. *CJP*, 2.

Chapter 3

1. Sligo to Glenelg, no. 470, 24 May 1836, enclosed letter of Special Justice William Hewitt, CO 137/215.

2. Demetrius Eudell, *The Political Languages of Emancipation in the British Caribbean and the US South* (Chapel Hill: University of North Carolina Press, 2002), 76.

3. Marshall, "We Be Wise", 17.

4. Litwack, *Been in the Storm*, 230.

5. Rebecca J. Scott, "Former Slaves: Responses to Emancipation in Cuba", in Beckles and Shepherd, *Caribbean Freedom*, 22.

6. See, for example, Litwack, *Been in the Storm*; Foner, *Reconstruction*; Gutman, *Black Family*; Marshall, "We Be Wise"; Brereton, "Family Strategies".

7. Brereton, "Family Strategies", 94.

8. Litwack, *Been in the Storm*, 230–31.

9. In the case of the United States, the sources show antecedents of reconstitution during slavery, such as reference to incidents of running away and the occasional approval of weekend visits by benevolent masters. However, the evidence of such occasions is infinitesimal compared to that of post-slavery efforts at reconstitution. See Litwack, *Been in the Storm*, 230–35.

10. Sligo to Glenelg, no. 182, 4 November 1835, enclosed report of T. Watkins Jones, CO 137/204.

11. Thome and Kimball, *Emancipation in the West Indies*, 103.

12. Smith to Glenelg, no. 210, 13 November 1837, enclosed *BTCM*, evidence of Jane Grove, 233, and Hamilton Brown, 234, CO 137/221.

13. Joseph Sturge and Thomas Harvey, *The West Indies in 1837, Being the Journal of a Visit to Antigua, Montserrat, Dominica, St Lucia, Barbados, and Jamaica; Undertaken for the Purpose of Ascertaining the Actual Condition of the Negro Population of those Islands* (London: Hamilton, Adams, 1838), lii, liii. For more on initiatives towards family reunions during slavery, see Bush, *Slave Women*, 108.

14. Smith to Glenelg, no. 210, 13 November 1837, enclosed *BTJW*, evidence of Peter William Atkinson, 166, William Mills, 167, Mr Senior, 170, Alexander Mills, 173, and James Finlayson, 176, CO 137/221.

15. Sligo to Glenelg, no. 103, 6 September 1835, enclosed report of Stipendiary Magistrate Cocking, CO 137/202.

16. Also prejudicial to apprentices' ability to visit family members was clause 27 of the local Abolition Act, December 1833, which punished as a vagabond any apprentice found wandering "beyond the limits of the plantation, without permission". For these laws, see *WAS*, appendix to the report, 14, 22.

17. Sligo to Spring Rice, no. 31, 12 September 1834, enclosures, CO 137/193.

18. Ibid.

19. Ibid.

20. Sligo to Spring Rice, no. 26, 29 August 1834, enclosed reply of Spring Rice to Sligo, CO 137/192.

21. Sligo to Glenelg, no. 316, 10 February 1836, enclosure, CO 137/209.

22. Smith to Glenelg, no. 128, 12 June 1837, enclosed letter of E.D. Baynes, CO 137/220.

23. Sligo to Glenelg, no. 470, 24 May 1836, enclosed letter of Special Justice William Hewitt, CO 137/215.

24. Smith to Glenelg, no. 131, 24 June 1837, enclosures, CO 137/220. The Imperial Act of Abolition, clause 9, prohibited the separation of families through the transfer of apprentices. However, this applied to attached praedial apprentices only, not to unattached praedials. Also, a transfer could only be carried out after this had been approved by a justice.

25. Smith to Glenelg, no. 3, 4 January 1838, enclosed letter of Special Justice J. Hulme, enclosed minute paper from Spedding to Stephen, CO 137/226.

26. *BTCM*, evidence of John James, 198, Eliza James, 198, and William Flemming, 198–99.

27. Smith to Glenelg, no. 128, 12 June 1837, enclosed report of Special Justice Thomas Davies, CO 137/220; Smith to Glenelg, no. 172, 8 September 1837, enclosed report of Special Justice James K. Dawson, CO 137/220.

28. *BTJW*, evidence of James Finlayson, 175–76.

29. Ibid.

30. Sligo to Charles Grant, no. 124, 5 June 1835, enclosed report on court proceedings by Special Justices Marlton, Walsh and Thomas, enclosed letter of Stipendiary

Magistrate Jackson, CO 137/199. Also see Sligo to Charles Grant, no. 27, 22 June 1835, enclosed valuation return, CO 137/199.

31. Sligo to Glenelg, no. 158, 13 October 1835, CO 137/203.

32. Litwack, *Been in the Storm*, 230.

33. For references to apprentices' priorities regarding the purchasing of their relatives' freedom, see Smith to Glenelg, no. 128, 12 June 1837, enclosed report of Special Justice Thomas Davies, CO 137/220; Smith to Glenelg, no. 172, 8 September 1837, enclosed report of Special Justice James K. Dawson, CO 137/220.

34. Sligo to Glenelg, no. 532, 13 July 1836, enclosed valuation report of Special Justice Hawkins, CO 137/216; Sligo to Glenelg, no. 499, 23 June 1836, enclosed valuation return of Special Justice Higgins, CO 137/216.

35. Higman, "Slave Family and Household", 271.

36. Sligo to Glenelg, no. 470, 24 May 1836, enclosed valuation report of Special Justice Moresby, CO 137/215.

37. Sligo to Charles Grant, no. 27, 22 June 1835, enclosed valuation return, CO 137/199.

38. Sligo to Glenelg, no. 129, 21 September 1835, enclosed valuation return, CO 137/202.

39. Sligo to Charles Grant, no. 27, 22 June 1835, enclosed valuation return, CO 137/199.

40. Sligo to Glenelg, no. 129, 21 September 1835, enclosed valuation return, CO 137/202.

41. Sligo to Glenelg, no. 499, 23 June 1836, CO 137/216.

42. For these reports from Lyon, see Sturge and Harvey, *West Indies in 1837*, appendix, lxxxvii, lxxxviii.

43. Smith to Glenelg, no. 54, 26 January 1837, enclosed report of Special Justice James Harris, CO 137/225.

44. Brereton, "Family Strategies", 82.

45. Litwack, *Been in the Storm*, 235.

46. Smith to Normanby, no. 110, 27 May 1839, enclosed report of a public meeting, Falmouth, CO 137/238.

47. Brereton, "Family Strategies", 94.

48. Smith to Glenelg, no. 74, 6 April 1839, enclosed reports of Stipendiary Magistrates Fishbourne and Hewitt, CO 137/238.

49. Smith to Glenelg, no. 182, 24 September 1838, enclosed report of Stipendiary Magistrate John Daughtrey, CO 137/232.

50. *Report of the Select Committee of the House of Commons on the West India Colonies*, 1842 (hereafter cited as *WIC*), evidence of Hinton Spalding, PP 1842 (479) 13, minute nos. 5648–5654.

51. Ibid., minute nos. 5525–35.

52. See Verene Shepherd, "The Effects of the Abolition of Slavery on Jamaican Livestock Farms (Pens), 1834–1845", *Slavery and Abolition* 10, no. 2 (September 1989): 196–202.

53. Smith to Normanby, no. 160, 16 August 1839, enclosed report of Stipendiary Magistrate Fishbourne, CO 137/239.

54. Swithin Wilmot, *Freedom in Jamaica, Challenges and Opportunities, 1838–1865* (Kingston: Jamaica Information Service, 1997), 6, 11.

55. James M. Phillippo, *Jamaica: Its Past and Present State* (London: John Snow, 1843), 336.

56. Sligo to Glenelg, no. 48, 7 July 1835, enclosed report of Stipendiary Magistrate John Daughtrey, CO 137/200.

57. Phillippo, *Jamaica*, 231–32. The conclusion that there was an increase in marriages among blacks when compared to the period of enslavement rests largely on stipendiary, missionary and other source-related reports of an increased number of marriages. See Metcalfe to Russell, no. 129, 20 November 1840, enclosure; *Extracts from Papers Printed by Order of the House of Commons, 1839, relative to the West Indies*, PP 1839, no. 107, part 1 (3) in Smith to Normanby, 3 July 1839, CO 137/250; Elgin to Stanley, no. 79, 2 September 1845, enclosed report of Stipendiary Magistrate Hall Pringle, CO 137/284; Metcalfe to Russell, no. 50, 30 March 1840, CO 137/248; Smith to Normanby, no. 141, 19 July 1839, enclosed report of Dr Sam Stewart, CO 137/239; *WIC*, evidence of Samuel Barrett, minute nos. 5263–64, and Alexander Geddes, minute no. 6912.

58. Addington to Stephen, no. 2770 Jamaica, 26 October 1847, enclosed letter from British consul general in Cuba, Joseph Crawford, CO 137/294.

59. Charles Grey to Earl Grey, no. 64, 7 July 1848, enclosed letter from H. Evelyn and enclosed report from Thomas Hylton, CO 137/299.

60. Addington to Merivale, no. 9292 Jamaica, 8 November, 1851, enclosed reply of Lord Grey to Sir Charles Grey, CO 137/312.

61. Charles Grey to Earl Grey, no. 51, 22 May 1847, enclosed petition of Cuffee Kelson, CO 137/292.

62. Ibid. Clause 1 of the 1806 Foreign Slave Trade Abolition Act declared that the removal of a slave to a foreign possession thereafter was illegal and would result in "the forfeiture of such slave to the Crown".

63. Ibid., enclosed petition of Cuffee Kelson.

64. Consul General Crawford to Aberdeen, "Slave Trade" no. 35, 8 November 1844, CO 137/281.

65. Dr R.R. Madden, "late Superintendent at the Havana", to James Stephen, 1 June 1841 (copy to the governor of Jamaica, 22 June 1841), CO 137/260.

66. Aberdeen to Crawford, "Slave Trade" no. 2, 31 January 1846, CO 137/290.

67. Elgin to Stanley, no. 100, 4 December 1845, CO 137/285. Although Elgin made reference (by jottings in the margin of this despatch) to the transmission of the 1845 affidavits of Cuffee and Nat Kelson, these were never located, either in subsequent despatches or in the Foreign Office correspondence. Cuffee's affidavit of 1845,

according to Elgin, was his first petition. These affidavits were sent in the original to Lord Stanley and were clearly never copied and placed in the sources. A subsequent mention by Governor Charles Grey in 1847 of "the matter" having been "brought by Lord Elgin to the notice of Lord Stanley in the Despatch no. 100 of December 4th, 1845 to which . . . no reply has been made", verified that Lord Stanley had been informed of the case at that point. Charles Grey to Earl Grey, no. 51, 22 May 1847, CO 137/292. Thus, in the absence of this first petition/affidavit of Cuffee Kelson, I had to rely on his second petition (from 1847) for important information about his case. Although this is a limitation of the source, there is no reason to believe that what Cuffee had to say about his family in the second petition would have differed significantly from what he said in the first. Thus, the validity of any conclusions drawn on the basis of the second petition should not be an issue.

68. Charles Grey to Earl Grey, no. 51, 22 May 1847, enclosed petition of Cuffee Kelson, CO 137/292.

69. Consul General Crawford to Aberdeen, no. 23, 10 December 1845, CO 137/290.

70. Aberdeen to Turnbull, no. 168 Jamaica, 31 January 1846, CO 137/290.

71. Aberdeen to Crawford, "Slave Trade" no. 2, 31 January 1846, CO 137/290.

72. Consul General Crawford to Aberdeen, no. 23, 10 December 1845, CO 137/290; Aberdeen to Crawford, "Slave Trade" no. 2, 31 January 1846, CO 137/290.

73. Aberdeen to Turnbull, no. 168 Jamaica, 31 January 1846, CO 137/290.

74. Charles Grey to Earl Grey, no. 51, 22 May 1847, enclosed petition of Cuffee Kelson, CO 137/292.

75. Elgin to Stanley, no. 52, 1 December 1842, enclosed deposition of Wellington, CO 137/264.

76. Elgin to Stanley, no. 16, 20 July 1842, CO 137/263.

77. Strangways to Stephen, no. 378 Jamaica, 13 February 1839, enclosed letters of Palmerston and de Onis, CO 137/245.

78. Ibid., enclosed letter of the Earl of Clarendon.

79. Elgin to Stanley, no. 16, 20 July 1842, enclosures, CO 137/263.

80. Elgin to Stanley, no. 52, 1 December 1842, enclosed deposition of Wellington, CO 137/264.

81. Elgin to Stanley, no. 16, 20 July 1842, enclosed letters of Turnbull, Charles Clarke and Crawford, CO 137/263.

82. Addington to Stephen, no. 2419 Jamaica, 26 November 1842, enclosed letter of Charles Clarke, CO 137/265.

83. Elgin to Stanley, no. 34, 3 October 1842, CO 137/264; Elgin to Stanley, no. 52, 1 December 1842, CO 137/263.

84. Elgin to Stanley, no. 34, 3 October 1842, CO 137/263.

85. Elgin to Stanley, no. 52, 1 December 1842, enclosed deposition of Wellington, CO 137/264.

86. Ibid.

87. Addington to Stephen, no. 2770 Jamaica, 26 October 1847, enclosed letter of Consul General Crawford, CO 137/294.

88. Ibid.

89. Charles Grey to Earl Grey, no. 106, 21 November 1848, CO 137/298.

90. The only other "black boys" from Jamaica referred to by the sources as being enslaved in Cuba by 1848 were Saulman and William. No evidence of their being found was located in the sources.

91. Addington to Merivale, no. 331 Jamaica, 12 January 1849, and enclosed minute papers, CO 137/305.

92. Earl Grey to Charles Grey, no. 250, 31 January 1849, CO 137/298.

93. Charles Grey to Earl Grey, no. 113, 27 December 1851, enclosed circular from US consul in Jamaica Robert Harrison and enclosed letter from British consul to New York Anthony Barclay, CO 137/311.

94. Ibid., enclosed letter from Consul Barclay; Addington to Merivale, no. 9292 Jamaica, 8 November 1851, CO 137/312.

95. For details on the boys' kidnapping, see Palmerston to Lord Grey, no. 9399 Jamaica, 11 November 1851, enclosed letter of British consul to New York Anthony Barclay, CO 137/312.

96. Charles Grey to Earl Grey, no. 113, 27 December 1851, enclosed letter from Consul Barclay, CO 137/311.

97. Darling to Newcastle, no. 63, April 1860, enclosed letter from Stipendiary Magistrate Richard Chamberlaine, CO 137/349; Darling to Newcastle, no. 74, 23 May 1860, enclosed deposition of Margaret Vassal Williams, CO 137/349.

98. Darling to Newcastle, no. 74, 23 May 1860, enclosed deposition of Sarah Campbell, CO 137/349.

99. Ibid., enclosed deposition of Penelope Campbell.

100. Darling to Newcastle, no. 63, 30 April 1860, enclosed extract from the *Philadelphia Inquirer*, CO 137/349.

101. Hammond to Fortesque, no. 4601 Jamaica, 7 May 1860, enclosures, CO 137/352.

102. Howard Hughes was kidnapped from Antigua when he was ten years old by a foreign captain who sold him into slavery in Puerto Rico. See the *Colonial Standard*, Friday, 10 September 1852.

103. Foner, *Reconstruction*, 84.

Chapter 4

1.   *CJP*, appendix A, evidence of Rev. George Sargeant, 115.

2.   Charles Grey to Earl Grey, no. 68, 28 July 1851, enclosed petition, CO 137/310.

3.   Moore and Johnson, *Neither Led nor Driven*, 209–11, 318.

4.   Eudell, *Political Languages*, 17.

5.   Long, *History of Jamaica*, 2:353, 414–5. See also Carmichael, *Domestic Manners*, 1:269–71; Edwards, *History of the British Colonies*, 2:148.

6.   Sir Henry Barkly to the Duke of Newcastle, no. 24, 21 February 1854, enclosed report of Stipendiary Magistrate R. Emery, CO 137/322; Eyre to Cardwell, no. 90, 19 April 1865, CO 137/390.

7.   Bryan, *Jamaican People*, 124.

8.   Litwack, *Been in the Storm*, 238, 366.

9.   Thome and Kimball, *Emancipation in the West Indies*, 114.

10. Miller, *Men at Risk*, 130–36, 167; Patterson, *Sociology of Slavery*, 167–68; Ladner, "Racism and Tradition", 276.

11. Froude, *English in the West Indies*, 198.

12. Sligo to Glenelg, no. 374, 10 March 1836, enclosed report of Dr S.H. Cooke, CO 137/215.

13. Sligo to Glenelg, no. 401, 20 April 1836, enclosed report of Special Justice Gregg, CO 137/215.

14. Sligo to Glenelg, no. 119, 18 September 1835, enclosed report of Stipendiary Magistrate Palmer, CO 137/225.

15. Sligo to Glenelg, no. 401, 20 April 1836, enclosed report of Stipendiary Magistrate Cocking. See also reports by Stipendiary Magistrates Fishbourne and Dawson, CO 137/215.

16. Sligo to Glenelg, no. 339, 19 February 1836, enclosed reports of T. McCornock and Custos Bernard, CO 137/209.

17. Sligo to Glenelg, no. 401, 20 April 1836, enclosed report of Stipendiary Magistrate Lyon, CO 137/215.

18. Smith to Glenelg, no. 51, 28 March 1838, CO 137/226.

19. Sligo to Glenelg, no. 182, 4 November 1835, enclosed report of Special Justice J. Daughtrey, CO 137/204.

20. Smith to Glenelg, no. 128, 12 June 1837, enclosed report of Special Justice J. Daughtrey, CO 137/220.

21. Berkeley to Gladstone, no. 17, 23 July 1846, enclosed report of Stipendiary Magistrate Bell, CO 137/289. See also reports of Stipendiary Magistrates Cocking, Ramsay and Walsh. For more reports on "parental apathy", see Elgin to Stanley, no. 197, 20 December 1843, enclosures, CO 137/275.

22. Elgin to Stanley, no. 8, 9 January 1844, CO 137/278.

23. Elgin to Gladstone, no. 52, 6 May 1846, CO 137/288.

24. For references to clauses of the act, see CO 137/310, Charles Grey to Earl Grey, no. 68, 28 July 1851, enclosures; Trestrail to Earl Grey, no. 5526 Jamaica, 23 June 1851, enclosed letter to Earl Grey from the Committee of the Protestant Dissenting Deputies, CO 137/313.

25. Charles Grey to Earl Grey, no. 68, 28 July 1851, enclosed petitions, CO 137/310. Among the groups which petitioned for disallowance of the act were the Baptist congregations of East Queen Street and Hanover Street in Kingston; Salter's Hill in St James; St Ann's Bay, Ocho Rios and Coultart Grove in St Ann; and dissenting congregations in Sturge Town, Salem, Brown's Town and Bethany, St Ann.

26. Trestrail to Earl Grey, no. 5526 Jamaica, 23 June 1851, enclosed letter from Hull Terrell and minute papers, CO 137/313.

27. Charles Grey to Earl Grey, no. 68, 28 July 1851, CO 137/310.

28. Bell to Labouchere, no. 58, 25 November 1856, enclosed report of Stipendiary Magistrate Richard Hill, CO 137/332.

29. Bell to Labouchere, no. 24, 24 March 1857, enclosed report of Stipendiary Magistrate Charles Lake, CO 137/334.

30. For these references to the Industrial Schools' Act of 1857, see Waddington to Merivale, no. 4908 Jamaica, 15 May 1858, enclosed report by Turner, CO 137/341. Although the Industrial Schools' Act used the phrases "reformatory" and "industrial schools" to imply the existence of these as separate institutions, before 1858 both were commonly referred to as "reformatories". After 1858, the two terms were used interchangeably in the sources. Reformatories, because of their emphasis on industrial training, were to all intents and purposes industrial schools. Governor Darling, for example, used the terms interchangeably (Darling to Labouchere, no. 40, 11 March 1858, CO 137/336). Also, "industrial schools" should not be confused with "industrial education", the latter being a reference to curriculum choices and the former being a reference to the institution.

31. Ibid. See also Darling to Labouchere, no. 40, 11 March 1858, CO 137/336.

32. Darling to Newcastle, no. 4, 21 January 1861, enclosed report of the Kingston and St Andrew's Reformatory for Girls, CO 137/353.

33. Darling to Newcastle, no. 28, 28 January 1860, enclosed report of St George's Reformatory, CO 137/348.

34. Darling to Newcastle, no. 12, 20 January 1862, CO 137/364.

35. *Report of the Commissioners of Inquiry upon the Government Reformatory at Stony Hill*, 1877 (hereafter cited as *CGR*), 17.

36. Grant to Buckingham, no. 63, 23 March 1868, enclosed report on the boys' reformatory, CO 137/432.

37. Eyre to Cardwell, no. 90, 19 April 1865, enclosed report of the Royal Society of Arts in Jamaica, CO 137/390.

38. Grant to Granville, no. 84, 8 April 1869, CO 137/441.

39. *CGR*, 2.

40. Cardwell to Storks, no. 47, 29 January 1866, CO 137/388.

41. Grey to Carnarvon, no. 222, 22 December 1876, enclosed report on evidence taken before the Reformatory Committee, CO 137/482.

42. *CJP*, appendix A, evidence of Rev. C. Douet, 82–83.

43. Grant to Granville, no. 186, 7 August 1869, enclosed letter from the superintendent of the boys' reformatory, CO 137/443.

44. *CGR*, 3.

45. Grant to Granville, no. 186, 7 August 1869, enclosed letter from the superintendent of the boys' reformatory, CO 137/443.

46. Newton to Hicks Beach, no. 365, 18 December 1879, CO 137/491.

47. One of the weaknesses of reformatory practice had been the housing of "criminal children" in the same institution as "destitute" children. This had strengthened the opposition of parents to their children being sent to reformatories. The colonial state was concerned that parents continued to view the reformatory as "a place of punishment rather than as a place for reformation". Thus, both the Commission of Inquiry on the Government Reformatory at Stony Hill and the Commission on the Juvenile Population recommended separation of these two categories of children into different institutions. Law 34 of 1881 provided for the establishment of two government industrial schools (for non-criminal children), one in Montego Bay and one in Kingston. Separate accommodation was to be provided for boys and girls. The law also provided for the reintroduction of certified private institutions. Musgrave to Kimberley, no. 23, 29 January 1881, enclosed reply of Kimberly to Musgrave, no. 79, 31 March 1881, and minute papers, CO 137/499.

48. For details on Law 34 of 1881, see *Laws of Jamaica, from Law 1 of 1880 to Law 20 of 1886* (University of the West Indies, Main Library, Mona); see also Musgrave to Kimberly, no. 23, 29 January 1881, CO 137/499. For references to the recommendations of the commissioners, see *CJP*, 7.

49. Ibid., with reference to Law 34 of 1881. For references to the views of witnesses before the commission, see *CJP*, appendix A, evidence of Bicknell, 19. For increased reports of "excessive punishment" of children, see the *Trelawny and Public Advertiser*, 2 August 1880, and *Colonial Standard,* 6 April 1875.

50. *CJP*, appendix A, evidence of Henry John Bicknell, 18, Joseph Reid, 91–92, and Rev. Pierce, 102.

51. For details on Law 34 of 1881, see *Laws of Jamaica*; also, Musgrave to Kimberley, no. 23, 29 January 1881, CO 137/499.

52. For reports on the tendency of some children to assert their independence, see *CJP*, minutes of evidence taken in St Thomas-in-the-East, evidence of James Harrison, 14, 18, and Arthur James, 22. For reference to expectations of returns on money spent, see *CJP*, 8. Note, however, that while this issue was of relevance to the thesis, it was not the focus of this chapter and therefore was not discussed in detail.

53. Musgrave to Hicks Beach, no. 234, 4 December 1878, enclosed report of the superintendent of the reformatories, CO 137/488.

54. Berkeley to Gladstone, no. 17, 23 July 1846, enclosed reports of Stipendiary Magistrates Walsh, Ramsay, Bell, Cocking and Kelly, CO 137/289.

55. Charles Grey to Earl Grey, no. 91, 20 September 1847, enclosed letter from John Salmon, CO 137/293.

56. Barkly to Newcastle, no. 24, 21 February 1854, enclosed report of Stipendiary Magistrate Dillon and enclosed reply of Newcastle, CO 137/322.

57. Barkly to George Grey, no. 101, 18 September 1854, CO 137/324.

58. Ibid., enclosed report of Stipendiary Magistrate Richard Hill.

59. Ibid.

60. Rushworth to Granville, no. 131, 21 May 1870, enclosed report of government inspector for schools for 1869, CO 137/449.

61. Grant to Kimberley, no. 103, 4 August 1871, CO 137/457. Model schools were the government's attempts at establishing institutions in which the emphasis was placed on industrial education. Reports that the Port Antonio model school was doing well may have been the result of a decision to remit the school fees of all the children who joined the industrial classes.

62. *CJP*, appendix A, evidence of Nuttall, 13. Regarding these recommendations of the commissioners, see page 9 of the report.

63. Musgrave to Kimberley, no. 138, 16 June 1880, enclosed report of inspector of schools John Savage, CO 137/495.

64. Musgrave to Kimberley, no. 138, 16 June 1880, CO 137/495.

65. Kimberley to Musgrave, no. 104, 11 September 1880, CO 137/495.

66. Musgrave to Kimberley, no. 283, 16 October 1880, CO 137/496.

67. Kimberley to Musgrave, no. 180, 14 December 1880, CO 137/496.

68. Musgrave to Kimberley, no. 267, 17 August 1881, enclosed rules for poor relief, CO 137/501. There were many in need who refused to apply for relief because of the stigma attached.

69. *CJP*, 3.

70. *CJP*, minutes of evidence, appendix A, evidence of William Lee, 47.

71. Barkly to George Grey, no. 32, 20 March 1855, enclosed report of Stipendiary Magistrate Charles Lake, CO 137/326. For references to orphaned black children being adopted by other family members or others, see Charles Grey to Earl Grey,

no. 16, 26 February 1851, CO 137/309; Charles Grey to Earl Grey, no. 68, 28 July 1851, enclosed petition of members of the East Queen Street Baptist Church, CO 137/310.

72. Eyre to Cardwell, no. 60, 22 March 1865, CO 137/388. For the comparable American philosophy, see Litwack, *Been in the Storm*, 237.

73. Cardwell to Eyre, no. 213, 1 June 1865, CO 137/388.

74. Cardwell to Storks, no. 47, 29 January 1866, CO 137/388.

75. Musgrave to Kimberley, no. 63, 1 March 1881, enclosed observations on Law 3 of 1881, CO 137/499. See also *Laws of Jamaica*.

76. Barkly to Newcastle, no. 24, 21 February 1854, enclosed report of Stipendiary Magistrate Thomas Witter Jackson, CO 137/322; Grant to Kimberley, no. 66, 23 April 1873, enclosed report on education, CO 137/470.

77. Froude, *English in the West Indies*, 198.

78. It was not possible, as a general procedure, to consistently disaggregate the concept of "parents" in this chapter, as the sources related to this discussion did not usually separate the male and female parental roles from each other in relation to the colonial state's attempts to assert control over children.

Chapter 5

1. *JRC*, part 2, evidence of Grace Cherrington, 272–73.

2. For emphasis on socio-economic causation, see Douglas Hall, *Free Jamaica, 1838–1865: An Economic History* (New Haven: Yale University Press, 1959); for discussion of causation and the roles of "Bogle and his men", see Don Robotham, " 'The Notorious Riot': The Socio-Economic and Political Bases of Paul Bogle's Revolt", Working Paper no. 28 (Kingston: Institute of Social and Economic Research, 1981), 27–97; for a focus on the roles of women in this event, see Wilmot, "Females of Abandoned Character", 290–92; for political developments in the aftermath of Morant Bay, see Roy Augier, "Before and After 1865", in Beckles and Shepherd, *Caribbean Freedom*, 170–80. For an example of a general treatment of the impact of the suppression, see Michael Craton, "Continuity Not Change: The Incidence of Unrest among Ex-Slaves in The British West Indies, 1838–1876", in Beckles and Shepherd, *Caribbean Freedom*, 196–98.

3. Clinton Hutton, " 'Colour for Colour, Skin for Skin': The Ideological Foundation of Post-Slavery Society, 1838–1865, the Jamaican Case" (PhD diss., University of the West Indies, 1997); Gad Heuman, *"The Killing Time": The Morant Bay Rebellion in Jamaica* (Knoxville: University of Tennessee Press, 1994).

4. Augier, "Before and After 1865", 174.

5.   Victor I. Reus, "Mental Disorders", in *Harrison's Principles of Internal Medicine*, ed. Anthony S. Fauci et al., 14th ed. (Columbus: McGraw-Hill, 1998), 2490.

6.   *JRC*, index to minutes of evidence, vi, vii, viii. However, 9 black family witnesses were deducted from the original 217 witnesses called, as they were repeat witnesses. Likewise, the original total of black family members was reduced by 9, from 106 to 97, for the same reason.

7.   The evidential base for this analysis is drawn only from *JRC*, part 2, section C, "Witnesses as to Deaths" (in all areas covered by the commission), and section D, "Witnesses as to Destruction of Property by Burnings". Excluded from the data collection was the section entitled "Witnesses as to the Suppression in Morant Bay and the Plantain Garden River District", as a survey of these witnesses showed that most were not black, nor were they, for the most part, victims of the suppression. Although their statements contained references to others who were flogged, shot or otherwise executed, it was not usually possible to determine the family connections of the victims mentioned. Therefore, a decision was taken not to utilize this section. Estimates must also be conservative because they do not reflect all those who were affected but did not come forward to give statements.

8.   Reus, "Mental Disorders", 2489.

9.   *JRC, part 2,* evidence of Henrietta Bailey, 969.

10.   Ibid., evidence of Maria Robinson, 938–39.

11.   Ibid., evidence of Francis Wilson, 352–53.

12.   Ibid., evidence of Eliza Berry and Mary Berry, 283–84. The Berry and Bryan families were examples of the persistence of extended family networks and of the continued practice of establishing contiguous or adjacent homes (discussed in chapter 1).

13.   Ibid., evidence of George Bryan, 147–49, and Mary Bryan, 149–50.

14.   Ibid., evidence of Grace Cherrington, 272–73.

15.   Ibid., evidence of Sarah Tyne, 961–62.

16.   Ibid., evidence of Susannah McGregor, 961–62.

17.   Ibid., evidence of Rebecca Telford, 499–500.

18.   Ibid., evidence Thomas Duncan, 528–29.

19.   Ibid., evidence of Hannah Aspitt, 484–85.

20.   Joy Lumsden, "'A Brave and Loyal People': The Role of the Maroons in the Morant Bay Rebellion in 1865", in Shepherd, *Working Slavery*, 484.

21.   *JRC*, part 2, evidence of Sarah McKindo, 500–502.

22.   Ibid., evidence of Charlotte Ross, 932–33.

23.   Ibid., evidence of Sophia Bates, 427–28.

24.   Ibid., evidence of Rosa Johnson, 487.

25.   Ibid., evidence of Robert Davis, 571.

26.   Ibid., evidence of John McLaren, 245–46.

27. Wilmot, "Females of Abandoned Character", 291–92. Also see *JRC*, evidence of David McBean, 529.

28. *JRC*, part 2, evidence of George Mac Murray, 248.

29. Ibid., evidence of Sophia Davis, 249–50.

30. The elitist stereotype of the chaotic and short-lived black union was illustrated by the views of Edward Long, who argued that "their notions of love are that it is free and transitory". Long, *History of Jamaica*, 415.

31. *JRC*, part 2, evidence of Lianta Logan, 954.

32. Ibid., evidence of Ann Mitchell, 102–4.

33. Ibid., evidence of Lucretia Mullens, 953.

34. Ibid., evidence of Catherine Johnson, 968–69.

35. Ibid., evidence of Isabella Francis, 575.

36. Ibid., evidence of Ann Cargill, 943.

37. Ibid., evidence of Rosey Young, 943.

38. Ibid., evidence of Henrietta Bailey, 969.

39. Ibid., evidence of Ann Weddorman, 250–51.

40. Ibid., evidence of Mary Ann Williams, 463–64.

41. Reus, "Mental Disorders", 2490.

42. *JRC*, part 2, evidence of Jane Brown, 466–67.

43. Ibid., evidence of Sarah McKindo, 500–502. For another reference to family members made sick by the events of the suppression, see *JRC*, part 2, evidence of Phoebe Ennis, 470–71.

44. *JRC*, part 1.

45. Abraham H. Maslow, *Toward a Psychology of Being* (New York: D. Van Nostrand, 1968), 527–34.

46. *JRC*, part 2, evidence of Ann Mackenzie, 317.

47. Ibid., evidence of Jane Wilson, 146–47.

48. Ibid., evidence of Ann Ogilvie, 975–76.

49. Ibid., evidence of Henrietta Piercy, 572.

50. Ibid., evidence of Rosa Johnson, 487.

51. Ibid., evidence of Esther Williams, 564–65.

52. Ibid., evidence of Agnes Stewart Davis, 390.

53. Ibid., evidence of Sophia Davis, 249–50.

54. Ibid., evidence of Betsy Buckley, 577.

55. Ibid., evidence of John William Hamilton, 570.

56. Ibid., evidence of Abraham Francis, 428–29, and Susannah McGregor, 433–34.

57. Ibid., evidence of Thomas Worgs, 573, and Mary Worgs, 565–66.

58. Ibid., evidence of Ann Rock, 574, Amelia Scott, 573, and Jane Wilson, 146–47.

59. Ibid., evidence of Lianta Logan, 954, and Gilbert Francis, 456–57.

60. Ibid., evidence of Phoebe Ennis, 470–71.
61. Ibid., evidence of George Mac Murray, 247–48.
62. Ibid., evidence of James Stewart, 311–13, and Sophia Davis, 249–50.
63. Ibid., evidence of Ann Mackenzie, 317.
64. Ibid., evidence of Catherine Wilson, 368–70.
65. Ibid., evidence of Rebecca Telford, 499–500, and Stephen Telford, 432–33.
66. Ibid., evidence of John Hamilton, 570, and George Mac Murray, 247–48.
67. Ibid., evidence of Sarah McKindo, 500–502, Lewis Orr, 419–20, and Sophia Davis, 249–50.
68. Ibid., evidence of Elizabeth Millet, 978–79.
69. Ibid., evidence of George Mac Murray, 247–48.
70. Ibid., evidence of Charles Walker, 307–9.
71. Ibid., evidence of William Christy Jr, 112–13, William Christy Sr, 113–14, and James Graham, 298–99.
72. Ibid., evidence of Sarah McKindo, 500–502, and Chloe Munroe, 932.
73. Ibid., evidence of John Hamilton, 570, and Grace Cherrington, 272–73.
74. Ibid., evidence of Cecelia Victoria Stewart, 271–72, Rebecca Telford, 499–500, Charlotte Ross, 932–33, and Henrietta Bailey, 938–39.
75. Ibid., evidence of Mrs Eleanor Shortridge, 38–41.
76. Grant to Carnarvon, no. 6, 22 August 1866, CO 137/406.
77. Grant to Carnarvon, no. 33, 24 October 1866, enclosed extract from the *Jamaica Guardian*, CO 137/407.
78. Grant to Carnarvon, no. 6, 22 August 1866, CO 137/406.
79. Storks to Cardwell, confidential, 23 February 1866, CO 137/399.
80. Storks to Cardwell, confidential, 10 March 1866, CO 137/401.
81. Grant to Carnarvon, no. 33, 24 October 1866, CO 137/407.
82. Carnarvon to Grant, no. 15, 16 November 1866, CO 137/407.
83. Storks to Cardwell, confidential, 18 February 1866, CO 137/399.
84. Grant to Carnarvon, no. 72, 24 December 1866, CO 137/408.
85. For all these cases, see Grant to Carnarvon, no. 72, 24 December 1866, enclosed depositions, CO 137/408; Grant to Carnarvon, no. 34, 24 October 1866, CO 137/407. A finding of "no bill" meant that there was not sufficient evidence to carry the prosecution forward. See Dalby, *Crime and Punishment*, 18.
86. Storks to Cardwell, no. 94, 20 April 1866, CO 137/404.
87. Grant to Buckingham, no. 269, 20 November 1868, CO 137/437.
88. Grant to Kimberley, no. 58, 8 May 1871, CO 137/456. For references to compensation claims by William Groves, see Grant to Buckingham, no. 18, 10 February 1868, enclosed letter of William Groves and enclosed letter of James Moore Ross, CO 137/430; Grant to Buckingham, no. 76, 15 April 1867, enclosed letter of James

Ross, CO 137/423. For Mrs G.W. Gordon's request for compensation, see Grant to Granville, no. 275, 3 December 1869, CO 137/444. See also Granville to Grant, no. 176, 8 October 1869, enclosed memorial from Mrs Gordon, CO 137/446.

89. For all references to William Kelly Smith and his attempts to gain compensation, see Grant to Kimberley, no. 58, 8 May 1871, enclosed petition from William Kelly Smith, CO 137/456; memorial of Smith to the Earl of Kimberley, 21 October 1871, CO 137/461.

90. Augier, "Before and After 1865", 174.

Chapter 6

1. Eyre to Cardwell, no. 90, 19 April 1865, enclosed letter of Rev. H. Clarke, CO 137/390.
2. *WAS*, iii–ix.
3. Ibid.
4. Metcalfe to Russell, no. 77, 2 May 1840, CO 137/249; Elgin to Stanley, no. 97, 10 August 1844, enclosures, CO 137/280.
5. Phillippo, *Jamaica*, 231–32. See also Elgin to Stanley, no. 79, 2 September 1845, enclosed report of Stipendiary Magistrate Hall Pringle, CO 137/284. For other reports of an upsurge in Christian marriage among blacks in the immediate post-slavery period, see Metcalfe to Russell, no. 50, 30 March 1840, CO 137/248; Metcalfe to Russell, no. 129, 20 November 1840, enclosure, CO 137/250; *WIC*, evidence of Samuel Barrett, minute nos. 5263–64, and Alexander Geddes, minute no. 6912.
6. For a sample of these explanations, see *CJP*, appendix A, evidence of Rev. Reinke, 106, and W. Bancroft Espeut, 122–23, and appendix C, evidence of Robert Pitters, 45.
7. Elgin to Stanley, no. 79, 2 September 1845, enclosed report of Stipendiary Magistrate Hall Pringle, CO 137/284.
8. Musgrave to Hicks Beach, 2 April 1879, no. 101, enclosed report of the attorney general on Law 15, CO 137/489. Also see *Laws of Jamaica*.
9. Newton to Hicks Beach, 7 September 1879, no. 270, CO 137/491.
10. *Laws of Jamaica*.
11. Darling to E.B. Lytton, no. 158, 24 December 1858, CO 137/340.
12. Grant to Kimberley, confidential, 22 August 1871, CO 137/458.
13. *CJP*, appendix B, evidence of Rev. Josias Cork, 27.
14. *Colonial Standard*, 17 February 1879. Note, however, that for the elite, divorce, though highly improbable, was not impossible. See, for example, Burnard, "A Matron in Rank", for a discussion on the Manning Divorce of 1741.
15. "Incestuous adultery" within the context of this law was that committed with a woman with whom (if the man's wife was dead) he could not legally contract marriage

because she was within the prohibited degrees of blood ties. For all details on the Divorce Law, see Musgrave to Hicks Beach, 10 December 1878, no. 240, enclosed copy of the Divorce Bill, CO 137/488.

16. Ibid.

17. Reports of the registrar general, quoted in Moore and Johnson, *Neither Led nor Driven*, 329; Bryan, *Jamaican People*, 102.

18. Bush, *Slave Women*, 100–101; Long, *History of Jamaica*, 421; Gardner, *History of Jamaica*, 182.

19. Bryan, *Jamaican People*, x, 280.

20. Elgin to Stanley, no. 1, 5 January 1846, CO 137/287.

21. Wages paid for estate labour were reduced by as much as 50 per cent from an average of one shilling and sixpence to one shilling after the passing of the Sugar Duties Act in 1846. There was also uncertainty in the payment of wages. See Wilmot, "Emancipation in Action", 53.

22. Elgin to Stanley, no. 1, 5 January 1846, enclosed letter of William Ramsay, CO 137/287.

23. Darling to E.B. Lytton, no. 134, 25 October 1858, enclosed report of Stipendiary Magistrate Hill, CO 137/339.

24. Ibid.

25. Eyre to Cardwell, no. 23, 8 February 1865, CO 137/388.

26. The Bastardy and Maintenance Laws of 1881 observed a subtle distinction between the terms "bastard" and "illegitimate". Whereas "illegitimate" referred to children born of parents living together in concubinage, "bastard" referred specifically to the illegitimate child of a man and woman who were not living together. For more discussion on these terms, see Brian L. Moore and Michele A. Johnson, " 'Little Black Bastards': Perceptions of Illegitimacy in Jamaica, 1865–1920" (paper delivered at the Social History Project Symposium, University of the West Indies, Mona, 4 May 2002).

27. Eyre to Cardwell, no. 90, 19 April 1865, CO 137/390.

28. Ibid.

29. Grant to Earl Granville, no. 262, 8 November 1869, CO 137/444; Grant to Kimberley, no. 250, 19 December 1870, CO 137/452.

30. Ibid. This clause of the Maintenance Law therefore incorporated the principle behind bastardy legislation.

31. Grant to Earl Granville, no. 262, 8 November 1869, CO 137/444.

32. See *CJP*, appendix A, evidence of Bicknell, 19–20, Rev. C. Douet, 82, and Rev. Pierce, 103–4.

33. *CJP*, report and minutes of evidence, 2, and appendix A, evidence of Henry Bicknell, 16–18.

34. Foner, *Reconstruction*, 88.

35. *Colonial Standard*, 17 October 1873.

36. *Colonial Standard*, 23 July 1877. For examples of similar cases, see *Colonial Standard*, 27 July 1875; 27 May 1876; 8 November 1876; 14 March 1877; 22 May 1878.

37. For example, see *CJP*, appendix C, evidence of Dr Gerrard, 50, and Rev. Richards, 5–6; appendix B, evidence of Jasper Gruber, 28.

38. *Laws of Jamaica*.

39. Ibid.

40. Ibid.

41. Musgrave to Kimberley, no. 146, 3 May 1881, enclosures, CO 137/500.

42. *Laws of Jamaica*.

43. *CJP*, appendix A, letter from Rev. Reinke, 106, and evidence of William Lee, 50.

44. Unwitting Eurocentric testimony pointed to the important role of the extended family in this respect. *CJP*, appendix A, evidence of William Lee, 50, and evidence of Nuttall, 14.

45. As explained in note 26, the 1881 bastardy and maintenance legislation established a legal distinction between "bastards" and "illegitimate children". The Maintenance Law excluded fathers of "bastards", dealing only with fathers living in "concubinage" and married fathers. Thus, the penalties prescribed under this law did not apply to fathers of "bastards".

46. Grant to Buckingham, no. 62, 23 March 1868, enclosures, CO 137/432.

47. Musgrave to Carnarvon, no. 188, 2 November 1877, enclosed report of the attorney general, CO 137/485.

48. Musgrave to Kimberley, no. 305, 23 September 1881, enclosed report of the attorney general, CO 137/501; *Laws of Jamaica*.

49. O. Nigel Bolland, "'The Hundredth Year of Our Emancipation': The Dialectics of Resistance in Slavery and Freedom", in Shepherd, *Working Slavery*, 335.

50. *CJP*, report, 7.

51. See, for example, Smith to Glenelg, no. 210, 13 November 1837, enclosed *BTJW*, evidence of Amelia Lawrence and Amaryllis Gale, 163–69, CO 137/221.

52. For this issue of a reported upsurge in Christian marriages in the immediate post-slavery period, see note 5 of this chapter as well as note 57 of chapter 3 of this work. See also Phillippo, *Jamaica*, 231–32; Sligo to Glenelg, no. 401, 20 April 1836, enclosures, CO 137/215; Metcalfe to Russell, no. 50, 30 March 1840, CO 137/248. Also see *CJP*, appendix C, evidence of Arthur Cecil James, 22.

53. *CJP*, appendix C, evidence of Nathaniel Beckford, 43.

54. Ibid., appendix A, evidence of Rev. Enos Nuttall, 14, and Rev. George Sargeant, 114.

55. *Annual Report of the Registrar General's Department*, 1881, 1882, quoted in Bryan, *Jamaican People*, 98. This trend among blacks in particular was also evident in the

1861 census. Although that census did not classify marriages and non-marriages according to race, the fact that the number of unmarried couples was far greater than that of married couples suggests that the predominant black population, as a rule, did not embrace legal, Christian marriage. See Higman, *Jamaican Censuses*, 18.

56. Eyre to Cardwell, no. 90, 19 April 1865, enclosed letter of Rev. M. Hine, CO 137/390.

57. *CJP*, appendix A, evidence of Rev. E. Reinke, 106, and Bancroft Espeut, 122–23; appendix C, evidence of Robert Pitters, 45; appendix A, evidence of E. Goldson, 29. See also Bush, *Slave Women*, 102.

58. *CJP*, appendix A, evidence of Rev. E. Reinke, 105–6.

59. Litwack, *Been in the Storm*, 243.

60. Bush, *Slave Women*, 94.

61. *Colonial Standard*, 25 November 1878; *Annual Report of the Registrar General's Department, Births*, 1881–82.

62. See, for example, *CJP*, appendix A, evidence of Rev. C. Douet, 81, and Joseph Reid, 93. For reports of economic distress, see Musgrave to Kimberley, no. 345, 23 November 1880, enclosed letters to the custos of St Mary, CO 137/497.

63. The theme of support for familial welfare is fundamental to this work. For specific references to the maintenance of elderly family members among blacks, see Thome and Kimball, *Emancipation in the West Indies*, 101; *CJP*, appendix A, evidence of Rev. George Sargeant, 116, and Rev. William Griffiths, 55.

Concluding Thoughts

1. Michel de Certeau, *The Practice of Everyday Life*, trans. Steven F. Rendall (Berkeley: University of California Press, 1984), quoted in Bolland, "The Hundredth Year", 321–22.

2. Bolland, "The Hundredth Year", 322.

3. Ibid.

4. Scarano, "Slavery and Emancipation", 268.

5. Scott, "Exploring Freedom", 417–18.

6. Marshall, "We Be Wise", 15, 20.

7. Litwack, *Been in the Storm*, 230.

8. Sudarkasa, "African Heritage", 43.

9. For a non-statistical approach, see Hutton, "Colour for Colour", and Heuman, "*Killing Time*".

10. *CJP*, appendix A, evidence of Nuttall, 7, and William Lee, 50.

11. Bush, *Slave Women*, 105–8.

12. *CJP*, appendix A, evidence of John Cassis, 68, and John Walker, 65.

13. Bush, *Slave Women*, 100–102.

14. Scarano, "Slavery and Emancipation", 269–70; Sabean, "History of the Family", 167.

15. On the continued discourse on the marginalization of the black male, see Errol Miller, *Marginalization of the Black Male: Insights from the Development of the Teaching Profession* (Kingston: Institute of Social and Economic Research, University of the West Indies, 1986); Miller, *Men at Risk*. Also see Keisha Lindsay, "Caribbean Male: Endangered Species?" Working Paper no. 1, ed. Patricia Mohammed (Mona: Centre for Gender and Development Studies, University of the West Indies, October 1997), 1–20; Barrow, "Men, Women and Family", 149–63; Barrow, "Masculinity and Family", 339–76; Beckles, "Black Masculinity"; Brodber, *Standing Tall*.

16. Brodber, preface to *Standing Tall*, xx.

17. Beckles, "Black Masculinity", 4–5.

18. Bridget Brereton, "General Problems and Issues in Studying the History of Women", in Mohammed and Shepherd, *Gender in Caribbean Development*, 120.

19. See the introduction and chapter 5 of this work for a discussion on the methodological and source-related challenges posed by the use of testimonies. Some historians who are engaged in this project of examining the past through the lens of the formerly oppressed include Alvin O. Thompson, John Lean and Trevor Burnard, Rebecca Scott, Verene Shepherd and Swithin Wilmot. See Thompson, *Unprofitable Servants*; Lean and Burnard, "Hearing Slave Voices"; Scott, "Exploring Freedom"; Shepherd, "Resisting Representation"; Wilmot, "Females of Abandoned Character".

20. Bolland, "The Hundredth Year", 336.

Bibliography

Primary Sources

Manuscripts

Jamaica Archives, Spanish Town

St Ann Parish Registers, Church of England, baptisms, 1826–48. 1B/11/8/2.
Trelawny Parish Registers, Church of England, baptisms, 1826–40. 1B/11/8/15/2.
Trelawny Parish Registers, Church of England, baptisms, 1841–54. 1B/11/8/15/3.
Vere Parish Registers, Church of England, baptisms, 1838–42. 1B/11/8/4.

West Indies and Special Collections, Main Library, University of the West Indies, Mona Library, Jamaica (Microfilmed Sources)

Colonial Office Records (microfilm). CO 137, vols. 192 (January 1834) to 507 (December 1882), inclusive. Governors' Correspondence, Public Offices, Miscellaneous and Individuals, 1834–1882. Originals of the Colonial Office Records are located in the Public Record Office, National Archives, London.
Correspondence of London Missionary Society (Council for World Mission)(microfilm). Incoming letters, West Indies, Jamaica. No. 919. 1830–1843. Originals located at School of Oriental and African Studies, University of London.
Despatches from US consuls in Kingston, Jamaica, 1796–1906 (microfilm). No. 273. 10 January 1835 to 1 December 1837; 12 January 1838 to 7 December 1838. Originals located at National Archives, Washington.
Ackroyd Papers, Hulme, Jamaica Magistracy (microfilm). D538/MI/1–8. Originals located in Staffordshire County Record Office, United Kingdom.

PRINTED SOURCES

Parliamentary Papers

1836 (560) 15. *Report of the Select Committee of Parliament Appointed to Inquire into the Working of the Apprenticeship System in the Colonies, with the Minutes of Evidence, Appendix and Index.*

1839 (107) 3. *Extracts from Papers Printed by Order of the House of Commons, 1839, Relative to the West Indies. Section I, Progress of Industry and General Condition of Society Since 1st August, 1838.*

1842 (479) 8. *Report of the Select Committee of the House of Commons on the West India Colonies, Together with the Minutes of Evidence, Appendix and Index, 25 July 1842.*

1866 4, part 1; 5, part 2. *Report of the Jamaica Royal Commission, 1866, along with the Minutes of Evidence and Appendix.*

Jamaica Government Sources

University of the West Indies, Mona Library, Jamaica

Annual Report of the Registrar General's Department, printed in annual *Department Reports.* Births. 1881, 1882.

Jamaica, Statutes and Laws. Vol. 4, *21 Victoria to 29 Victoria, 1857–1866.*

Laws of Jamaica. Vol. 2, *1 Victoria to 10 Victoria, 1837–1847.*

Laws of Jamaica, from Law 1 of 1875 to Law 39 of 1879.

Laws of Jamaica, from Law 1 of 1880 to Law 20 of 1886.

Report of the Commissioners of Inquiry upon the Condition of the Juvenile Population of Jamaica, with the Evidence Taken and an Appendix. Kingston: Government Printing Establishment, 1879.

Report of the Commissioners of Inquiry upon the Government Reformatory at Stony Hill, with the Evidence Taken and an Appendix. Kingston: General Penitentiary, 1877.

ECCLESIASTICAL SOURCES

Baptist Missionary Society. *Christian Missions in the East and West in Connection with the Baptist Missionary, 1792–1873.* London: Yates and Alexander, 1873.

NEWSPAPERS

Colonial Standard and Jamaica Despatch. 1851–1881.

Falmouth Post. 1835–1860.

Gleaner and De Cordova's Advertising Sheet. Kingston, 1867.

Jamaica Witness, Falmouth. 1877–1879.

St Jago de la Vega Gazette. 1839–1840.

Trelawny and Public Advertiser. 1871–1876.

Eighteenth- and Nineteenth-Century Works

Bigelow, J. *Jamaica in 1850, or The Effects of Sixteen Years of Freedom on a Slave Colony.* New York: George Putnam, 1851.

Candler, John. *The West Indies: Extracts from the Journal of John Candler While Travelling in Jamaica.* London: Thomas Ward, 1851.

Carmichael, Mrs A.C. *Domestic Manners and Social Condition of the White, Coloured, and Negro Population of the West Indies.* 2 vols. London: Whittaker, Treacher, 1833; reprint, Negro Universities Press, 1969.

Davy, John. *The West Indies, Before and Since Slave Emancipation, Comprising the Windward and Leeward Islands' Military Command; Founded on Notes and Observations Collected during a Three Years' Residence.* London: W. and F.G. Cash, 1854. Reprint, London: Frank Cass, 1971.

Duncan, P. *A Narrative of the Wesleyan Mission to Jamaica, with Occasional Remarks on the State of Society in that Colony.* London: Partridge and Oakey, 1849.

Edwards, Bryan. *The History, Civil and Commercial, of the British Colonies in the West Indies.* 5 vols. London: J. Stockdale, 1793.

Froude, James Anthony. *The English in the West Indies, Or, The Bow of Ulysses.* London: Longmans, Green, 1888.

Gardner, William James. *A History of Jamaica from Its Discovery by Christopher Columbus to the Present Time: Including an Account of Its Trade and Agriculture; Sketches of the Manners, Habits, and Customs of All Classes of Its Inhabitants; and a Narrative of the Progress of Religion and Education in the Island.* London: E. Stock, 1873.

Gosse, P.H. *A Naturalist's Sojourn in Jamaica.* London: Brown, Green and Longmans, 1851.

Gurney, Joseph John. *A Winter in the West Indies, Described in Familiar Letters to Henry Clay of Kentucky.* London: n.p., 1840.

Harvey, Thomas, and William Brewin. *Jamaica in 1866: A Narrative of a Tour through the Island, with Remarks on Its Social, Educational and Industrial Condition.* London: A.W. Bennett, 1867.

Lee, W. *A Supplement to the Digest of the Laws of Jamaica, Containing Those Passed in the Year 1869.* Kingston: M. DeCordova, McDougall, 1870.

Long, Edward. *The History of Jamaica, or General Survey of the Antient and Modern State of that Island: With Reflections on Its Situations, Settlements, Inhabitants, Climate, Products, Commerce, Laws, and Government.* 3 vols. London: T. Lowndes, 1774.

Madden, Richard R. *A Twelvemonth's Residence in the West Indies during the Transition from Slavery to Apprenticeship.* Vol. 2. Philadelphia: n.p., 1835.

Marwick, William. *William and Louisa Anderson: A Record of Their Life and Work in Jamaica and Old Calabar.* Edinburgh: Andrew Elliot, 1897.

Matthews, John, *A Voyage to the River Sierra-Leone.* London, 1788.

Minot, J. *A Digest of the Laws of Jamaica from 33 Charles II to 28 Victoria.* Kingston, 1865.

Phillippo, James M. *Jamaica: Its Past and Present State.* London: John Snow, 1843.

Sewell, William G. *The Ordeal of Free Labour in the British West Indies.* New York: Harper and Brothers, 1861.

Sligo, Howe Peter, Marquis. *Jamaica under the Apprenticeship.* London, 1838.

Sturge, Joseph, and Thomas Harvey. *The West Indies in 1837, Being the Journal of a Visit to Antigua, Montserrat, Dominica, St Lucia, Barbados, and Jamaica; Undertaken for the Purpose of Ascertaining the Actual Condition of the Negro Population of those Islands.* London: Hamilton, Adams, 1838. Reprint, London: Frank Cass, 1968.

Thome, James A., and J. Horace Kimball. *Emancipation in the West Indies: A Six Months' Tour in Antigua, Barbados, and Jamaica, in the Year 1837.* New York: American Anti-Slavery Society, 1838.

Underhill, Edward Bean. *The West Indies: Their Social and Religious Condition.* London, 1862. Reprint, Westport, CT: Negro Universities Press, 1970.

———. *The Tragedy of Morant Bay: A Narrative of the Disturbances in the Island of Jamaica in 1865.* London: Alexander and Shepheard, 1895.

Williams, James. *A Narrative of Events since the First of August, 1834, by James Williams, an Apprenticed Labourer in Jamaica.* London: J. Rider, 1837.

Winterbottom, Thomas. *An Account of the Native Africans in the Neighbourhood of Sierra Leone.* 2 vols. London: C. Whittingham, 1803.

Secondary Sources

MODERN BOOKS

Barrow, Christine. *Family in the Caribbean: Themes and Perspectives.* Kingston: Ian Randle, 1996.

Barrow, Christine, ed. *Portraits of a Nearer Caribbean: Essays on Gender Ideologies and Identities.* Kingston: Ian Randle, 1998.

Beckles, Hilary McD. *Centering Woman: Gender Discourses in Caribbean Slave Society* Kingston: Ian Randle, 1999.

Beckles, Hilary McD., and Verene Shepherd, eds. *Caribbean Freedom: Economy and Society from Emancipation to the Present.* Kingston: Ian Randle, 1993.

Blake, Judith. *Family Structure in Jamaica: The Social Context of Reproduction.* New York: Free Press of Glencoe, 1961.

Brathwaite, Edward (Kamau). *The Development of Creole Society in Jamaica, 1770–1820.* Oxford: Clarendon, 1971.

Brereton, Bridget, and Kevin Yelvington, eds. *The Colonial Caribbean in Transition: Essays on Postemancipation Social and Cultural History.* Kingston: University of the West Indies Press, 1999.

Brodber, Erna. *Standing Tall: Affirmations of the Jamaican Male – 24 Self-Portraits.* Kingston: Sir Arthur Lewis Institute of Social and Economic Studies, University of the West Indies, 2003.

Bryan, Patrick. *The Jamaican People, 1880–1902: Race, Class and Social Control.* Kingston: University of the West Indies Press, 1991.

Burn, W.L. *Emancipation and Apprenticeship in the British West Indies.* London: Jonathan Cape, 1937.

Bush, Barbara. *Slave Women in Caribbean Society, 1650–1838.* London: James Currey, 1990.

Chilungu, Simeon, and Sada Niang, eds. *African Continuities/L'Héritage Africain.* Toronto: Terebi, 1989.

Clarke, Edith. *My Mother Who Fathered Me: A Study of the Family in Three Selected Communities in Jamaica.* 2nd ed. London: George Allen and Unwin, 1970.

Cobley, Alan Gregor, and Alvin O. Thompson, eds. *The African-Caribbean Connection: Historical and Cultural Perspectives.* Bridgetown: Department of History, University of the West Indies, Cave Hill, and the National Cultural Foundation, 1990.

Cole, Johnnetta B., ed. *Anthropology for the Eighties: Introductory Readings.* New York: Free Press, 1982.

Crahan, Margaret E., and Franklin W. Knight, eds. *Africa and the Caribbean: The Legacies of a Link.* Baltimore: Johns Hopkins University Press, 1979.

Craton, Michael. *Empire, Enslavement and Freedom in the Caribbean.* Kingston: Ian Randle, 1997.

Curtin, Philip D. *The Atlantic Slave Trade: A Census.* Madison: University of Wisconsin Press, 1969.

———. *Two Jamaicas: The Role of Ideas in a Tropical Colony, 1830–1865.* Westport, CT: Greenwood, 1968.

Dalby, Jonathan. *Crime and Punishment in Jamaica: A Quantitative Analysis of the Assize Court Records, 1756–1856.* Kingston: Social History Project, Department of History, University of the West Indies, 2000.

De Certeau, Michel. *The Practice of Everyday Life.* Translated by Steven F. Rendall. Berkeley: University of California Press, 1984.

Eisner, Gisela. *Jamaica, 1830–1930: A Study in Economic Growth.* Manchester: Manchester University Press, 1961.

Engerman, Stanley, and Robert Fogel. *Time on the Cross: The Economics of American Negro Slavery*. Boston: Little, Brown, 1974.

Engerman, Stanley, and Eugene Genovese, eds. *Race and Slavery in the Western Hemisphere: Quantitative Studies*. Princeton: Princeton University Press, 1975.

Eudell, Demetrius. *The Political Languages of Emancipation in the British Caribbean and the US South*. Chapel Hill: University of North Carolina Press, 2002.

Fadipe, N.A. *The Sociology of the Yoruba*. Nigeria: Ibanan University Press, 1970.

Fauci, Anthony S., et al., eds. *Harrison's Principles of Internal Medicine*. 14th ed. Columbus: McGraw-Hill, 1998.

Foner, Eric. *Nothing but Freedom: Emancipation and Its Legacy*. Baton Rouge: Louisiana State University Press, 1983.

―――. *Reconstruction: America's Unfinished Revolution, 1863–1877*. New York: Harper and Row, 1988.

Frazier, E. Franklin. *The Negro Family in the United States*. 2nd ed. Chicago: University of Chicago Press, 1966.

Goveia, Elsa. *Slave Society in the British Leeward Islands at the End of the Eighteenth Century*. New Haven: Yale University Press, 1965.

Green, William A. *British Slave Emancipation: The Sugar Colonies and the Great Experiment, 1830–1865*. Oxford: Oxford University Press, 1976.

Greenfield, Sidney. *English Rustics in Black Skin: A Study of Modern Family Forms in a Pre-Industrial Society*. New Haven: College and University Press, 1966.

Gutman, Herbert G. *The Black Family in Slavery and Freedom, 1750–1925*. New York: Pantheon, 1976.

Hall, Catherine. *Civilising Subjects: Metropole and Colony in the English Imagination, 1830–1867*. Cambridge: Polity, 2002.

Hall, Douglas. *Free Jamaica, 1838–1865: An Economic History*. New Haven: Yale University Press, 1959.

―――. *In Miserable Slavery: Thomas Thistlewood in Jamaica, 1750–1786*. London: Macmillan, 1989.

Henriques, Fernando. *Family and Colour in Jamaica*. London: Eyre and Spottiswoode, 1953.

Herskovits, Melville. *The Myth of the Negro Past*. 2nd ed. Boston: Beacon, 1958.

Herskovits, Melville, and Frances Herskovits. *Trinidad Village*. New York: Knopf, 1947.

Heuman, Gad. *"The Killing Time": The Morant Bay Rebellion in Jamaica*. Knoxville: University of Tennessee Press, 1994.

Higman, Barry W. *Montpelier, Jamaica: A Plantation Community in Slavery and Freedom, 1739–1912*. Kingston: University of the West Indies Press, 1998.

―――. *Slave Population and Economy in Jamaica, 1807–1834*. Kingston: University of the West Indies Press, 1995.

———. *Slave Populations of the British Caribbean, 1807–1834*. Baltimore: Johns Hopkins University Press, 1984.

Higman, Barry W., ed. *The Jamaican Censuses of 1844 and 1861: A New Edition, Derived from the Manuscript and Printed Schedules in the Jamaica Archives*. Kingston: Social History Project, Department of History, University of the West Indies, 1980.

———. *Methodology and Historiography of the Caribbean*. Vol. 6 of *General History of the Caribbean*. London: UNESCO, 1999.

Hollingsworth, T.H. *Historical Demography*. London: Camelot, 1969.

Holt, Thomas. *The Problem of Freedom: Race, Labor and Politics in Jamaica and Britain, 1832–1938*. Kingston: Ian Randle, 1992.

Jowitt, Earl, and Clifford Walsh, eds. *Jowitt's Dictionary of English Law*. Vol. 1, *A–K*. 2nd ed. London: Sweet and Maxwell, 1977.

July, Robert W. *A History of the African People*. 5th ed. Long Grove, IL: Waveland, 1998.

Litwack, Leon F. *Been in the Storm So Long: The Aftermath of Slavery*. New York: Knopf, 1981.

Lovejoy, Paul E., ed. *Identity in the Shadow of Slavery*. London: Continuum, 2000.

Mair, Lucille Mathurin. *A Historical Study of Women in Jamaica, 1655–1844*. Edited and with an introduction by Hilary McD. Beckles and Verene A. Shepherd. Kingston: University of the West Indies Press, 2006.

Marwick, Arthur. *The Nature of History*. London: Macmillan Education, 1989.

Maslow, Abraham H. *Toward a Psychology of Being*. New York: D. Van Nostrand, 1968.

Mbiti, John S. *African Religions and Philosophy*. 2nd ed. Oxford: Heinemann, 1989.

McAdoo, Harriette Pipes, ed. *Black Families*. 2nd ed. Newbury Park, CA: Sage, 1988.

McGlynn, Frank, and Seymour Drescher, eds. *The Meaning of Freedom: Economics, Politics, and Culture after Slavery*. Pittsburgh: University of Pittsburgh Press, 1992.

Miller, Errol. *Marginalization of the Black Male: Insights from the Development of the Teaching Profession*. Kingston: Institute of Social and Economic Research, University of the West Indies, 1986.

———. *Men at Risk*. Kingston: Jamaica Publishing House, 1991.

Mohammed, Patricia, and Catherine Shepherd, eds. *Gender in Caribbean Development*. 2nd ed. Kingston: Canoe, 1999.

Moore, Brian L., and Michele A. Johnson. *Neither Led nor Driven: Contesting British Cultural Imperialism in Jamaica, 1865–1920*. Kingston: University of the West Indies Press, 2004.

Moore, Brian L., and Swithin Wilmot, eds. *Before and After 1865: Education, Politics, and Regionalism in the Caribbean*. Kingston: Ian Randle, 1998.

Olivier, Lord [Sydney Haldane]. *Jamaica: The Blessed Island*. London: Faber and Faber, 1936.

Paton, Diana. *No Bond but the Law: Punishment, Race, and Gender in Jamaican State Formation, 1780–1870*. Durham: Duke University Press, 2004.

Patterson, Orlando. *Freedom in the Making of Western Culture.* Vol. 1 of *Freedom.* London: I.B. Tauris, 1991.

———. *Slavery and Social Death: A Comparative Study.* Cambridge: Harvard University Press, 1982.

———. *The Sociology of Slavery: An Analysis of the Origins, Development and Structure of Negro Slave Society in Jamaica.* London: McGibbon and Kee, 1967.

Phillips, Arthur, ed. *Survey of African Marriage and Family Life.* London: Oxford University Press, 1953.

Phillips, Ulrich Bonnell. *Life and Labour in the Old South.* Boston: Little, Brown, 1929.

Roberts, George W. *The Population of Jamaica*, 2nd ed. New York: Kraus-Thomson Organization, 1979.

Satchell, Veront. *From Plots to Plantations: Land Transactions in Jamaica, 1866–1900.* Kingston: Institute of Social and Economic Research, University of the West Indies, 1990.

Scott, Rebecca J. *Slave Emancipation in Cuba: The Transition to Free Labor, 1860–1899.* Princeton: Princeton University Press, 1985.

Shepherd, Verene, ed. *Working Slavery, Pricing Freedom: Perspectives from the Caribbean, Africa and the African Diaspora.* Kingston: Ian Randle, 2002.

Shepherd, Verene, and Hilary McD. Beckles, eds. *Caribbean Slavery in the Atlantic World.* Kingston: Ian Randle, 2000.

Shepherd, Verene, Bridget Brereton and Barbara Bailey, eds. *Engendering History: Caribbean Women in Historical Perspective.* Kingston: Ian Randle, 1995.

Smith, Michael G. *The Plural Society in the British West Indies.* Berkeley: University of California Press, 1965.

———. *West Indian Family Structure.* Seattle: University of Washington Press, 1962.

Smith, Raymond T. *The Negro Family in British Guiana: Family Structure and Social Status in the Villages.* 2nd ed. London: Routledge and Kegan Paul, 1971.

Steady, Filomina Chioma, ed. *The Black Woman Cross-Culturally.* Cambridge, MA: Schenkman, 1981.

Terborg-Penn, Rosalyn, Sharon Harley and Andrea Benton Rushing, eds. *Women in Africa and the African Diaspora.* Washington, DC: Howard University Press, 1987.

Thomas-Hope, Elizabeth, ed. *Perspectives on Caribbean Regional Identity.* Liverpool: Centre for Latin American Studies, University of Liverpool, 1984.

Thompson, Alvin O., ed. *In the Shadow of the Plantation: Caribbean History and Legacy.* Kingston: Ian Randle, 2002.

———. *Unprofitable Servants: Crown Slaves in Berbice, Guyana, 1803–1831.* Kingston: University of the West Indies Press, 2002.

Willigan, J. Dennis, and Katherine A. Lynch. *Sources and Methods of Historical Demography.* New York: Academic Press, 1982.

Journal Articles and Chapters in Books

Alleyne, Mervyn. "African Roots of Caribbean Culture". In Cobley and Thompson, *African-Caribbean Connection*, 107–22.

Altink, Henrice. "To Wed or Not to Wed? The Struggle to Define Afro-Jamaican Relationships, 1834–1838". *Journal of Social History* 38, no. 1 (Fall 2004): 88–111.

Augier, Roy. "Before and After 1865". In Beckles and Shepherd, *Caribbean Freedom*, 170–80.

Barrow, Christine. "Masculinity and Family in the Caribbean: 'Marginality' and 'Reputation' Revisited". In Barrow, *Portraits of a Nearer Caribbean*, 339–76.

———. "Men, Women and Family in the Caribbean: A Review". In Mohammed and Shepherd, *Gender in Caribbean Development*, 149–63.

Beckles, Hilary McD. "Caribbean Anti-Slavery: The Self-Liberation Ethos of Enslaved Blacks". In Shepherd and Beckles, *Caribbean Slavery*, 869–78.

Besson, Jean. "Family Land and Caribbean Society: Toward an Ethnography of Afro-Caribbean Peasantries". In Thomas-Hope, *Perspectives on Caribbean Regional Identity*, 57–83.

Blassingame, John W. "Using the Testimony of Ex-Slaves: Approaches and Problems". *Journal of Southern History* 41, no. 4 (November 1975): 473–92.

Bolland, O. Nigel. " 'The Hundredth Year of Our Emancipation': The Dialectics of Resistance in Slavery and Freedom". In Shepherd, *Working Slavery*, 320–39.

———. "The Politics of Freedom in the British Caribbean". In McGlynn and Drescher, *Meaning of Freedom*, 113–43.

Brereton, Bridget. "Family Strategies, Gender and the Shift to Wage Labour in the British Caribbean". In Brereton and Yelvington, *Colonial Caribbean in Transition*, 77–107.

———. "General Problems and Issues in Studying the History of Women". In Mohammed and Shepherd, *Gender in Caribbean Development*, 119–35.

Bryan, Patrick. "The Black Middle Class in Nineteenth-Century Jamaica". In Beckles and Shepherd, *Caribbean Freedom*, 284–95.

Burnard, Trevor. " 'A Matron in Rank, a Prostitute in Manners': The Manning Divorce of 1741 and Class, Gender, Race and the Law in Eighteenth-Century Jamaica". In Shepherd, *Working Slavery*, 133–52.

Caldwell, John, Pat Caldwell and I.O. Orubuloye. "The Family and Sexual Networking in Sub-Saharan Africa: Historical Regional Differences and Present-Day Implications". *Population Studies* 46, no. 3 (November 1992): 385–410.

Campbell, Carl. "Social and Economic Obstacles to the Development of Popular Education in Post-emancipation Jamaica, 1834–1865". In Beckles and Shepherd, *Caribbean Freedom*, 262–68.

Castaneda, Digna. "The Female Slave in Cuba during the First Half of the Nineteenth Century". In Shepherd, Brereton and Bailey, *Engendering History*, 141–54.

Chilungu, Simeon. "Marriage, Family and Kinship Ties in Africa". In Chilungu and Niang, *African Continuities*, 61–118.

Craton, Michael. "Changing Patterns of Slave Families in the British West Indies". *Journal of Interdisciplinary History* 10, no. 1 (Summer 1979): 1–35.

———. "Continuity Not Change: The Incidence of Unrest among Ex-slaves in the British West Indies, 1838–1876". In Beckles and Shepherd, *Caribbean Freedom*, 192–206.

Desrochers, Robert E. Jr. "'Not Fade Away': The Narrative of Venture Smith, an African American in the Early Republic". *Journal of American History* 84, no. 1 (June 1997): 40–66.

Gordon, Shirley. "Schools of the Free". In Moore and Wilmot, *Before and After 1865*, 1–12.

Hall, Catherine. "White Visions, Black Lives: The Free Villages of Jamaica". *History Workshop* 36 (Autumn 1993): 100–132.

Hall, Douglas. "The Flight from the Estates Reconsidered: The British West Indies, 1838–1842". In Beckles and Shepherd, *Caribbean Freedom*, 55–63.

Higman, Barry W. "African and Creole Slave Family Patterns in Trinidad". In Crahan and Knight, *Africa and the Caribbean*, 41–64.

———. "The Development of Historical Disciplines in the Caribbean". In Higman, *Methodology and Historiography*, 3–18.

———. "Household Structure and Fertility on Jamaican Slave Plantations: A Nineteenth-Century Example". *Population Studies* 27, no. 3 (1973): 527–50.

———. "The Slave Family and Household in the British West Indies, 1800–1834". *Journal of Interdisciplinary History* 6, no. 2 (Autumn 1975): 261–87.

———. "Theory, Method and Technique in Caribbean Social History". *Journal of Caribbean History* 20, no. 1 (1985–86): 1–29.

Hoetink, Harry. "The Cultural Links". In Crahan and Knight, *Africa and the Caribbean*, 20–40.

Johnson, Howard. "Historiography of Jamaica". In Higman, *Methodology and Historiography*, 478–530.

Klein, Herbert S., and Stanley L. Engerman. "Fertility Differentials between Slaves in the United States and the British West Indies: A Note on Lactation Practices and Their Possible Implications". *William and Mary Quarterly*, 3rd series, 35, no. 2 (April 1978): 357–74.

Ladner, Joyce. "Racism and Tradition: Black Womanhood in Historical Perspective". In Steady, *Black Woman*, 269–88.

Lean, John, and Trevor Burnard. "Hearing Slave Voices: The Fiscal's Reports of Berbice and Demerara-Essequibo". *Archives* 27, no. 107 (Oct. 2002): 120–33.

Lindsay, Keisha. "Caribbean Male: Endangered Species?" Working Paper no. 1. Edited by Patricia Mohammed. Mona: Centre for Gender and Development Studies, University of the West Indies, October 1997.

Lumsden, Joy. "'A Brave and Loyal People': The Role of the Maroons in the Morant Bay Rebellion in 1865". In Shepherd, *Working Slavery*, 467–89.

MacGaffey, Wyatt. "Lineage Structure, Marriage and the Family amongst the Central Bantu". *Journal of African History* 24 (1983): 173–87.

Marks, Shula, and Richard Rathbone. "The History of the Family in Africa: Introduction". *Journal of African History* 24 (1983): 145–61.

Marshall, Woodville. "Notes on Peasant Development in the West Indies since 1838". In Beckles and Shepherd, *Caribbean Freedom*, 99–106.

———. "'We Be Wise to Many More Tings': Blacks' Hopes and Expectations of Emancipation". In Beckles and Shepherd, *Caribbean Freedom*, 12–20.

Mintz, Sidney. "The Origins of Reconstituted Peasantries". In Beckles and Shepherd, *Caribbean Freedom*, 94–98.

———. "History and Anthropology: A Brief Reprise". In Engerman and Genovese, *Race and Slavery*.

Mohammed, Patricia. "The Caribbean Family Revisited". In Mohammed and Shepherd, *Gender in Caribbean Development*, 164–75.

Patterson, Orlando. "The Constituent Elements of Slavery". In Shepherd and Beckles, *Caribbean Slavery*, 32–41.

Reus, Victor I. "Mental Disorders". In Fauci et al., *Harrison's Principles of Internal Medicine*, 2485–503.

Ripley, C. Peter. "The Black Family in Transition: Louisiana, 1860–1865". *Journal of Southern History* 41, no. 3 (August 1975): 369–80.

Robotham, Don. "'The Notorious Riot': The Socio-Economic and Political Bases of Paul Bogle's Revolt". Working Paper no. 28. Kingston: Institute of Social and Economic Research, University of the West Indies, 1981.

Sabean, David Warren. "The History of the Family in Africa and Europe: Some Comparative Perspectives". *Journal of African History* 24 (1983): 163–71.

Scarano, Francisco. "Slavery and Emancipation in Caribbean History". In Higman, *Methodology and Historiography*, 233–82.

Scott, Rebecca J. "Exploring the Meaning of Freedom: Postemancipation Societies in Comparative Perspective". *Hispanic American Historical Review* 68, no. 3 (August 1988): 407–28.

———. "Former Slaves: Responses to Emancipation in Cuba". In Beckles and Shepherd, *Caribbean Freedom*, 21–27.

Sekora, John. "Black Message/White Envelope: Genre, Authenticity, and Authority in the Antebellum Slave Narrative". *Callaloo* 10 (1987): 482–515.

Sheller, Mimi. "Quasheba, Mother, Queen: Black Women's Public Leadership and Political Protest in Post-emancipation Jamaica, 1834–1865". *Slavery and Abolition* 19, no. 3 (December 1998): 90–113.

Shepherd, Verene A. "The Apprenticeship Experience on Jamaican Livestock Pens, 1834–38". *Jamaica Journal* 22, no. 1 (February–April 1989): 48–55.

———. "The Effects of the Abolition of Slavery on Jamaican Livestock Farms (Pens), 1834–1845". *Slavery and Abolition* 10, no. 2 (September 1989): 187–211.

———. "Gender, Migration and Settlement: The Indentureship and Post-indentureship Experience of Indian Females in Jamaica, 1845–1943". In Shepherd, Brereton and Bailey, *Engendering History*, 233–57.

———. "Gender and Representation in European Accounts of Pre-emancipation Jamaica". In Shepherd and Beckles, *Caribbean Slavery*, 702–11.

———. "'Petticoat Rebellion'? The Black Woman's Body and Voice in the Struggles for Freedom in Colonial Jamaica". In Thompson, *In the Shadow of the Plantation*, 17–38.

———. "The Politics of Migration: Government Policy towards Indians in Jamaica, 1845–1945". In Moore and Wilmot, *Before and After 1865*, 177–89.

Shepherd, Verene A., with Ahmed Reid. "Rebel Voices: Testimonies from the 1831–32 Emancipation War in Jamaica". *Jamaica Journal* 27, nos. 2–3 (2004): 54–63.

Sheridan, Richard. "From Chattel to Wage Slavery in Jamaica, 1740–1860". *Slavery and Abolition* 14, no. 1 (April 1993): 13–40.

Steady, Filomina Chioma. "African Feminism: A Worldwide Perspective". In Terborg-Penn, Harley and Rushing, *Women in Africa*, 3–24.

Sudarkasa, Niara. "African and Afro-American Family Organization". In Cole, *Anthropology for the Eighties*, 132–60.

———. "Female Employment and Family Organization in West Africa". In Steady, *Black Woman*, 49–63.

———. "Interpreting the African Heritage in Afro-American Family Organization". In McAdoo, *Black Families*, 37–53.

———. "'The Status of Women' in Indigenous African Societies". In Terborg-Penn, Harley and Rushing, *Women in Africa*, 25–41.

Wilmot, Swithin. "Black Labourers and White Missionaries: Conflict on the Estates in Hanover, Jamaica, 1838–47". *Jamaican Historical Review* 14 (1984): 18–27.

———. "Emancipation in Action: Workers and Wage Conflict in Jamaica, 1838–1840". In Beckles and Shepherd, *Caribbean Freedom*, 48–54.

———. "'Females of Abandoned Character'? Women and Protest in Jamaica, 1838–65". In Shepherd, Brereton and Bailey, *Engendering History*, 279–95.

———. "Not 'Full Free': The Ex-slaves and the Apprenticeship System in Jamaica, 1834–1838". *Jamaica Journal* 17, no. 3 (1984): 2–10.

Zacek, Natalie. "Voices and Silences: The Problem of Slave Testimony in the English West Indian Law Court". *Slavery and Abolition* 24, no. 3 (December 2003): 24–39.

Conference Papers, Published Lectures and Theses

Beckles, Hilary McD. "Black Masculinity in Caribbean Slavery". Occasional Paper 2:96 (St Michael, Barbados: Women and Development Unit, University of the West Indies, 1996), 1–15.

Carter, Henderson. "Labour, Resistance and Protest in Barbados, 1838–1904". PhD dissertation, University of the West Indies, Cave Hill, 2000.

Francis, Cavell. "Breaking the Silence: Voices of the Enslaved in the Production of the Past". Paper presented to the Staff/Graduate Seminar, Department of History and Archaeology, University of the West Indies, Mona, November 2004.

Hutton, Clinton. " 'Colour for Colour, Skin for Skin': The Ideological Foundation of Post-Slavery Society, 1838–1865, the Jamaican Case". PhD dissertation, University of the West Indies, Mona, 1993.

Jemmott, Jenny. "The Family in Post-Emancipation Jamaica". Paper presented to the Staff/Postgraduate Seminar, Department of History, University of the West Indies, Mona, 30 January 1992.

———. "The Family during the Apprenticeship Period in Jamaica: Impact and Adjustment". Paper presented to the Social History Project Symposium, University of the West Indies, Mona, 21 April 2001.

———. "Black Family Advocacy in Jamaica, 1834–1838". Paper presented to the Staff/Graduate Seminar, Department of History and Archaeology, University of the West Indies, Mona, 30 April 2004.

Moore, Brian L., and Michele A. Johnson. " 'Little Black Bastards': Perceptions of Illegitimacy in Jamaica, 1865–1920". Paper presented to the Social History Project Symposium, Department of History and Archaeology, University of the West Indies, Mona, 4 May 2002.

Robertson, James. "Ventriloquizing Slaves' Voices in Mid-Eighteenth-Century Jamaica". Paper presented to the Social History Project Symposium, Department of History and Archaeology, University of the West Indies, Mona, 4 May 2002.

Rodney, Walter. "From Nigger Yard to Village". From a talk given in December 1978 on Plantation Society in Guyana. *Reform: A Caribbean Journal of Rural Development* (pamphlet, May 1988).

Shepherd, Verene A. "Locating Enslaved Women's Voices in the Colonial Caribbean: The Promises and Pitfalls of 'Ventriloquism' ". Position paper presented to the First Text and Testimony Collective Workshop, Dartmouth College, Hanover, New Hampshire, 18–20 May 2001.

———. "Resisting Representation: The Problem of Locating the Subaltern Woman's Voice". Paper presented to the Second Conference on Caribbean Culture, University of the West Indies, Mona, 9–12 January 2002.

Wilmot, Swithin. "Freedom in Jamaica: Challenges and Opportunities, 1838–1865". (Pamphlet.) Kingston: Jamaica Information Service, 1997.

Index

Sabean, David, 3–4, 17, 200

St Ann, 69

St Catherine's Hall estate, 82–83

St Elizabeth, 70, 95

St George, 94–95, 96

St George's Industrial Home and Reformatory for Boys, 125, 126, 128

St Joseph, 69–70

St Thomas-in-the-East, 40, 117–18; after Morant Bay Rebellion, 142–43, 151, 198

Salmon, John, 70

Samuels (local justice), 90

Sarah (Orange Valley estate), 50

Satchell, Veront, 61

Saulman (abducted boy), 104–5

Saunders, Janette, 46

Savage, John, 71, 134–35

Saxham estate, 86–87

Scarano, Francisco, 3, 4, 5, 200

Schawfield estate, 65–66

schools: attendance decline, 121, 132, 134; built by families, 39, 48–49, 70–71; on estates, 118, 119; industrial, 118–19, 120–32; *in loco parentis,* 125; model (government), 134, 225n61; "ragged", 180; reformatory, 125–28, 129; terms for, 223n30. *See also* education

Scott, Charlotte, 164

Scott, Rebecca, 6, 37–39

Scott, William, 61

self-help, 39, 165, 194–95

Senior (Penshurst estate), 59, 89

separation (marital), 173, 174–75

Seraphine (Lovely Grove estate), 62

Shann, William, 148

Shaw, Rosie, 65

Sheller, Mimi, 49–50, 58

shelter. *See* homes

Shepherd, Verene, 8, 33

shopkeepers, 158

Shortridge, Eleanor, 162

Shortridge, Samuel, 162

Sicard family (York Castle estate), 91

Silvera (debt collector), 72

Simpson (Trafalgar estate attorney), 51

slavery, 38, 47; abusive treatment under, 41–42, 56–57; and family structure, 14, 22, 33. *See also* kidnap victims

Sligo, Howe Peter Browne, Marquess of, 50–51, 59, 87, 90; and judicial abuses, 42, 44, 53, 57

smallpox, 136–37

Smith, Charles (Richmond estate attorney), 66, 67

Smith, Charles and Euphemia, 65–66

Smith, Evalina, 53

Smith, Lionel, 46, 57, 58–59, 119

Smith, M.G., 1, 13

Smith, Raymond, 13

Smith, William Kelly, 165

social control: apprenticeship (traditional) as, 136, 137–38; of children, 113–14, 115–16, 120–38; churches as, 113–14, 120; government mechanisms, 113–14, 115–16, 126–27, 181–83, 196–97; legislation as, 168–69, 187–88, 199. *See also* education; legislation

Spain, 100–101, 103, 107. *See also* Cuba

Spalding, Hinton, 94–95

special justices. *See* magistrates

Spring Mount estate, 50

Spring Rice, Thomas, 85

Stainsby, W. (magistrate), 106

Stanley, Edward, 14th Earl of Derby, 101

Steelfield estate, 48

Sterling, Ann, 91

Stewart (Holland estate overseer), 151

Stewart, Amelia, 147

Stewart, Cecelia Victoria, 160I

Stewart, Charles, 48

Printed in the USA
CPSIA information can be obtained
at www.ICGtesting.com
LVHW070025120923
757844LV00003B/257

9 789766 405069